Mastering Teaching

Mastering Teaching

Thriving as an Early Career Teacher

Edited by Moira Hulme, Rebecca Smith,
and Rachel O'Sullivan

 Open University Press

Open University Press
McGraw-Hill Education
8th Floor, 338 Euston Road
London
England
NW1 3BH

email: enquiries@openup.co.uk
world wide web: www.openup.co.uk

and Two Penn Plaza, New York, NY 10121-2289, USA

First edition published 2021

A catalogue record of this book is available from the British Library

ISBN-13: 9780335250356
ISBN-10: 0335250351
eISBN: 9780335250363

Library of Congress Cataloging-in-Publication Data
CIP data applied for

Typeset by Transforma Pvt. Ltd., Chennai, India

Praise Page

"A key strength of this book, apart from its coverage of key aspects of pedagogy and what it means to be a teacher, is that it is written by a wide range of educators, from researchers and lecturers to senior leaders and teachers in a variety of schools. The presentation, with its vignettes of good practice and prompts for reflection, is accessible and ideal for dipping into by those who seek ideas and guidance or background reading for assignments. The style is engaging and there is a very good balance between theory and research-informed practice. An excellent addition to the thinking educator's bookshelf."
—Dr David Waugh, Professor of Education, Durham University

"The distinctive challenges facing Early Career Teachers are identified and addressed with a clear focus on developing the adaptive expertise which is the foundation and sustenance of success in this demanding profession. Each chapter is co-authored by experienced teacher educators drawn from both university and school-based settings."
—Professor Linda Clarke, Ulster University

"This is a book that is sorely needed to support the flourishing of teachers during the demanding early stages of their careers. It is also likely to be heavily used by providers of teacher induction support and other professional development courses. Among its great strengths are both the comprehensive coverage of the important issues and concerns that early career teachers encounter and the way in which it combines critical insights from the best research with focused practical advice. I anticipate that the book will have a very positive impact on teachers and on the learners in their classrooms for many years to come."
—Ian Menter, Emeritus Professor of Teacher Education, University of Oxford, Former President of the British Educational Research Association (2013-15)

"Mastering Teaching is a core, comprehensive, credible and cutting-edge introduction to early career teacher learning. This 'industry standard' volume is written with clarity and expertise by a formidable team of school and university-based teacher educators. Based on contemporary understandings of how teachers learn to ensure excellent learning for

children and young people in today's diverse classrooms, this volume understands how the professional teacher's relationships with other colleagues build evidence-based approaches to teaching; and how relationships with parents and carers is vital in understanding the personal context in which each child or young person learns."

—*Dr Beth Dickson, University of Glasgow*

Contents

Contributors

Steph Ainsworth is Senior Lecturer (Primary) and co-leads the Doctor of Education programme at Manchester Metropolitan University

Reihana Aitken is Assistant Headteacher at the Abraham Moss Community School, a multicultural all-through school in North Manchester

Joe Barber is Senior Lecturer (English) in Education at the School of Teacher Education at Manchester Metropolitan University

Joanna Baynham is Senior Lecturer (Geography) in Education at the School of Teacher Education at Manchester Metropolitan University

Gary Beauchamp is Professor of Education and Associate Dean Research at Cardiff School of Education and Social Policy, Cardiff Metropolitan University

Charlotte Booth is the Programme Lead for PGCE Primary Education at the School of Teacher Education at Manchester Metropolitan University

Helen Borley is Headteacher of Mount Stuart Primary School in Cardiff

Aidan Brierley teaches at Acre Hall Primary School, Trafford

Tony Brittain is Deputy Headteacher, Sale Grammar School. He is responsible for teacher education, induction, and the development of newly and recently qualified teachers

Geraldine Carter teaches at Sandbach Primary Academy & Research School, Cheshire, where she is a Specialist Leader in Cultural Education

Majella Dalton-Bartley is Senior Lecturer (Religious Education) at the School of Teacher Education at Manchester Metropolitan University

Mike Dore is Deputy Headteacher at Parrs Wood High School, Manchester

Nansi Ellis is Assistant General Secretary of the National Education Union

Joanne Formosa is Assistant Headteacher at River View Primary School, Salford

Hannah Frank teaches Geography at the Simon Balle all-through School, Hertford

Dominic Griffiths is Senior Lecturer in Inclusive Education at the School of Childhood, Youth and Education Studies, Manchester Metropolitan University

Chris Hanley is Senior Lecturer (English) in Education and co-leads the Doctor of Education programme at Manchester Metropolitan University

Moira Hulme is Professor of Teacher Education at the Education and Social and Research Institute, Manchester Metropolitan University

Irene Leach is a freelance educator/researcher and specialist teacher with twenty-five years' experience working with neurodiverse groups across a range of phases and settings

Rachel Marsden is a teacher of English at King George V College, Southport

Jennifer McGahan is a Lecturer in Psychology at the Department of Psychology, Manchester Metropolitan University

Karen Meanwell is Associate Head of the School of Teacher Education at Manchester Metropolitan University

Clare Nelson is a Year 2 teacher, History Lead, Geography Lead, and School Librarian at Cheadle Catholic Infant School

Rachel O'Sullivan is Senior Lecturer in Education at Manchester Metropolitan University

Nigel Pritchard is a class teacher and Digital Competence Lead in Mount Stuart Primary School in Cardiff

Rachael Rivers leads Continuing Professional Development at the Learning for Life Partnership, a multi-academy trust based in East Cheshire

Helen Ryan-Atkin is Senior Lecturer (Primary) in Education at Manchester Metropolitan University

Mark Sackville-Ford is Assistant Trust Director of SEND, Laurus Trust, Cheadle Hulme

Rebecca Smith is Headteacher of Sale Grammar School. She has 20 years' experience in a range of different types of schools and provides school-to-school support to senior leaders and headteachers

Corinne Woodfine is BA primary Education Programme Lead and Departmental Disability Coordinator at Manchester Metropolitan University

Ben Wye is Senior Lecturer (primary) in Education at Manchester Metropolitan University.

Figures and tables

Introduction

This book proceeds from the premise that teaching is a complex and intellectually demanding professional undertaking. We know that the quality of teaching is the most influential within-school factor affecting outcomes for children and young people. Supporting teachers well in the early stages of their career has the potential to reduce turnover and attrition, benefitting the schools and communities they serve. Uniquely, teaching often makes the same demands of novices and experienced teachers. We maintain that the needs of new teachers are different from those of their more experienced colleagues. Experienced educators know that initial preparation is rarely sufficient to provide the knowledge and repertoire of skills necessary to teach well in a variety of contexts. Compared with other professions, teachers' early career development and support stops too soon.

This book starts from a commitment to the development of adaptive expertise and an appreciation of the policy and institutional contexts in which new teachers forge their careers. It is based on extensive consultation with school leaders, early career teachers and their mentors. *Mastering Teaching* responds to the challenges novice teachers face so that they might continue to grow professionally. In writing this book, we aim to support the transition into teaching, enhance new teacher confidence and effectiveness in the primary and secondary classroom, and promote a culture of collaborative professionalism that lays the foundation for career-long professional growth.

Teaching is a demanding profession and although individuals surround you all day, there can be limited time spent with other colleagues or space to reflect. The following chapters provide an insight into the perspectives, experiences, and research of other professionals and are written in such a way as to encourage rich dialogue between colleagues across a wide range of themes, different sectors of education, and national policy contexts. The opportunity to reflect together and to discuss your own experiences, alongside those of fellow teachers and those shared within the vignettes, will encourage teachers to further hone their beliefs and think deeply about teaching. The importance the book places on research also challenges the reader to consider how and which research can influence their practice, thus further developing and challenging their practice, the climate they create within their classrooms, and the difference they can make. Throughout each chapter, the inclusion of research reminds practitioners, that no matter what stage you are in your career, to explore research and test out its relevance within your own setting. It provides an important reminder that great teaching not only instils in others the importance of and desire for lifelong learning, but also requires that of those who choose to teach.

Who is this book for?

This book is designed to meet the development needs of early career teachers, that is, teachers who are within five years of gaining their first teaching post. The content is appropriate for beginning and recently qualified teachers, and the professionals who support them in school, including formal and informal mentors, school leaders, and induction coordinators. The collection includes rich illustrative examples from UK primary and secondary schools. The collection includes chapters that address different curriculum areas and phases of education. The issues and debates addressed are relevant across the four national education systems of the UK. The text is also relevant to those aspiring to teach who are undertaking courses in education studies, education psychology, or teacher education. The book contains material and activities that will be useful to coordinators of professional learning in school.

The writing team

This collection is distinctive in that it draws on the combined expertise of a team of more than thirty experienced educators working in schools and universities. Each chapter is co-authored by school-based and university-based teacher educators, modelling a collaborative approach to teacher development. Each academic–practitioner pairing has grown from sustained engagement in the field and reflects strong partnership work in supporting new teachers. Through our collaboration, we model the partnership work that is integral to professional learning in the workplace.

The chapters draw on the professional experience of lead practitioners who work in a wide range of education settings: nursery, primary, secondary, all-through schools, sixth forms, and special education. The team encompasses professional perspectives from faith schools and single-sex schools, as well as multicultural, multilingual urban settings. Practitioner contributors are accomplished teachers with senior leadership roles in schools and Multi-Academy Trusts. The writing team includes educationists with experience as school inspectors, advisory roles, school and MAT curriculum leaders, special/inclusive education and professional learning leads. Collectively, the practitioner team commands over one hundred years of experience in supporting teachers. Practitioners have worked with their academic co-authors to identify priorities, select examples, and direct the reader to further resources and networks. Lead practitioners bring rich examples and vignettes to illustrate key challenges reported by early career teachers and offer strategies for reflection and development.

Our team of accomplished practitioners collaborated with a number of academics – professors, senior lecturers, and lecturers with a range of specialisms in educational research, psychology, and primary and secondary teacher education. Most of these co-authors are employed at the Faculty of Education, Manchester Metropolitan University, one of the largest providers of initial teacher education in the United Kingdom. Each year the university prepares over 1000 new teachers, working in close partnership with over 1500 schools.

How to use this book

Individual chapters are intended to support self-study and reflection, and to stimulate professional dialogue. Each chapter contains prompts for reflection to be used in professional conversations with mentors, peers, and critical friends. Every chapter contains an accessible precis of research that synthesises key messages for a practitioner audience and identifies print and online sources for further reading. Conceptual language and key terms are addressed succinctly in the end-of-book Glossary. The terms included in the Glossary appear in bold upon first mention in the text. Each chapter has a number of feature boxes containing illustrative examples from authentic practice contexts to help to bridge the knowledge–practice gap.

Overview of the book

The structure of *Mastering Teaching* is underpinned by four principles grounded in existing knowledge about how early career teachers are best supported to become committed and effective professionals over time (Table 0.1). This design creates a coherent pathway that provides challenge and support regardless of an early career teacher's starting point, phase, or subject specialism.

Chapter 1, 'The professional knowledge of teachers', outlines the different types of knowledge required by teachers: content knowledge, pedagogical knowledge, and curriculum knowledge. Particular attention is afforded to Shulman's theory of knowledge (1986) and especially to pedagogical content knowledge (PCK). PCK represents the distinctive knowledge base of teaching and supports our belief that teaching is a profession. Accessible examples are used from primary and secondary geography to develop your command of theory-through-practice. Throughout the chapter prompts for reflection are provided to help you learn from experience and to support your future planning. Developing PCK is a

Table 0.1 Professional learning principles and book structure

Principle	Chapter focus
Deepening intellectual quality: understanding how children and young people learn	*Professional knowledge of teachers* *Modelling curriculum design* *Understanding memory*
Enhancing connections between theory and practice: linking professional knowledge and action with changing work contexts and needs	*Developing positive behaviour* *Wellbeing of children and young people* *Digital classrooms: Pedagogy and practice*
Valuing diversity and differences: setting ambitious expectations for success for all and building strong family–school relations	*Inclusive pedagogy* *Setting ambitious expectations* *Relationships with parents and carers*
Growing professionally as a new teacher: embracing peer support, collaboration, and mentoring challenge	*Developing through reflection and enquiry* *Teacher wellbeing and resilience* *Becoming research literate*

challenge for all early career teachers. This initial exploration of professional knowledge is developed further in the following chapter on curriculum design.

Chapter 2, 'Modelling curriculum design', takes a conceptual approach to curriculum development. If teachers are to be curriculum builders, as well as deliverers, then it is important to foster a deep understanding of the principles and purposes of curriculum design. This chapter draws on the notion of threshold concepts (Meyer and Land, 2003, 2005) to explore disciplinary (academic subject matter), pedagogic (teacher skills and knowledge), and pupil-centred curriculum development. Each of these three strands is exemplified through practice examples drawn from secondary English literature. Importantly, pupils are positioned as active agents in their own learning. Readers are asked to reflect on their own experiences of learning a difficult subject or practice to understand how many pupils feel when they encounter challenging aspects of the curriculum. The authors emphasise that having a detailed curriculum plan will be insufficient without attention to how the curriculum is experienced by pupils. Collaborative curriculum enquiry is also a feature of Chapters 5, 10, and 12.

Chapter 3, 'Understanding memory', aims to develop your understanding of the two memory systems, working and long-term memory. The relationship between working memory and school performance has received a great deal of attention in recent years. This chapter provides a comprehensive and very accessible introduction to the psychology of memory. Applying cognitive load theory, that is, how learning is compromised when the demands of a task exceed processing capacity (Sweller, 2010), the chapter presents a series of strategies to help you reduce cognitive load in your classroom. Attention then turns to practical ways to help pupils retrieve information using illustrative examples from primary history and geography. The chapter ends with consideration of metamemory: the self-monitoring and self-control of memory processes. You are shown how to integrate metamemory activities in the primary classroom.

Chapter 4, 'At the crossroads: A roadmap for navigating the complexities of behaviour management', aims to support the early career teacher to think deeply about the nature of behaviour and the associated concept of behaviour management within a school setting. The chapter outlines a holistic model that integrates a conceptual understanding of behaviour, with praxis (putting theory into practice) and teacher values. You will explore approaches to behaviour management in school that range from 'indulging' to 'guiding' to 'controlling'. A series of prompts for reflection will guide your engagement with the material, which is applicable to both primary and secondary settings. The authors caution against over-reliance on recipe knowledge, quick fixes and short cuts that may work in the short term, and encourage early career teachers to think deeply about how to foster a 'supportive and inclusive environment' for learning and wellbeing. It may be helpful to read this chapter in conjunction with Chapters 5, 7, and 8.

Chapter 5, 'Wellbeing of children and young people', aims to develop your understanding of the multiple domains that comprise pupil wellbeing, and the pastoral, curricular, and pedagogical strategies used to promote wellbeing in school. Wellbeing has attracted increased attention in response to the poor performance of the UK on measures of wellbeing in childhood and adolescence (The Children's Society, 2020a). The chapter opens with consideration of how wellbeing is defined and measured. This matters because different definitions of wellbeing lead to different orientations within wellbeing-focused education policy and school-level programmes. A range of policy frameworks and case studies is used to illustrate how pupil wellbeing is instantiated in the school curriculum, Teachers' Standards, and school development planning, including school responses to (pandemic-induced) school closure. The chapter concludes with consideration of pedagogical approaches to the development of social and emotional skills. A wide range of sources of support and resources is provided for the early career teacher interested in learning more about wellbeing policy and practice.

Chapter 6, 'Digital classrooms: Pedagogy and practice', explores how digital technology can be used to promote effective online, hybrid, and face-to-face learning. The affordances of learning technologies include speed, automation, retrieval capacity, interactivity, and an ability to 'play' imaginatively with content in a variety of forms. This chapter encourages a judicious approach with careful thought given to educational purpose (learning goals) and not simply availability. It is easy to be dazzled by the impressive range and capability of digital technologies. Using examples from within and beyond classrooms, early career teachers are supported to consider when it is appropriate to use digital technology. Examples of promising practice are used to encourage early career teachers to take measured risks with new technologies. Risk-taking should proceed alongside collegial inter-professional and home–school communication, and evaluation of impact. (For a further example of considerations in the transition to online learning during Covid-19 school closures, see Chapter 5.)

Chapter 7, 'Inclusive pedagogy: Using Universal Design for Learning', aims to help you develop your practice through an appreciation of neurodiversity. The authors maintain that 'inclusive pedagogy is about recognising the diversity of your learners and making a positive commitment to gradually developing your practice to become more flexible and responsive to this diversity'. Seeing practice through a neurodiversity lens means moving away from deficit-focused approaches to Special Educational Needs and Disabilities (SEND) that focus on labels. In contrast, the authors argue, 'we are all neurodiverse' and advocate focusing on the individual strengths of different learners. The chapter introduces Universal Design for Learning (UDL) as a framework for inclusive whole-class lesson planning rather than 'bolt-on' differentiation activities. A cycle of lesson planning is used to develop your grasp of UDL as an iterative and reflective process. Practice examples from secondary geography and art are used to exemplify the UDL approach. This chapter encourages early career teachers to celebrate neurodiversity and to consider how they can develop a more inclusive pedagogical approach in their own practice.

Chapter 8, 'Setting ambitious expectations', outlines a number of strategies that early career teachers can use to build a culture of expectation, aspiration, and success for all their pupils. The deleterious effect of negative labelling and negative self-fulfilling prophecies are well known. Using Dweck's (2007) comparison of a growth and fixed mindset, this chapter helps teachers appreciate the importance of instilling in their pupils a belief that improvement is always possible. A number of strategies are outlined to support ambitious expectations. These include the use of benchmarking through peer observation, visualisation of expectations, modelling behaviour for learning or 'living' out these expectations, with empathy, and positive behaviour management. It may be helpful to read this chapter in conjunction with Chapters 4 and 7.

Chapter 9, 'The role of emotion in relationships with parents and carers', supports the early career teacher in an area of practice that is under-explored. This chapter contains stimulus material and prompts for reflection for use by early career teachers and their supporters/mentors. Three key concepts are used to examine how emotion influences relationships between parents/carers and teachers: autobiographical experience, unconscious bias, and cultural myths surrounding education. These concepts are addressed through three vignettes, or stories from practice, that capture atypical and potentially emotive scenarios involving parents/carers and early career teachers. This contribution to the collection foregrounds the relational dynamics of work in schools and teachers' emotional labour. The authors conclude by arguing that an effective teacher and parent/carer relationship is one that is 'dialogic, where both parties are co-constructors of knowledge about the child'. For examples of how schools foster home–school relations in response to specific needs, revisit Chapter 5.

Chapter 10, 'Developing through reflection and collaborative enquiry', starts from an appreciation that teachers are, first and foremost, learning professionals. Primary teachers at different stages in their professional learning journey discuss how they use models of reflection from Dewey (1933) and Schon (1983), to Kolb (1984) and Gibbs (1988), to support their continuing learning. We are reminded that reflection and 'professional vision' are skills that demand 'intentional noticing' (Goldman and Grimbeek, 2014; Mason, 2001) and a commitment to explicating hidden bias through 'assumption hunting' (Brookfield, 2017). The chapter argues that investment in professional learning should not be viewed as a 'personal commodity' but a 'shared resource' that supports the development of the teaching community. Four approaches to collaborative professional learning are outlined: guided viewing of video, Lesson Study, learning rounds, and collaborative curriculum enquiry. These strategies can be trialled by pairs or groups of teachers working together to address self-identified priorities, or as a whole school or cluster of schools with common development priorities. Importantly, the chapter considers the conditions conducive to professional growth and the affective dimensions of professional learning that are significant for all teachers and especially those at an early career stage. It will be helpful to read this chapter in conjunction with Chapters 11 and 12.

Chapter 11, 'Teacher wellbeing and resilience', offers a social ecological approach to a professional problem that is often presented as an individual responsibility. The concept of teacher resilience is subjected to critical examination and the factors that contribute to teachers' sense of wellbeing are investigated. In offering a social ecological approach, the authors argue that resilience should not be seen as 'a characteristic of the individual, but rather as a complex interaction between factors within the individual and their environment'. The chapter uses semi-fictional vignettes based on teachers' everyday experiences to explore key themes from the research literature. Factors important for teacher resilience include self-esteem, life orientation (how optimistic you are as a person), emotional intelligence, self-care, conflict between beliefs and practice (the extent to which you feel you are expected to teach in a way that is inconsistent with your professional values), workload, and conditions of employment. The authors conclude that multi-level strategies (peer-to-peer, school-wide, middle tier, national agencies, and professional associations) are needed to develop a sense of collective agency and public responsibility for educator wellbeing.

Chapter 12, 'Becoming research literate', argues that all teachers should be supported to engage in professional enquiry as knowledge producers and discerning consumers of pedagogical research. Education research is a pluri-disciplinary field that encompasses research by practitioners as well as those engaged in empirical and disciplinary enquiry (psychology, neuroscience, sociology, history, philosophy). The chapter offers an overview of the various iterations of the evidence movement in education in the United Kingdom. Drivers and barriers to greater research engagement by teachers and schools are identified. In addition to deliberation on effectiveness, educators are encouraged to consider whether promising interventions that have worked well elsewhere are appropriate, feasible, and defensible in the proposed context of use. The reader is introduced to theories of change and logic models in improvement planning. Ground rules are provided for appraising research, and ethical issues in conducting research in educational settings are addressed. Links are provided to networks that support teachers' engagement with, and in, collaborative enquiry. This chapter reiterates the importance of informed judgement by learning professionals.

Through the following chapters we encourage you to invest in your own learning and professional development. We invite you to think deeply and differently and we call upon you to interrogate your practice, to experiment and take risks as you seek solutions to the challenges you face in your own classroom or teaching space. Every day teachers are surrounded by rich research opportunities. Stenhouse (1981) challenged all teachers to experiment in their 'laboratories' and reject being positioned as the researched but instead be active in researching their own practice. It is through interrogating your own practice and developing reflective, critical curiosity that you will be best positioned to gain a fuller understanding of what you do and why you do it, moving from the position of passive consumer to empowered, agentic professional. Deeper understanding of your practice will enable you to respond effectively to the needs of all your pupils. There is overwhelming evidence that the quality of teaching is the most influential within-school factor affecting outcomes for children and young people (Barber and Mourshed, 2007; Coe et al., 2014; Hattie, 2013; OECD, 2005). It is therefore the responsibility of all teachers to examine and advance their personal pedagogy, to seek opportunities to share best practice, work collaboratively, and find solutions to the challenges they face. The themes woven through the chapters of this book will, we believe, enable you to develop the art, craft, and science of your pedagogy (Pollard et al., 2014) and in so doing become more effective in your practice and more secure in your teacher identity.

Moira Hulme, Rachel O'Sullivan, and Rebecca Smith, Editors

1 The professional knowledge of teachers

Joanna Baynham and Hannah Frank

Introduction

This chapter proceeds from an understanding of teaching as a complex intellectual activity. The knowledge base of teachers is contested. The chapter introduces different ways of classifying the types of knowledge needed by teachers in the classroom. Shulman's theory of **pedagogical content knowledge** (PCK) is used as a way of making sense of what new teachers need to know and do. You will engage with different types of knowledge for teaching, such as content knowledge, pedagogical knowledge, and curriculum knowledge, and consider what this means for skilful teaching and practice enhancement. In addition, careful consideration will be given to knowledge of the learner, educational contexts, and educational ends, purposes, and values. The discussion is supported by illustrative examples from secondary geography but key themes are equally applicable to other subjects and stages of education.

Shulman's theory of knowledge

Shulman's theory of knowledge (1986) helps us to make sense of what we mean by professional knowledge, especially in the context of dynamic school curricula where the emphasis can change between skills and knowledge. The knowledge teachers need is not just about the subject matter they are teaching, there is a wealth of knowledge needed to be a successful teacher. Shulman (1987: 8) organises the professional knowledge base of teaching into seven types: content knowledge, general pedagogical knowledge, curriculum knowledge, pedagogical content knowledge, knowledge of learners and their characteristics, knowledge of educational contexts, and knowledge of educational ends, purposes, and values.

It is important to consider all of these knowledges and reflect on what this means for you, as an early career teacher. We also need to be aware that this knowledge base is not fixed and final. It offers a broad outline that can and will continue to evolve. Your professional knowledge will develop across the career course and as you move between settings.

Content knowledge

This is sometimes seen as the most important form of knowledge, since the traditional view of teaching is the teacher imparting their own knowledge to a group of pupils. We know good subject knowledge is important. Whatever phase you

Table 1.1 Examples of how content knowledge can be organised within a subject

Bloom's **cognitive taxonomy**	This is a way of organising knowledge according to higher-order and lower-order cognitive skills. This can help both the teacher and the pupils make sense of the level of challenge of different knowledge within the subject area. Bloom's Taxonomy has been used in many ways to support teaching and learning since it was first introduced in 1956. More recently, a revised taxonomy has updated the categories to include remember, understand, apply, analyse, evaluate, create (Anderson et al., 2014).
Schwab's structures of knowledge	Schwab (1978) refers to the **substantive** and **syntactic** structures of a subject, or in other words the literacy and grammar of a subject. What language does a pupil need to know in order to be able to articulate a particular subject matter?

teach, pupils ask questions and they look to you for the answers. Although a teacher can know a lot about a subject, can they know everything? In a primary classroom, can you be an expert in all subject areas? We know from our experience as geography teachers that the very nature of our subject is dynamic, and the subject knowledge needed changes with it. In addition to this, a teacher must also be able to tell a pupil why something is important and valid within a subject. They will know how to organise theory in their subject **discipline** and understand the syntax of the subject. There are many different ways to organise this subject content knowledge (for further guidance, see Chapter 2 on 'Modelling curriculum design'). Table 1.1 describes two examples of how content knowledge can be organised within a subject.

When starting to teach a new topic, or if you are less secure about content knowledge, where do you acquire this information? In the vignette below, Hannah reflects on teaching cold environments in sixth-form geography for the first time and how she gained that knowledge.

Vignette 1

Having studied glaciation as part of my degree, I was confident in my understanding of the range of systems and processes operating in cold environments. However, once I had read the A level curriculum in preparation for planning my lessons, it quickly dawned on me that there was a big gap between the terminology students were expected to know and what I knew. To add to the challenge, I was teaching cold environments to a group of students who lived in Hertfordshire, many of whom had never visited a cold environment. To overcome this, I read A level textbooks alongside other glaciation textbooks to ensure I was using the correct terminology to meet the specification of the exam board. Making sense of the content knowledge before beginning to consider how to teach it was really important. Once I had the knowledge of what I needed to teach and the language I needed to use, I had to consider HOW I would get this information across to my students. When I first started teaching, I wanted to basically tell the students what I knew but with experience I learnt that this did not work with all students, in fact most of the students I taught. They would be quiet in a lesson and they would complete tasks I set but when I tested their knowledge, the recall was not always there. I was fortunate that I could try different ways of teaching and learning with my classes. Virtual field trips as well as decision-making activities were used to help students visualise and bring to life what a glaciated landscape looks and feels like. I found this has more successful outcomes and by working with more experienced teachers to plan collaboratively, we planned much more engaging lessons which ultimately led to better outcomes for students.

To overcome the initial lack of content knowledge, Hannah had to really consider what knowledge the pupils needed to know and then how she would transfer that knowledge to the pupils. The difference between a teacher of a subject and another subject specialist is that the teacher also needs to understand why that knowledge is important, the circumstances for that belief, and the language and literacy of the specific subject. The terminology, words, and phrases that are specific to the subject are a really important aspect of teaching the content. When you start teaching, the content knowledge may be clear but the nuances of that knowledge specific to the age and curriculum may not come easily but you will learn quickly what the expected content is. This is where you may feel like a subject disciplinary expert but as a teacher you use **adaptive expertise** to respond to the pupils and how they learn. You adjust to different ways of thinking about the subject content.

Prompt for reflection

Think back to the first lesson you taught in your training year. You were most probably given a specific piece of content knowledge to teach to the class.

- Where did you get the content knowledge from?
- What process did you go through to learn that knowledge?
- How did you decide how you would teach that knowledge to the pupils?

Now consider a lesson you have taught where the knowledge needed was entirely new to you. Did you go through the same steps or did you do something different?

General pedagogical knowledge

Towards the end of vignette 1, Hannah is beginning to try to make sense not only of *what* to teach when teaching the topic of cold environments but also the *how*. As a teacher, pedagogical knowledge is key. How do we teach? What **pedagogy** are we using? You may have fallen into the 'Google trap' where you are asked to teach a lesson for the first time and spend hours trying to find a 'fun' activity which doesn't always fit with the content you are due to teach.

General pedagogical knowledge is knowledge about teaching and ways of teaching. Shulman (1986) refers to this as the broad principles and strategies of classroom management and organisation that appear to transcend subject matter. It is difficult to define, as the knowledge is very much context specific and what works well in one context may not work in another. **Early career teachers** can find this hard when they start at a new school. As they reflect back to their experiences whilst training, what may be regarded as good pedagogical knowledge in an earlier setting may not be valued in the same way in another. As a result, many early career teachers think they are getting it wrong and get confused. Context is discussed later in the chapter, but this could be the school, the class or even one child, and that context is an important part of a teacher's pedagogical knowledge. Varying the general pedagogical knowledge you have in your classroom can also help to keep students – and the teacher – more engaged and interested in what is happening in the classroom. Try to avoid using the same methods over and over again. Becoming a professional means not only honing routine strategies, but developing the capacity to respond well to new or unexpected situations. This is what is meant by adaptive expertise.

Curriculum knowledge

This is knowledge of what is needed to be taught for a particular subject, class, age, etc. That might be in the context of your school, or as part of a national curriculum or examination specification. It is then about breaking down the curriculum into smaller chunks as part of long-, medium-, and short-term planning. An experienced teacher will be familiar with a range of curricular methods to teach a specific topic to ensure that the students can understand it. They will be aware of common misconceptions, alternative texts, and so on. One example that resonates for us as experienced geography teachers is teaching the San Andreas fault. Most pupils know about this fault line from Hollywood movies but in many commonly used textbooks there are errors in the diagrams. If you are an early career teacher, you may assume that the book is correct but always check!

There is also value in being aware of the curriculum knowledge students are learning in other subjects at the same time, and what they have learnt in earlier stages in their school career. Sometimes in the primary phase, the class teacher is responsible for teaching the whole curriculum, but if you teach in a school with multiple-form entry, or are working part time with a job share and at secondary level, you have to be more proactive and seek out what each subject team is doing. Being able to appreciate the whole curriculum can have real benefits, as you are able to draw on this in your own lessons and help pupils make sense of all the knowledge they are learning. Read vignette 2 where Hannah describes why this understanding of curricular knowledge is important.

Vignette 2: The need for cross-curricular knowledge

In most schools, weather and climate is part of a Key Stage 3 unit of work (ages 11–14). We teach it to our Year 7s (age 11–12). Students often have a good understanding of weather from primary school and learn the key words and concepts relatively quickly. I remember planning a lesson on climate graphs; students had to draw climate graphs based on data from two different locations. I then set questions that students would answer to compare the two graphs. After introducing the task, I let the students have a go. After five minutes, and nearly every hand going up asking for help, I realised the whole class needed to stop. It was not my geography teaching or the way I explained the task that was the problem. The students did not know how to draw bar and line graphs together, some did not know how to scale an axis. After the lesson had finished, I had a discussion with the maths department who explained that the skill of drawing a climate graph was something not expected until much further on in their maths journey. I expected the students to be able to do this along with a number of other mathematical skills, such as pie charts, percentages, ratios, logarithmic scales, without knowing when and how it was taught in maths. This made me realise the importance of knowing what students are learning in other subjects. In the new curriculum for A level, the emphasis on statistics means I need to liaise much more closely with the maths department so I can prepare students for the statistical methods needed for A level geography.

Furthermore, I now realise that it's not just about knowing the skills students do and do not know. It is also good to understand what process and theories they are being taught in other subjects that are covered in the geography curriculum. There is often a crossover with science where different names can be given to the same processes and they can teach physical geography differently, which often leads to confusion. Being aware of this makes it much easier for the students.

Prior experiences the teacher brings to the curriculum are really important. Where subject knowledge is inadequate there may be a tendency to use published teaching packs of materials (that are designed to be 'teacher-proof') without any analysis of whether the material is suitable for the purpose and context in which it will be used.

Prompt for reflection

Think about a topic or subject you are going to teach and consider how you will teach it? Do the resources you have access to (textbooks, online material, physical artefacts) have sufficient information and activities in them? What criteria are you using to assess the value of resources? For example, relevance, recency, cost, accessibility, potential to adapt to individual needs. What can you do to make that learning experience more beneficial for all pupils? Can you do this for every lesson you teach?

Very early on in my career, someone told me that you can't be a good teacher until you have been in the classroom for a few years. I remember feeling quite cross about that, but I do know what they meant. Experience is important, but so too is creativity and innovation through sustained enquiry. You need to have a go at teaching topics and concepts before you know how to judge the most effective strategies in a particular set of circumstances. Don't be too hard on yourself. Reflect on what and how you did, and then think about what you'd do differently next time – just like you were asked to do when training.

Pedagogical content knowledge

This is the most important type of knowledge for educators. Shulman describes pedagogical content knowledge (PCK) as 'that special amalgam of content and pedagogy that is uniquely the province of teachers, their own special form of professional understanding' (1987: 8). It brings together both content knowledge and pedagogical knowledge. Pedagogical content knowledge is the distinct professional knowledge base of teachers. Teachers must be able to make informed decisions about the important ideas and skills in their subjects, as well as how promising new ideas are tested and older less effective ways of working are rejected. (See also Chapter 12 on 'Becoming research literate'.)

Pedagogical content knowledge goes beyond the subject content itself and considers the subject knowledge needed for teaching. This is where a teacher is expected to know not only the common content knowledge needed to teach the subject, but also the usual representations of that knowledge and the best way to teach it. The teacher will need to have to hand a variety of different methods in order to be able to choose the most appropriate way of representing a concept, whether through experience, professional dialogue or research. It is these pedagogical methods that develop in the training year and beyond. For Shulman, PCK is a combination of: 'The most regularly taught topics in one's subject area, the most useful forms of representations of those ideas, the most powerful analogies, illustrations, examples, explanations and demonstrations' (1986: 9). Pedagogical content knowledge also takes into account an understanding of what makes learning a particular topic easy or difficult, the conceptions and preconceptions at different ages, and the backgrounds of the children (Shulman, 1987).

> Teachers do not tell students what they know about the subject matter but they transform it in ways that are understood by learners. The transformation of preparation, representation, selection, adaptation and tailoring to student characteristics require combinations or ordering of these processes. (Reitano and Harte, 2016: 281)

Shulman states that these forms of transformations 'are the essence in the act of pedagogical reasoning, of teaching as thinking, and of planning – whether explicitly or implicitly – the performance of teaching' (1987: 16).

As an early career teacher you need to be able to demonstrate that you have a good understanding of PCK and you are developing from an expert in a subject to an expert teacher. You need to be able to demonstrate that you understand how to represent the content whilst considering the pedagogy of a particular topic or concept, and how you adapt this to the context in which – and with whom– you are working. This is very much an active process rather than a checklist you can go through.

Prompt for reflection

Consider how you can share and articulate your developing understanding of PCK. Can you reflect on a lesson you taught whilst training and a lesson on a similar topic you have taught recently? How were the lessons different? How were they similar? How do you think understanding PCK may have supported this development in your teaching?

Knowledge of learners and their characteristics

When you start your first teaching job, getting to know your students can seem like an impossible task, but it is vital to really gain an understanding of the complexity and needs of each individual. We divide the knowledge of learners into two parts: social and cognitive knowledge of learners (Turner-Bisset, 1999).

Social knowledge of learners means what children of a particular age range are like: how they behave, their interests and preoccupations. Cognitive knowledge of learners consists of knowledge of child development that informs practice, and knowledge that is context-bound to a particular group of learners. This kind of knowledge develops as the teacher gets to know the pupil(s), and is linked to Shulman's idea of adaptation (1987: 17) where material is adapted and represented in a way that the specific child can interpret and understand. In education in the UK, we would refer to this as 'differentiation'. This is something that all teachers find challenging but particularly early career teachers, as they have to get to know pupils quickly in order to be able to adapt curricular material for the specific needs of either individuals or the whole class.

Knowledge of educational contexts

This is the knowledge of all settings where learning takes place (Shulman, 1986). This could be the size and location of the school, the quality of the support, the amount of feedback early career teachers receive, or even the quality of communication and relationships in the school as well as the expectations of senior leaders. Having a good understanding of your educational context is really important.

Prompt for reflection

How does your own education and schooling compare to the school you are now working in? Think about the similarities and differences? Consider the context of your own education and how this will affect learning and teaching in your classroom. What sources of information (secondary and primary, numerical and descriptive) are available to you about your current setting – performance data, wellbeing policies, inter-professional working, inspection reports, school handbook and policies, curriculum records, socio-economic data about the area? How much have you accessed these and used this information in your approach? Which sources of information were most useful and why?

Knowledge of educational ends, purposes, and values

In many studies, this type of knowledge appears to be implicit rather than explicit and is therefore harder to capture both in the sense of short-term goals for a lesson or long-term goals in a series of lessons. Many of you will do this without thinking but sometimes it does need more explicit consideration. Why are we teaching what we teach? Who is telling us to teach this? For example, the reforms to the geography national curriculum in 2014 were debated extensively in England – should climate change be included or not? Who decides? The notion of moral purpose is important and as an early career teacher do take time to really think about this. In terms of the national curriculum, moral purpose is an underpinning rationale guiding curriculum design in Wales, Scotland, and Northern Ireland but less visible in official policy deliberation on the formal curriculum in England.

In all four home nations the state decides what knowledge is included in – and excluded from – the curricula. Bernstein (2000) uses three main fields of knowledge: production (the development of new knowledge), re-contextualisation (how this knowledge is interpreted), and reproduction (how it is then pedagogically transferred in schools). He sees these fields as a hierarchy of knowledge. This links back to the curricula in considering who tells us what and potentially how to teach. In England, the work of Hirsch (2016) around cultural literacy and core knowledge forms part of this discussion on what core knowledge is. Hirsch's research is based in the United States and argues that all pupils should have access to the same core knowledge to allow them to participate successfully in society. Young (2008) refers to this as 'powerful knowledge'. What makes knowledge powerful and who decides?

Prompt for reflection

Why does your curriculum include the knowledge it does? Where has that come from? Who has decided that it is important/powerful? What knowledge is excluded? How has content changed over time? Are there spaces for teachers to use professional discretion?

Knowledge of self

This is not included in Shulman's original list but features in the work of others as an important part of teacher knowledge (see, for example, Alsup, 2006; Beauchamp and Thomas, 2010; Bibby, 2011; Schutz et al., 2018). Your sense of self will have started in your training year and will continue to develop as you gain more experience. This can be particularly challenging if others within the system (your peers, mentor or line manager) hold different beliefs about what constitutes professionalism in teaching. When you are training you are constantly asked to reflect on your own practice but through the early career phase and beyond you have more independence and fewer formal opportunities to do this. To continue to grow professionally, it is important that you continue to reflect on your sense of self and your identity as a teacher.

Alternatives to Shulman's model

Whilst Shulman's model continues to be a good base for considering the professional knowledge of teachers, it is not the only model. Bennett and Turner-Bissett (2002) argued that it was impossible to distinguish between content knowledge and PCK because in the very act of teaching, all knowledge is presented pedagogically in some way. Pedagogical content knowledge may appear to be an incontestable construct according to much of the literature surrounding it but there is also an argument that PCK does not allow for a variety of teaching models and that it is only relevant when the teaching is didactic and teacher-led and therefore does not seem to encompass different ways of teaching (Meredith, 1995). Most teachers embrace a wide range of teaching and learning styles and a skilled teacher will know the PCK of their subject so that they can select the most appropriate method for that particular concept. Teachers usually do this without realising that is what they are doing. As an early career teacher this can be more challenging, especially if your school has a particular way of teaching. Try to keep in mind your own professional knowledge and do not be afraid to try out and evaluate new ways of doing things!

In the subject discipline of geography, the Geographical Association (one of the subject-specific teaching associations for teachers of geography) has argued for a 'core knowledge curriculum'. The Association (2011) distinguishes between three types of knowledge in the professional knowledge base for geography teachers.

1. *Core knowledge*: the world of geography knowledge that can be derived from maps and globes.
2. *Content knowledge*: the main content of the geography curriculum – its key concepts, ideas, and generalisations.
3. *Procedural knowledge*: 'thinking geographically', which is a distinctive procedure – it is not the same as thinking historically, or scientifically, or mathematically.

The Geographical Association has suggested that when selecting what to teach, all three knowledges are important and should be considered. The choices teachers make on what to include and what not to include reflects professional judgement (Brooks, 2015).

Prompt for reflection

Reflect on your own practice using the following headings and note your strengths, areas for development, and how you can move forward.

- Your subject area – both as an academic discipline and a school subject
- Your knowledge of your students
- Your knowledge of pedagogy.

Conclusion

Whilst this chapter has focused on Shulman's professional knowledge bases, it is clear that the professional knowledge needed by teachers is subject to debate. We can see this in how the Professional Standards for teachers in different jurisdictions value different aspects of professional practice (DfE, 2011; GTCNI, 2011; GTCS, 2012; Welsh Government, 2017). Shulman's model offers a starting point that has been reviewed and adapted by others. The general consensus is that PCK represents the distinctive knowledge base of teaching and strengthens its claim to professional status. Developing PCK is a challenge for all early career teachers and the experiences you already have will help your knowledge base to grow. Seek out support and advice from your subject associations and more experienced teachers in school who will be able to help you make sense of these different knowledge bases – and do not be afraid to ask for support.

Further reading and resources

Anderson, L.W., Krathwohl, D.R., Airasian, P.W., Cruikshank, K.A., Mayer, R.E., Pintrich, P.R. et al. (2014) *A Taxonomy for Learning, Teaching, and Assessing: A revision of Bloom's Taxonomy of Educational Objectives*, Pearson New International edition. Harlow: Pearson.

Department for Education (DfE) (2011) *Teachers' standards*. London: DfE. Available at: https://www.gov.uk/government/publications/teachers-standards.

General Teaching Council for Northern Ireland (GTCNI) (2011) *Teaching: The reflective profession*. Belfast: GTCNI. Available at: https://gtcni.org.uk/professional-space/professional-competence/teaching-the-reflective-profession.

General Teaching Council for Scotland (GTCS) (2012) *Standards for registration*. Edinburgh: GTCS. Available at: https://www.gtcs.org.uk/professional-standards/standards-for-registration.aspx.

Guerriero, S. (ed.) (2017) *Pedagogical knowledge and the changing nature of the teaching profession*, Educational Research and Innovation. Paris: OECD Publishing. Available at: http://www.oecd.org/education/pedagogical-knowledge-and-the-changing-nature-of-the-teaching-profession-9789264270695-en.htm.

Welsh Government (2017) *Professional standards for teaching and leadership*. Cardiff: Welsh Government. Available at: https://hwb.gov.wales/professional-development/professional-standards/.

Modelling curriculum design: A conceptual approach

Chris Hanley and Mike Dore

Introduction

This chapter outlines a *conceptual* approach to curriculum development. The key theoretical resource is Meyer and Land's notion of *threshold concepts* (Land et al., 2005; Meyer and Land, 2003, 2005), which is developed with reference to other scholarly texts. A **methodological approach** to curriculum development is presented that is concerned with three interconnected strands: *what* is being taught, *how* it is taught, and *how* it is received. For an early career teacher, these are perhaps the most fundamental questions to consider, as they form the basis of every learning episode. The three strands are governed by three conceptual areas. These are *disciplinary, pedagogic*, and *pupil-centred. The disciplinary* is concerned with academic subject matter. The *pedagogic* relates to teacherly skills and knowledge. The *pupil-centred* is concerned with how curriculum content is experienced by learners.

There is a discussion of how each strand connects with key learning experiences, or *thresholds*. With reference to a vignette about teaching practice, and opportunities for critical reflection, the chapter models thinking about **curriculum** that is relevant to practice. The chapter offers a detailed example of curriculum development in English Literature while reflecting upon the ongoing challenges for curriculum makers in general. Thus, the chapter offers rich resources to both new entrants to the teaching profession and established practitioners.

Research summary: Threshold concepts

This section is concerned with the distinctive character of threshold concepts. It provides valuable context for the subsequent discussion of three strands of curriculum development: *disciplinary, pedagogic*, and *pupil-centred.*

Meyer and Land define a threshold concept as 'akin to a portal, opening up a new and previously inaccessible way of thinking about something' (2003: 1). In addition to being *transformative*, threshold concepts are *irreversible* and *integrative*. Once learned they are not easily unlearned; they also reveal the 'previously hidden interrelatedness of something' (2003: 5). They are also *bounded* in the way they connect to other 'conceptual areas', and potentially *troublesome* (2003: 6) in that they are difficult to understand and may create a deeper challenge to the pupil's identity. Meyer and Land provide a range of examples of threshold concepts in operation, linked to different academic disciplines.

Land et al. also highlight the idea of **liminality**. They refer to a pre-liminal state as concerned with 'the ways in which students approach, or come to terms with, a threshold concept' (2005: 58). They are concerned with fundamental knowledge and how it is experienced by learners. They argue that as students acquire threshold concepts, and extend their use of language in relation to those concepts, there occurs a shift in the learner's subjectivity. Therefore, threshold concepts lead not only to transformed thought but to a transfiguration of identity and adoption of an extended discourse (Meyer and Land, 2005: 374–375). For example, there will be things you remember doing at school and have never forgotten. These episodes changed you or the way you see the world, and extended your ability with language in that area and perhaps others.

Meyer and Land talk about *ways of thinking and practising*, or WTP, as a crucial 'threshold function' (2003: 12). WTP refers to the characteristic ways of thinking and doing within a discipline, so that problems and their solutions appear in particular sequences and are amenable to certain kinds of analytical and conceptual treatment. WTP is also concerned with pupils being able to see connections between thought and action in their discipline and corresponding issues in the real world (2003: 12).

A key point is that teachers need to be responsive to the different ways in which students struggle to understand. Meyer and Land cite the work of Elizabeth Ellsworth, which encourages teachers in, 'cultivating a third ear that listens not for what a student knows ... but for the terms that shape a student's knowledge, her not knowing, her forgetting, her circles of stuck places and resistances' (Ellsworth, 1997: 71, cited in Meyer and Land, 2005: 378).

The key implication is that troubles with knowledge and identity cannot be simply overcome with more efficient curriculum planning of outcomes (Meyer and Land, 2005). The aim is rather to create a 'framework of engagements' (Land et al., 2005: 57), which is *recursive*. This means that the pupil approaches the threshold material in a number of different ways, not by rote; by doing so she is inducted into the WTP of the subject area. A key insight seems to be that the pupil is moving towards the deeper patterns, or conceptual understandings, that integrate the subject matter in that discipline. For example, understanding the basic processes of algebra in mathematics opens up new aspects of mathematical knowledge that were previously unavailable: inequalities, exponents, polynomials, radical and rational expressions.

It is here where the notion of narrative is so critical. Fox writes about some pupils' 'strong resistance to this induction into the symbolic order' and how narrative can bridge the gap between 'direct experience' and the 'printed page' (1998: 145). By crafting a path through curriculum as a story of discovery and adventurous framing, you can aim to make the learning as experiential and exciting as possible. Consider this as an example. Imagine if I was teaching about the effects of sugar upon teeth in Science. I could present the learning as an academically forbidding challenge through my vocabulary and approach, and switch off many pupils in the process. This is not to suggest that the academic core ideas need to be abandoned, rather that they must come after the hook of personal interest and experiential learning. If I present my lesson as 'today we are investigating the aetiology of dental caries', all I am really asking is how does sugar cause tooth decay. How much more interesting could I make this? Some tooth decay images? How much is too much sugar quiz? A dynamic experiment? It is through this apprenticeship of independence (Birtwistle, 1998) that pupils can begin to feel a shift in their subjectivity: as someone who can and does find learning new things and acquiring new skills exciting, rewarding, and ultimately transformative. Ultimately, the teacher makes a decision that eases understanding and opens up the topic by hooking on to something that the student knows, understands or finds compelling.

Discipline

In this chapter, we draw out three aspects of conceptual thresholds, as identified by Meyer and Land. These are *disciplinary*, *pedagogic*, and *pupil-centred*. These strands are connected. The *disciplinary* strand relates to concepts in an academic subject like history, mathematics or English literature. Different subjects have different kinds of connection with the pupils' 'common-sense' apprehension of the world and the 'everyday' language that describes it. It might be possible in humanities and arts subjects to acquire a great deal of knowledge in 'everyday' language and concepts, but this is less possible in mathematics and the natural sciences (White, 2018). This reminds us that pupils enter classrooms with a variety of resources for making sense of demanding, obscure, complex or 'troublesome' knowledge (Meyer and Land, 2003). Teachers need to think carefully about how they will introduce specialist vocabulary in ways pupils can understand, and how this will connect with distinctive *ways of thinking and practising* in that subject. It is worth considering here what specialist vocabulary is relevant to your subject or phase and how you can introduce it at appropriate levels to meet the needs of the learners. You could also reflect upon the challenge of moving *between* specialist vocabularies (moving between subjects).

Example of discipline: English Literature

A key *way of thinking and practising* in English Literature concerns the context of the literary work. This means understanding how the literary work has been produced and shaped by its context of production and reception. If pupils merely learn some historical information, they run the risk of having superficial conceptual knowledge that creates 'false proxy, leading students to settle for the naïve version' (Land et al., 2005: 61). Take Shakespeare's *Macbeth* (1606), for example. Knowing about seventeenth-century witchcraft, religious separatism, and gender politics is not sufficient to fully conceptualise the play's context. What is needed is a deeper interconnected and applied knowledge about the political messages of the play and the consequences of such messages. In another example, J.B. Priestley's *An Inspector Calls* was written in 1945, but set in 1912. Pupils can be encouraged to critique the prevailing discourses in pre-Titanic 1912 and post-war 1945. What distinguishes this from mere 'exploration of context' is when both the historical and *contemporary* operation of power is questioned: pupils begin to consider how power, privilege, and responsibility co-exist in their own time.

This process of challenge and critique applies to the pupils themselves. Pupils read literary texts; literary texts also 'read' pupils. What we think about a character reveals much about our attitudes, values, and beliefs as readers. Perhaps the biggest challenge in the English classroom is to take account of and make allowance for the individuality of pupil responses and the creative independence and uniqueness of pupil readings of the chosen literature.

Prompt for reflection

When you are thinking about what you want to teach or 'upskill' in your pupils, first reflect upon *your* knowledge and experience. What makes you competent in a given topic or subject area? Think about ...

- What have I experienced and what do I know that is useful?
- What tacit knowledge do I possess and how can I recall and communicate it?
- How can I shape my knowledge into building blocks of competence that I can teach, practise, and reinforce?
- What is the school's vision for teaching and learning?
- What examples can I share with the class and how can I explain things in lots of different ways to widen my net of success?

To illustrate, let us consider how we could teach historical context to generate readings of Shakespeare's *Macbeth*. By historical context, we mean an understanding of the era in which the text was written and set. Macbeth surrenders to greedy ambition (encouraged by his wife and the witches) and perpetrates murder to keep his immoral kingship.

A traditional reading may see the text as denouncing the evil of witchcraft and human ambition, thus upholding the morality of obedience and conformity. A more nuanced reading may see the play as a character study of the corruption of power and the moral malaise that follows lusty greed, encouraging the viewer to examine the recesses of their own 'black and deep desires' (Act I, Scene IV). A more transformative reading may see the text as breaking out of an ideology that kingship is divinely anointed. Also, that the ideology of kingship and power changes in the play, and that we are encouraged to see the human frailty that exists in us all, independent of power, status, and wealth. Finally, a challenging reading may see the play as discrediting the notion of monarchy entirely: as the errors of the powerful have rippling consequences for all. It may consider that a society without hierarchy would create less misery, as Ross mourns:

> Alas, poor country!
> Almost afraid to know itself. It cannot
> Be called our mother, but our grave, where nothing,
> But who knows nothing, is once seen to smile;

> Where sighs and groans and shrieks that rend the air
> Are made, not marked; where violent sorrow seems
> A modern ecstasy.
>
> (Macbeth, IV.III)

This then gives rise to modern parallels involving critiques of political hypocrisy, scandals, and injustices.

In reference to the 'Prompt for reflection' box above, the teacher preparing to teach *Macbeth* makes a series of judgements, informed by reflections about her current knowledge and previous experience. She might decide, for example, that 'ambition' is a universal human emotion and immediately accessible to the pupils; the teaching should begin here. Handled properly, she thinks this preparatory work will create a point of entry to the abstract ideas (hierarchy, ideology) she wants to address later. Her intention is to 'hook' the pupils via the initial grounding in character feelings and motivations; she thinks this will lead them to a better understanding of the abstract material.

This seems straightforward enough, but the notion of curriculum design being rooted in the stages of 'threshold concepts' presents many challenges. Meyer and Land (2003) use the analogy of Adam and Eve's new knowledge of shame to illustrate how perception passes from innocence to experience. Another analogy here could be that of the removal of a mask: when the world is seen through a new filter, the new perception of reality is not easily apprehended.

Similarly, they argue that seeing the world as a past version of yourself can be problematic. In other words, the most effective preparation for teaching concepts is to recollect, as well as you can, *your own* difficulties with mastering them. Empathising with how pupils could struggle places you in the best position to understand how you can help them achieve mastery and assimilation.

As Davies (2002) states: 'Integration is troublesome because you need to acquire the bits before you can integrate, but once you've got the bits you need to be persuaded to see them in a different way' (cited in Meyer and Land, 2003: 6). One method of acquiring these bits is through the scaffolding process, which Sherrington (2019) likens to stabilisers on a bike. However, these can become formulaic and mechanistic if a pupil becomes over-reliant on them or is unable to free themselves from the shackles of the formula.

With English Literature, rubrics demand that certain aspects are executed with competence and fluency. However, creativity and flair in expression and contextual appreciation are needed for higher grades, which a mechanistic formula constrains rather than enables. As Sherrington states, 'the whole point of scaffolding is that, eventually, it has to be taken down' (2019: 23). Such an approach can help you to frame a narrative or story around what pupils are learning to make the topics and principles more memorable and conceptual. If pupils are trying to assimilate and practise too many ideas at once, then this can lead to conceptual overload and pupils can struggle to put all the pieces back together. It is useful to consider concepts as jigsaw pieces: if a pupil can see the picture on the box and gets a chance to fully see what is on each piece, then the likelihood of re-assimilation increases.

Pedagogy

Pedagogy is concerned with the distinctive character of teacherly skills and knowledge. Pupils will approach thresholds in a number of ways, and their understanding will take a number of forms. A key aspect of the teacher's *pedagogy* relates to his or her understanding of when and how to use particular simplifications, and how these connect with the underlying conceptual architecture of the subject.

Rosenshine's principles of instruction

In his *Principles of Instruction* (2010), Rosenshine presents ten principles that are rooted in research with classroom examples. You should not misinterpret 'instruction' as just lecturing or telling, but instead consider 'instruction' as meaning 'practice'. In other words, Rosenshine writes about how teachers can maximise their efforts with a theoretical and practical basis. Perhaps one of the most compelling suggestions is to 'only present small amounts of new material at any time, and then assist students as they practise this material' (2010: 10; reprinted in Sherrington, 2019).

Sherrington points to the importance of a 'structured curriculum' where some of the content of a subject needs 'subject specific curriculum context' (2019: 13). This requires us as teachers to be clear about what we want pupils to learn, how we can assess it, the depth and stickiness of that knowledge, and how we can build in retrieval practice to ensure that the learning is retained and conceptually accessible for applying it later. Sherrington summarises the challenge in thinking about curriculum succinctly: there is 'a "curse of knowledge" that experts experience: we don't always know what we know; we accumulate a great deal of tacit knowledge from experience in our specialist areas and it requires some thought to map this out for our novice learners' (2019: 6). We should not underestimate the importance of pedagogical concerns in the enactment of curriculum aims: it is the map by which we navigate.

Prompt for reflection

One of the key principles in thinking about curriculum is the time that you will give to guiding pupil practice. Consider the following in light of your teaching:

A teacher can help this rehearsal process by asking questions … the quality of storage will be weak if pupils only skim the material and do not engage in 'depth of processing'. It is also important that all pupils process the new material and receive feedback. (Rosenshine, 2010: 69)

Think of a difficult topic or concept you will be teaching.

- How can you break it down into parts? Can you spend more time presenting the new material and give pupils time to have meaningful practice by using and applying it independently?

- Can you build in more rehearsal time? Rushing through a curriculum may tick boxes and make us feel we are 'getting through it', but meaningful connections and rehearsal are more important and more effective if we want pupils to retain and remember.
- Can you ask more effective questions to rehearse the learning: Why is this …? What are you struggling to understand? What is the main idea? How does this link with something you already know? Can you create your own question to show your understanding? What errors can we identify? What can you now do?

Pupil-centred

Pupil *agency* is concerned with the potential in a learning situation for pupils to act upon it and to affect the nature of that situation by exercising their creative and critical capacities. Manyukhina and Wyse remind us that pupils are active 'agents' or actors in educational situations. Moreover, their 'emotions … attitudes and beliefs … concerns, aspirations and interests' (2019: 225–228) create real effects and the suggestion is, although the issue of learner agency is complicated, the teacher is concerned with maximising opportunities for pupils to take 'an active role in directing the learning process, for example, making decisions, assuming control, taking an action or refraining from one' (2019: 228).

Vignette

English teacher Sarah is teaching a literature lesson about William Golding's novel, *Lord of the Flies.* She is taking the class towards a *threshold* of understanding, involving a number of concepts. She wants the class to be able to understand that a fictional text is a produced artefact, not just an extension of life.

She thinks that some of the class will struggle to cross this threshold, but in different ways. Equally, she does not want to mislead the class by over-simplifying the concepts. Her lesson plan highlights information for herself, information about the subject, and opportunities for pupil agency. She decides to begin with a discussion of *audience responses* to *character*. The bulk of the discussion centres on pupils' 'common-sense' responses to characters in the story. What are their motives and purposes? Who do you like? Where does responsibility lie? Pupils are encouraged to reflect critically upon the experience of friendship and rivalry and about character motives, to adopt a stance about the text's key messages, as long as they support it with evidence.

Her use of *audience response* and *character* reminds the class that a subject-specific technical vocabulary has to be learned and mastered. In an earlier lesson,

Sarah introduced information relating to the author's biography, the socio-political contexts that influenced the text's production, and its underlying motives and assumptions. She touches on this information during the dialogue, thus reminding the class that the text is a produced artefact.

Thus reassured, she switches with some confidence from 'common-sense' language and concepts into technical vocabulary like *audience, character, protagonist, antagonist, tension, ambiguity, ideology,* and *imperialism*. She expects that these concepts, judiciously employed, will enable the pupils to integrate what has already been discussed within a deeper, conceptual (generalisable) understanding about how the text functions.

Prompt for reflection

Imagine you are planning a scheme or unit of work for pupils. You are aiming to provide a series of engagements with the fundamental ideas or thresholds. You want the pupils to master these before moving on, but you are aware that there will be pre-liminal variation (Meyer and Land, 2005: 384). You will need to look and listen carefully, in order to discern the different ways in which pupils approach, or do not approach, thresholds in understanding.

Plan some lessons that revisit the key ideas in various ways. In each plan, it might be useful to consider these points with your mentor:

- *Disciplinary knowledge*: you need to know which concepts to teach, and how they connect with the underlying conceptual architecture of the subject.
- *Pedagogy*: you need to understand how the concepts will be taught to make them accessible, but not to the point of over-simplification.
- *Pupil agency*: you need to consider how to connect with pupils' interests, attitudes, and beliefs. Consider how and where pupils can exercise some autonomy or creativity or make decisions.

Consider with your mentor how to foster pupils' literacy skills (reading, writing, oracy) as a way of enabling engagement with fundamental ideas.

The Early Career Framework

The Early Career Framework (DfE, 2019a) in England details the Teacher Standards and support for those in their first two years of teaching. Amongst the core aims of 'Standard 3: demonstrating good subject and curriculum knowledge' are 'ensuring pupils master foundational concepts and knowledge' and 'drawing explicit links between new content and the core concepts and principles in the subject' (2019a: 12). The iterance of 'transfer', 'linking', and 'demonstrating' shows how the curriculum intent is focused upon providing a bridge and accessible paths to pupils with core skills and knowledge. Similarly, some of the core aims of 'Standard 4: plan and teach well-structured lessons' are to use 'guides, scaffolds, and worked examples' and 'starting expositions at the point of current pupil understanding' (2019a: 15). The focus on 'concrete representations of abstract ideas' and 'making the steps in a process memorable' addresses the core purposes of effective teaching.

It is perhaps useful here to remember that a curriculum plan is not an effective curriculum: the disciplinary content, pedagogical skills, and *ways of thinking and practising* developed should open up the possibilities of a rubric document and create episodic and iterative practice. A scheme of work on volcanoes only really fulfils its purpose when the classroom practice helps pupils to take ownership and charge of their learning through the unlocking of potentially forbidding concepts by you the subject and pedagogical expert. In order to remember what this feels like for pupils, think back to a time when you began your apprenticeship or induction into a difficult subject or practice. The lack of familiarity you felt with the jargon, the expert voices, and the academic code needing to be unlocked through assistance and considerable endeavour. This is how school feels for most pupils and if they are lacking in confidence, self-efficacy or positive reference points, then this induction can be even more problematic and forbidding. It is the exciting challenge of the teacher to be creative and positive to overcome these barriers.

In your career, you will need to make decisions about curriculum and align these with the school vision. Deciding *what* you will teach and *how* are two of the steps, but a more challenging and conceptual consideration would be: how can you break this down and reinforce it through lots of examples and analogies that will get pupils to take a personal interest in the topic?

Conclusion

The key learning points of this chapter can be summarised as follows:

- Threshold concepts are gateways to learning that open up other paths and change the way that we see the world.
- Disciplinary knowledge, pedagogy, and pupil agency are all connected.
- Approach curriculum design and enactment through the lens of the uninitiated expert and identify the core steps needed to master the skill/topic.
- Pupils should be seen as active agents in learning.
- Narratives, stories, connections, hooks, episodic learning, and analogy are all key to successful teaching and learning.

Further reading and resources

Manyukhina, Y. and Wyse, D. (2019) Learner agency and the curriculum: A critical realist perspective. *The Curriculum Journal*, 30 (3): 223–243.

Sherrington, T. (2019) *Rosenshine's Principles in Action*. Woodbridge: John Catt Educational.

White, J. (2018) The weakness of 'powerful' knowledge. *London Review of Education*, 16 (2): 325–335.

3 Understanding memory

*Jennifer McGahan, Clare Nelson,
and Joanne Formosa*

Introduction

In this chapter, the importance of memory within an educational setting will be explored. You will develop an understanding of how the memory system works through cognitive models of memory and related research. There is a current trend in education to develop learning activities that facilitate the integration of new knowledge into the **long-term memory** system more effectively. This chapter aims to inform your practice and show you how to maximise the amount of information your pupils remember using evidence from the learning sciences.

Before we jump to classroom implementation, it is important that you first develop a basic understanding of the memory system. 'Memory' is often thought of as one single process; in fact, 'memory' is an umbrella term for a number of functionally separate systems. The first distinction we must acknowledge is between *working* and *long-term* memory processes.

Long-term memory

Long-term memory refers to a cognitive process that allows us to perceive and process (encode), store and then subsequently retrieve information. The capacity of the long-term memory is theoretically limitless. The concept of memory remains strongly associated with learning and is something we all have a basic understanding of both within and outside the classroom. Whether we are revising for an exam, trying to remember pupils' names or just driving home, an intact long-term memory system is essential for normal everyday functioning.

Long-term memory is supported by two separate systems: *episodic* and *semantic*. Memory for factual information relies on the **semantic memory** system; when recalling how many wives Henry VIII had, or the capital of France, we use this system. Semantic memory can be measured via vocabulary, reading and writing ability, and comprehension – skills that develop steadily throughout childhood. Importantly, the recall of semantic information is context free, meaning that we do not recall when we learnt a particular fact, we simply recall the details of the fact. Recalling contextual information from past personal events or autobiographical information (for example, recalling where you ate breakfast this morning) relies on a different system, known as episodic memory. As children's brains develop, their **episodic memory** abilities increase, supporting better recall of information from events they have experienced. Studies have shown that there are sharp increases in episodic memory recall during middle childhood

(6–12 years). Asking pupils to recall what they did during the school holidays will be much more challenging for 4- and 5-year-olds compared to 8- or 9-year-olds due to an underdeveloped episodic memory system.

When pupils learn new information in your classroom, they may activate both the semantic and episodic memory systems. When asked to recall information from a topic covered previously, pupils may: (1) recall the lesson; (2) recall information taught in the lesson; (3) recall both the lesson and the information.

Working memory

Working memory refers to a system that stores and simultaneously processes information, and is different from the long-term memory system because it has a very limited capacity. The working memory system has various subsystems (phonological loop, visuospatial sketch pad, episodic buffer, and the central executive) and combines various processing mechanisms, including visual and auditory inputs (Baddeley, 2000; Baddeley and Hitch, 1974). Working memory is a limited capacity store both in terms of how *much* information is can hold (3–4 items) and also how *long* it can hold it for (15–20 seconds). This is important in the classroom because this system can easily become overwhelmed during learning activities. Working memory functions develop gradually from 4 years of age continuing into adolescence (Gathercole et al., 2004). Pupils' ability to hold and manipulate information will improve gradually throughout their schooling. In the classroom, pupils use their working memory system for many tasks, including copying work from the board, completing tasks with multiple instructions such as 'put your pen down, go to your tray, get out your reading book and turn to page 18', and reading.

Working memory and reading

The aim of reading is to comprehend a text. To do this, individuals must visually process the words, then match the words to existing knowledge in the long-term memory system (sounds, spellings, punctuation, meaning of words). Next, we combine this information with the context to understand the passage. Working memory keeps all of this relevant information available, whilst information is being retrieved from long-term memory, and then integrates all sources of information to comprehend the meaning.

Now that you have a good understanding of these two memory systems, it is time to consider how you can plan and deliver lessons that exploit these processes and improve learning in your pupils.

Prompt for reflection

When planning your lessons, do you consider the constraints of your pupils' memory abilities?

Cognitive load

Learning large amounts of new information can feel overwhelming and frustrating, a feeling every learner has experienced at some point. **Cognitive load** theory states that learning is compromised when the demands of a task exceed processing capacity (Sweller, 2010). This theory links into working memory and its limited capabilities. Learning a new topic with a lot of novel content, and completing complex tasks related to it, may overload a pupil's working memory system. For example, an introductory lesson on 'memory' will introduce new words (episodic, semantic), may refer to complex neuroanatomical structures (parahippocampal cortex), whilst alluding to abstract processes (**encoding** and **retrieval**). Holding all of this information in the working memory system exceeds capacity and ultimately interferes with the processing and storage of this new information (known as schema acquisition). Schemas are mental representations that refer to objects, ideas, groups of information on a topic, or concepts. Once a schema is acquired, more complex information can be added incrementally. You have hopefully added to your existing 'memory schema' after reading this first part of the chapter!

Crucially, schemas are stored in the long-term memory system where infinite amounts of information can be stored and retrieved. When required, schemas can be transferred back to working memory to support new learning. When this happens, schemas are processed by the working memory system as a single entity rather than its many constituent parts. This allows the working memory system to hold and advance complex constructs that would otherwise exceed its capacity. When you were reading the information at the start of the chapter, you activated your existing schema for 'memory' and whilst reading the information you (hopefully!) added more information to this representation. However, if you had no previous schema for 'memory' in your long-term memory, it is likely that your working memory system would become overwhelmed with this new concept and information. Similarly, setting a complex comprehension test for a pupil with a limited vocabulary will overwhelm their working memory systems very quickly, resulting in an inability to complete the task.

Here are some ideas on how to reduce cognitive load in your classroom:

Daily review. Starting lessons with a 'daily review' reduces cognitive load by retrieving schemas from the long-term memory (this is one of Rosenshine's principles of action; see 'Further reading and resources' for more information). This review can take place daily or at longer intervals, but crucially it should ask pupils to retrieve information from previous lessons that overlap with information you plan to teach. Retrieving this information from the long-term memory system frees up the working memory system when presenting new information during your lesson.

Instructions. Instructions given to pupils should reduce cognitive load; tasks with minimal guidance are less effective than tasks with clear instructions. When problem-solving, pupils who are shown a solution or the teacher 'thinks aloud' frequently outperform pupils who have to solve a problem for themselves. When a problem is modelled for pupils in the first instance, they are able to 'borrow' from existing information in their long-term memory and reorganise the schema to solve the problem. If teachers do not model a solution,

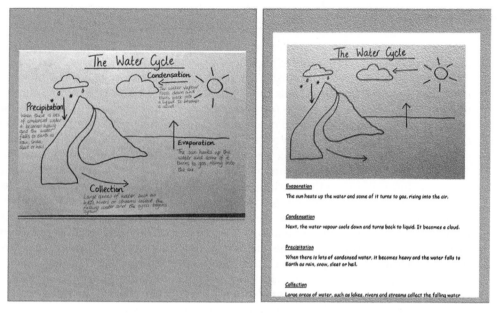

Figure 3.1 Example of split and integrated worksheets
Provided by Claire Nelson, Cheadle Catholic Infant School

there are huge demands on the working memory system; pupils are required to retain the instructions, generate solutions, and test procedures. Instead, adopt a fading procedure as pupils master a topic, with the level of teacher input decreasing as pupils' ability increases. As schemas become more complex, pupils will be more able to categorise new information and problems, requiring less support as they move from being a novice to an expert on specific tasks.

Presentation format. A task that requires pupils to split their attention between various sources creates additional cognitive load. Consequently, cognitive load is increased when the presentation of information is fragmented. This will occur, for example, if a worksheet has a diagram on one page and an explanation for the diagram on another page. It is preferable for diagrams and key information to be combined into a single figure rather than being presented side by side. When information is separate, pupils need to expend working memory reserves to integrate the different sources, reducing the capacity for learning the information (see Figure 3.1).

Prompts for reflection

When introducing a new topic, do you show pupils how you can reduce cognitive load? How could the resources in your lesson have a positive impact on cognitive load?

Retrieval practice

One way to increase long-term memory is by engaging in retrieval practice – in other words, testing yourself. This strategy is often referred to as the 'testing effect' (Roediger and Karpicke, 2006). It is important to differentiate the term 'retrieval' in this memory context from 'retrieval' often used in the classroom to refer to a reading skill using a text to find an answer. Testing improves learning more than re-studying information repeatedly because testing slows down the forgetting rate compared with re-study. Testing activates the long-term memory system during the search for, and retrieval of, an answer. During a test, pupils may activate their episodic system (to recall the lesson on that topic) and/or their semantic system (to recall a fact). Conversely, re-study involves encoding information multiple times (for example, reading or highlighting revision notes) with limited activation of the long-term memory system in an outward direction. Re-studying activities can create a false sense of familiarity for information, whereas testing is effortful and at times frustrating for the learner. This is the reason why, despite the indisputable benefits of testing, people frequently adopt re-studying as their preferred learning strategy. Studies have shown that most pupils will not spontaneously adopt test-based strategies. This leaves the responsibility with teachers to incorporate retrieval activities into lessons and homework. Teaching pupils about the substantial advantages of testing can be an effective way to encourage them to use testing as a learning tool (see the section on 'metamemory' below for more information).

The literature on the testing effect is extensive; however, implementing this approach effectively in the classroom can be problematic. Here are some things to consider:

Test format. Tests must require pupils to retrieve information without relying on notes, textbooks or wall displays. This retrieval can take the form of short-answer questions, mind maps or multiple-choice tests, all of which can result in improved learning. However, it is important to remember that multiple-choice tests include lures and this can lead to the creation of false knowledge, whereby pupils learn the wrong answer. Multiple-choice tests also offer pupils the option of guessing. To ensure that pupils retrieve information and do not just choose the 'familiar' answer, all multiple-choice options should have been encountered before. For example, answers to the question 'Which memory system supports the recall of facts?' could be: 'semantic / episodic / working'. All these options should feel equally familiar to the pupils; to answer the question correctly, they need to retrieve information that differentiates them.

The optimum test format utilises short-answer questions and includes corrective feedback to avoid pupils learning incorrect responses. The most effective way to test pupils and avoid false knowledge creation is to provide corrective feedback. Studies show that on multiple-choice tests delayed feedback is more effective than immediate feedback (correct answer presented after each question). Feedback also helps pupils to monitor their learning progress when using regular testing in the classroom. Retrieval practice combined with corrective feedback enhances individuals' motivation because they can evaluate their competence on a learning task (Abel and Bäuml, 2020).

Retrieval practice works best when pupils have to work hard to recall the information. One way to make it more difficult is to increase the length of time between tests. There is a large body of evidence that shows that spaced retrieval is much more effective than mass practice (cramming for an exam). Revisiting topics throughout the year via retrieval-based tests results in better long-term memory for a topic. Test content should avoid immediate retrieval (testing directly after an activity) and should instead cover content covered yesterday, last week or last term. An easy way to incorporate spaced testing is to set homework retrieval tasks based on previous classes instead of the current week.

Classroom environment. Testing pupils in the classroom may involve small group discussions or the teacher asking the whole class a question. When pupils are tested in this way, the benefits are not the same for everyone because listening to others recall information is not as beneficial as retrieving the information yourself. To make 'group' testing beneficial to everyone in the class, pupils who do not provide the answer should be asked to focus on their own retrieval performance rather than the pupil answering the question. You could ask everyone in the class to write down an answer. Selecting one pupil to answer a question in the classroom will not encourage this effortful process in other class members. As the teacher, you could try to make each student potentially responsible to provide an answer (Abel and Roediger, 2018). This can be achieved by randomly selecting pupils to answer questions, rather than asking a general question and selecting a willing pupil. Writing names on lolly sticks and drawing names at random to answer questions is one way to encourage everyone in the class to prepare an answer. Whole-class retrieval can also be adapted to decrease cognitive load by teachers writing down the answers from pupils on a whiteboard during this activity and expanding the answers as a group. Writing down responses provides pupils with a concrete reference point when processing new information offered by the teacher and other pupils. Utilising an **ABC questioning method** (**A**dd anything, **B**uild on the answer, **C**hallenge then answer) allows the teacher to create clear links between previous answers, reducing cognitive load.

Prompt for reflection

Do my class tests require pupils to retrieve information? How do I make sure that all pupils are engaged and have retrieved information during group teaching?

Below are two examples from practice. The first is an example of how one school introduced a new strategy for retrieval in their history lessons. The second example shows how one teacher worked to improve memory following a field trip.

Practice example 1: 'History mystery' box

Claire Nelson, Cheadle Catholic Infant School

As the history subject leader for my school, I identified that the facts Year 2 pupils (age 6–7) were learning during a topic were not easily recalled later in the year. The children did not naturally make connections between the historical topics they learnt and they only remembered the most obvious and basic facts once the topic had finished. I had created a scheme of work that lent itself to overlapping topics so that knowledge and skills could be built on from Year 1 to Year 2. I wanted an additional tool that would help children to revisit and make links between different historical topics, as well as aiding transition to the junior school. I decided to try a 'history mystery' box.

The box itself is nothing special, just a cardboard box that had been decorated. The box contained photographs/pictures of significant historical figures that the children had previously learnt about in Year 1 and 2 (Neil Armstrong, Grace Darling, Mary Anning, Kelly Holmes, Walter Tull, James Kirk, Gertrude Powicke, Fred Perry, and Sarah Storey). The aim was to start each history lesson with a quick retrieval activity using a prompt from the box, to ensure that pupils were regularly recalling information from previous topics. Some examples of the sort of activities we might ask the children to do in this ten-minute recap session are:

- with a partner write down at least three things you know about X
- tell me two things the same and two things that are different about X and X
- who do you think is the biggest hero, X or X? Say why.

The children would work either with a partner or alone and then would be randomly called upon (using names on lolly sticks) after five minutes to share what they had come up with. We noticed that after a few weeks the answers that children came up with started to become more sophisticated, as they became more comfortable with the expectations of the activity. Children began to organise their ideas (on whiteboards, without prompting) in different ways. For example, one pair put their comparison of Grace Darling and Mary Anning into a Venn diagram to demonstrate the similarities and differences, something we had done with different people in a previous history lesson three or four months earlier.

One history lesson I decided to do something different with the box. A small group of children asked me if they could look at the box by themselves. I was pleased that they had asked and took it as a sign that they were enjoying the sessions at the start of each lesson. I told them that they could use the box after their history lesson. Using whiteboards and pens the pupils were left to explore the box independently. Initially, the children wrote down facts they could remember about different people, then someone had an idea – by recalling information from previous lessons, the pupils worked together to create a timeline (see Figure 3.2). The children ordered the pictures in a justifiable chronological order from Grace Darling through to Sarah Storey.

It was amazing how much I learnt about these children's understanding as I watched them work together. I could see them question each other, recall facts,

C: I am going to make a timeline.

O: What? What can we use to make a timeline?

C: The people and heroes. We can try to put them in order and make a timeline.

(C started making a timeline and putting them into an order. This attracted other children who came to see what she was doing and they started to discuss whether the order was correct and who should go where)

F: The moon landing was 50 years ago and that's a really long time ago. That one should go first. Actually, we learnt about it in Year 1 so it must be 51 years ago now.

L: Yes, but look at the pictures. There is a photo of Neil Armstrong but only paintings of Grace Darling and Mary Anning, so they must go first on the timeline.

F: Oh! So where would this go?

B: What war was James Kirk in? Was it the First or the Second World War?

S: Well, Sarah Storey must go at the end of the timeline because she is still alive today.

N: Let's put Gertrude Powicke and James Kirk next to each other because they both were in the First World War.

L: Well Gertrude Powicke should go last because she died just a little bit after the war.

F: What about Fred Perry?

S: His photo is black and white so he must go near them (by which S meant other people with black and white photos). Before or after?

L: I think the war was before Fred Perry.

Figure 3.2 Conversation between pupils using the 'History Mystery' box

use sources, create a timeline, justify their ideas. One of the most gratifying things was the wide range of abilities working on this activity, and everyone was able to contribute and recall information relevant to the task in hand.

I would have loved to have added some historical events as well (they knew about the first moon landing and the Great Fire of London, so it would have been interesting to see how they fitted in too). We will be introducing history mystery boxes to Year 1 as well, so that the box can travel with them to Year 2. We also want the children to take the box with them to Year 3 so that their new teacher (in the junior school) will be able to see what they have learnt and will be able to build on their prior learning from Key Stage 1.

The history mystery box demonstrates that spaced retrieval throughout the year does improve long-term memory and results in detailed recall for each photograph; this would not have been a fun activity for the pupils if the information was difficult to retrieve or forgotten entirely. The pupils used the photographs to cue retrieval of rich, detailed information including names, dates, and events. By engaging in this activity, the pupils improved their long-term memory further.

Practice example 2: Geography field trip

Joanne Formosa, River View Primary School

Pupils aged 9–10 years were taken on a geography school trip to a local country park, where they would explore the features of a rural landscape and learn the names of trees, plants, and animals which grow/live there. The aim of the school trip was to improve pupils' understanding of contrasting urban and rural landscapes. Throughout the visit the children were engaged in discussions focused on these landscapes, and prompt sheets were used to assist children in exploring the environment and identifying plant and animal species. On the way back to school, the teacher began questioning the children about the trip; some children were unable to recall the name of the country park and had already forgotten some of the plants and trees that they had studied.

The same afternoon the teacher held a discussion with a random selection of eight mixed-ability pupils on a one-to-one basis. The questions asked ranged from specific ones such as 'Can you name some of the trees?', to open-ended questions such as 'Can you explain what a rural landscape is?' and 'Can you compare a rural and urban landscape?' It was clear that all of the pupils could only recall a limited amount of information even when prompted. Whilst half of the children recalled some of the specific species (e.g. a type of fungi or plant), none of them could remember with any clarity the differences between an urban and rural landscape. Interestingly, half of the children spoke about things that were not the focus of the visit at all, such as the story trail and the children's play park. To improve memory for this information the teacher developed a plan:

> **Review:** each geography lesson for five days following the trip would start with a daily review to reduce cognitive load.

> **Prompt sheet:** using the sheet from the trip as visual support, pupils were required to learn the species of plants, trees, and animals again. The following day the names of the trees and plants were removed from the prompt sheet and the class teacher used a range of strategies to review these including using vocabulary, images of the plants and trees, and photographs taken during the trip.

> **Modelling:** the teacher carefully modelled the information relating to urban and rural landscapes and used questioning to develop language, with the children having access to their vocabulary sheet. On day four, the teacher verbally modelled how to compare an urban landscape with a rural one. The following day the children worked in pairs to describe the differences between an urban and rural landscape. This learning took place in short intervals of no more than fifteen minutes each.

At the end of the five days following the trip, the same pupils took part in a discussion group and were questioned about rural and urban landscapes. This time all of the pupils showed a marked improvement in their ability to retrieve the names of trees, plants, and animals, and they were able to refer to the specific features of a rural landscape and use specific vocabulary. The children were able to make clear connections to the visit to the country park and could compare rural and urban landscapes with greater clarity. The learning was reviewed after four weeks and then again each half term; the children completed a paper-based quiz each half term and were able to answer questions on the test sheet and verbalise their learning during discussions.

Metamemory

Metamemory is a type of **metacognition** that involves the self-monitoring and self-control of memory processes, including knowledge of your own memory capabilities and strategies (highlighting my notes helps me to remember / I am brilliant at remembering the words to songs) as well an understanding of how the memory system works and varies between tasks and situations (e.g. I can overload my working memory system because it has a limited capacity). It involves decisions we make about the following: study time allocation, activities we select when we know we will have to remember something in the future (e.g. rehearsal), and what information we should focus on during learning activities (parts of the lesson you did enjoy or parts you found difficult). Metamemory also involves confidence judgements of our own abilities. Research shows that younger children greatly overestimate their memory capacity, but this metamemory judgement improves with age.

As a teacher, you want pupils to remember the information in your classes, but you also want them to develop lasting habits that will facilitate learning in other environments. Metamemory is central to this process; pupils need to develop an awareness of what effective strategies look like and when to employ them. Research shows that teaching pupils effective strategies will not necessarily improve memory performance. Instead, for improvement in learning, pupils need explicit encouragement and modelling of metamemory strategies. Even when pupils see the increased benefits of a particular memory strategy, transfer to other tasks is not spontaneous, particularly in young children. Teaching pupils to be autonomous learners is more relevant than ever since the reintroduction of linear GCSEs and A levels in England. Pupils are required to recall large amounts of information over extended periods to pass exams, thus monitoring and employing effective strategies is crucial. There are some important things to consider when developing metamemory in your pupils:

Control. Motivation is important for any behaviour change; it is crucial that pupils see successful remembering as something they control. Pupils who believe that effort and strategy result in successful learning do better on memory tests than pupils who believe successful learning happens by chance. Teachers can challenge beliefs by encouraging reflection and modification of strategies following a learning task. Reflection and monitoring teaches pupils that successful memory recall is within their control because deliberate memory strategies lead to more success.

Transfer. To be successful, a metamemory strategy must be transferable across tasks. Research has found that strategies were transferred when 7–8-year-old pupils were taught three monitoring skills: (1) *assessment* – to reflect on the success of a strategy; (2) *attribution* – to attribute success to a specific strategy; and (3) *selection* – compare various strategies and identify the best one. Selection was found to be crucial for transfer because it involved judgements on the effectiveness of strategies, rather than being told which one to use. Regular prompts instructing children to 'think back' to the monitoring training session were required to cue strategy use. Consistent prompts are especially important for younger pupils who may not retain or transfer strategies easily. When an elaboration technique (e.g. remember a dog and a hat are a pair by imagining the dog wearing the hat) was successfully taught to 5–6-year-olds, they identified it as more effective than rehearsal. However, spontaneous uptake and transfer of this strategy was uncommon in 5–6-year-olds. Conversely, children aged 10 years and above did adopt the elaboration strategy (Schneider, 1985).

Developmental differences. Metamemory abilities develop throughout childhood and adolescence as memory systems mature. It is important to remember that a strategy that will work for older pupils may not be effective for younger pupils. For example, on a list learning test younger children did not benefit from extra learning opportunities in-between trials (here is a list of the items you did not remember) because they could not differentiate between items they recalled and forgot. Older children (10 or 11 years of age) did benefit from the extra learning opportunity because they used this time to encode the items they missed. You can support young children with this type of activity by highlighting the missed items and encouraging use of this attentional strategy.

Successful recall of prose relies on pupils being able to differentiate between salient and trivial details. Studies show that directing attention to important aspects of the prose in this way is a metamemory strategy that gradually improves with age (from 7 years continuing into older adolescence). This has important implications for class activities; tests with younger pupils should avoid unstructured retrieval of information such as 'write down everything you can remember about the story'. Using specific questions about characters or concepts will help younger pupils to cue retrieval of important information. Older pupils, particularly those aged 11 and above, will be more able to select important information and will benefit from less structured tests that require the creation of their own cues. Reflection and self-regulation are at the crux of successful metamemory development. Pupils need to continually adapt their strategies as demands increase throughout their schooling.

Here is an example of how to integrate metamemory activities into a primary lesson.

Practice example 3: Metamemory in the classroom

Claire Nelson, Cheadle Catholic Infant School

Shapes is an area of mathematical learning that is difficult for children to remember, particularly when it has not been taught for a while. The names and properties of the shapes are often muddled and as shapes is taught less frequently than number facts and calculations, sometimes children struggle to retain what they have learnt. This is not surprising as a number of shapes are aesthetically and phonetically very similar (hexagon, pentagon, and heptagon). This makes it is a perfect opportunity to use metamemory techniques.

Lesson: 2D shapes
Objective: To identify and describe the properties of 2D shapes, including the number of sides.
Activity: Talk about the names of shapes and how many different sides they have. As a class talk about the shapes pupils remember easily and identify others that are harder to remember. Have a short discussion about how they remember shape names. At this point, introduce the idea that we use different memory 'tricks' to remember this kind of information. Explain that today they are going to explore the shapes and come up with a little story or connection that will help them to remember the number of sides for each shape.

As a class, work through one example and come up with a little story or visual image to go with an octagon. The teacher models the thought process and shows them how to do it by 'think talking', using a running commentary as they work (e.g. an octagon has eight sides, I am going to remember that fact by thinking about an octopus and it's eight legs and also starts with the sound 'oct').

Then, put the children into pairs or small groups. Each group has a small collection of 2D shapes (e.g. circle, hexagon, pentagon, octagon). The children are given time to look at, feel, and explore the shapes and then talk to each other about how they are going to remember the number of sides for each shape. It is important that each child generates their own unique memory cue for each shape. To ensure that this strategy is effective, pupils must be able to generate this cue later and they also need to retrieve their cue from both looking at that shape and hearing / reading the shape name. One great example provided by a Year 2 pupil was a pentagon – you hold a pen with five fingers in your hand and it has five sides. At intervals throughout the lesson, encourage children to share some interesting examples but stress that each strategy will probably be different, since everyone will remember it in different ways.

Importantly, this is not where this tasks ends. The teacher should revisit this information and encourage the children to recall their strategies in another lesson, combining both retrieval practice and practice of their strategies and cues. Pupils should reflect on the strategy and the teacher enquire about how useful it was for the children, where possible making direct comparisons to other strategies. Reference to the use of the memory strategies should be referred to before encouraging this technique again in subsequent lessons.

Integrating memory techniques into your lessons can involve relatively simple adjustments. Rather than trying to include each approach separately, we hope that the examples provided give you some ideas of how to combine the approaches. The shapes lesson, for example, involves developing metamemory strategies, retrieval activities, and reduction of cognitive load (via modelling and the elaboration strategy relying on existing schemas). Regular use of these techniques alongside explanations, justifications, and reflection will improve the amount of information your pupils encode, store, and retrieve from their long-term memory system.

Prompt for reflection

Which areas of learning could you apply this strategy to? How could you model metamemory techniques for the pupils in your class?

Conclusion

For most people, their long-term memory systems function effortlessly. We remember huge amounts of information with ease, only paying attention when it fails us. For many, this automaticity can be a barrier to learning because we consider memory an involuntary reflex that we have no control over. I hope that after reading this chapter you now feel that this is very much to the contrary. Raising your awareness of this extraordinary system is an empowering process and teaching your pupils how to monitor and manipulate this system will support lifelong learning. To quote the famous educational psychologist John Sweller, 'If nothing has changed in long-term memory, nothing has been learned' (2011: 5).

Further reading and resources

Brown, P.C., Roediger III, H.L. and McDaniel, M.A. (2014) *Make it Stick*. Cambridge, MA: Harvard University Press.

Doolittle, P. (2013) How your 'working memory' makes sense of the world, *TED Talk*, June. Available at: https://www.ted.com/talks/peter_doolittle_how_your_working_memory_makes_sense_of_the_world?language=en#t-548976.

Education Endowment Foundation (EEF) (2019b) *Metacognition and self-regulated learning*, Guidance report. Available at: https://educationendowmentfoundation.org.uk/tools/guidance-reports/metacognition-and-self-regulated-learning/.

Rosenshine, B. (2012) Principles of instruction: Research-based strategies that all teachers should know. *American Educator*, 36 (1): 12–19.

Sherrington, T. (2019) *Rosenshine's Principles in Action*. Woodbridge: John Catt Educational.

4 At the crossroads: A roadmap for navigating the complexities of behaviour management

Joe Barber and Mark Sackville-Ford

Introduction

The purpose of this chapter is to support you as an early career teacher to think deeply about the nature of behaviour and the associated concept of behaviour management within a school setting. We aim to offer a roadmap for the ways that behaviour is conceptualised and theorised. By considering the relatedness of three different domains, you will be in a more informed position to develop your own philosophy of behaviour by combining theory with **praxis**. At the same time, we encourage self-reflection on your experiences, values, and beliefs and how these will influence your approach to behaviour.

Figure 4.1 is used as a structure for the chapter, as we believe it helps to provide a roadmap for exploring and understanding the complexities of behaviour. Throughout the chapter, we hope that in each of the three domains you are able to reflect and work to understand how behaviour is operating in each area, and to map the congruency and disparity between them in your own educational world. We argue that by producing your own individual roadmap, you can identify ways to continue productively on your journey with 'behaviour'. The greater the congruency

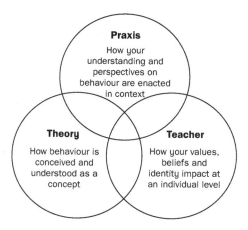

Figure 4.1 Holistic model for understanding behaviour

between the three domains, the more effective we believe your own understanding and practice of behaviour will be. Where there is a disparity, we encourage you to think about why this is problematic and how you might respond to it.

Praxis – that is, putting theory into practice – is an important word for you in considering the relationship between what approaches you are aware of, what you accept, reject, and implicate, and how you enact them in the context of your classroom. There can be a disconnect between an idea and the way in which we execute it practically. This might also involve us as teachers doing things in our classrooms without really thinking about how and why we do them.

Before we consider what you *do*, a useful and important place to begin is to consider how you frame the behaviours of children in the way that you *think*. Your initial teacher education (ITE) is likely to have introduced you to some debates about behaviour management, the typical ways that schools construct guidelines and routines to deal with unwanted behaviours, as well as offering you some strategies for dealing with 'low-level disruptions' or more challenging behaviours. You may have been trained as a newly qualified teacher (NQT) on the school's particular system, and you will no doubt be familiar with how to move through the striations and stratifications of it, as well as which school staff are key in its implementation.

This brings us to the final point in this introduction. We propose that there is not necessarily a correct way for schools to organise systems, structures, and policies around behaviour. For this reason, we will attempt to give examples of school practices that might align with certain standpoints. The authors have their own personal philosophies of behaviour that will naturally influence this chapter, but rather than explicitly talk to this, we encourage the reader to form their own or think critically about ours.

Once you begin teaching, the school's system will often become your principal means of dealing with pupils and it can easily become the totality of your understanding and skillset when it comes to being a teacher. You are unlikely to have much time to read many books or attend CPD sessions aimed at developing your practice, and if you do, the advice can seem competing, conflicting, and sometimes conceptual to the point of being impossible for you to implement within your own classroom and practice.

Prompt for reflection

Consider the following questions:

How does your school 'frame' pupil behaviour?
What counts as poor behaviour in classrooms?
How is this communicated to pupils in words and deeds?
What routines are insisted upon and what purposes do they serve?
How do you interpret a child's refusal to meet your expectations or follow rules?
What kinds of behaviours are likely to 'push your buttons'?
How aware are you of how this makes you feel?
What sort of responses do you usually give to these?

Praxis: How your understanding and perspectives on behaviour are enacted in context

As an early career teacher, you will have spent considerable time thinking about the practicalities of the management of behaviour in your classroom. Those of you who are primary teachers will have thought carefully about child development and the ages of the children you are supporting, and how to adapt your approach appropriately. Those of you who are teaching in a secondary school or college will have thought about the context of your subject, differences within and between classes, plus the impact of the timetable on engagement and motivation. You will have watched experienced teachers leading a classroom. You will have borrowed some of these techniques, some of which will have worked for you and some not. Thinking about why, or why not, in each case is important for your development.

Whilst we acknowledge the value of learning directly from others, we argue that too often behaviour is reduced to a set of approaches, strategies, tricks, and tips. Whilst there is evidence that some of these approaches work, particularly in the short term, it is not unusual for them to lack a theoretical underpinning, meaning that they are at best simplified, and at worst they counteract one another. This can result in a confusing set of policies and practices in schools that rely on outdated notions of authority and power, relationships and control.

We baulk at the idea of a 'toolbox' of strategies for behaviour management because it presents behaviour as a 'problem' that has an easy 'fix'. In other words, it is a reductive way to consider behaviour management, and is likely to limit the development of your practice because it underestimates the nuances of human behaviour and adult–child interaction. Such approaches can offer some valuable strategies, but we argue that these should be used to build upon a considered exploration and examination of pupil behaviour. Training courses on 'behaviour management' can be entertaining and engaging, but may ultimately offer an over-simplified notion of needing to 'manage' behaviour. This very typical and dominant approach aligns with the theory of behaviourism, which we return to in more detail later in the chapter.

This is not an attempt to eschew the tenets of behaviourism, but to help early career teachers become aware that many approaches fit within this paradigm, that they may not actually have concord with it (although their praxis indicates otherwise), and to open up other ways of framing children's behaviour in schools and classrooms. It should also be said that the authors have always maintained high expectations of children's behaviour with a view to maximal learning and development taking place within the classroom.

It is common for student and early career teachers to want more input on 'behaviour management' and to feel underprepared for entering the classroom. They often reject any value in learning about theory and want to cut straight to knowing how to maintain authority and assert control at all times. We suggest there is no short cut and instead adopting the three-domain approach will assist you in being active in your own development. The simple enactment of strategies is unlikely to develop your efficacy as a teacher and will typically lead to you feeling on the attack, under attack, or prepared for battle. Classrooms and schools should not be not battlegrounds whereupon the fight for control becomes the principal goal. Therefore, your practice cannot be seen in isolation from a theoretical and paradigmatic context – there *is* one at work in what you *do*. To consider your praxis in a more holistic way will develop your skill, your effectiveness, and your confidence as a teacher.

As an early career teacher, it is important to develop research and policy literacy – that is, to examine and evaluate the guidance you are offered. For example, in seeking to simplify the complexities of behaviour for the beginning teacher, the Early Career Framework in England relies on a set of approaches that are offered to teachers as the way to 'manage behaviour effectively'. It suggests that teachers should learn to:

- develop a positive, predictable, and safe environment for pupils
- establish effective routines and expectations
- build trusting relationships
- motivate pupils.

These four objectives are very sound suggestions. However, such simple imperatives are not without unhelpful complexities and take for granted a starting point that warrants theoretical discussion and debate. For instance, in establishing the 'correct' environment for pupils, teachers are told that they should do so 'by establishing a supportive and inclusive environment with a predictable system of reward and sanction in the classroom' (DfE, 2019a: 26). We will explore 'behaviourism' in more detail later in the chapter, but the concept of 'rewards and sanctions' is underpinned by a very definite theory of behaviour. It can be argued that the behaviourist approach might clash with the notion of a 'supportive and inclusive environment' that is offered in the same sentence. Consider for a moment a pupil who is experiencing an emotional crisis and whose behaviour leads to classroom disruption. How can this pupil be supported and made to feel safe at the same time as accepting a sanction? There is a need to develop an understanding of theoretical disparities between practices prescribed in policy.

Policy

The way that schools translate practice around behaviour is to put this into a policy document. Such systems can enable teachers and pupils to operate with transparency and consistency throughout the school but they can also erode the autonomy of the teacher in developing their own understanding of behaviour. Teachers can become overly reliant on the system and stall their own efficacy and impact on the development of productive and respectful relationships with pupils (Barber and Noble, 2020).

A key consideration of many policies is 'consistency'. However, this is much harder to achieve in practice. Teachers and students are social beings and human interaction cannot be reduced to a set of checklists or approaches, without them being interpreted and subtly adjusted. As a teacher, you are not piloting a ship or operating a machine. Instead, at an individual level, we view different pupils' behaviour differently, we build relationships with pupils differently, and teachers themselves are different. This is something we will explore more in the 'Teacher' domain later in the chapter.

You may feel that as an early career teacher you have little influence over policy and in order to fulfil the requirements of the Teachers' Standards, you might feel the need to evidence your competence by implementing national and local policy. As a longer-term professional aim, however, we encourage you to engage critically with approaches presented to you. Teachers have a professional responsibility to assess interventions that influence the education and care of children and young people. It is important to consider the knowledge base that informs the pedagogical strategies that are recommended to us. Are the principles guiding professional action political, ideological, philosophical, or evidence-based?

Prompt for reflection

Review the Early Career Framework. Can you identify the influence of behaviourism throughout Standard 7? Alongside this, look at Standard 1 and its emphasis on wellbeing, trust, and relationships. How might this lead to disparity in the classroom?

What would happen if we did not have a behaviour policy?

At this stage in your career, it is useful to ask difficult questions. It does seem reckless to propose the removal of behaviour policies. After all, this is a statutory requirement from central government. However, some schools are moving away from having a 'behaviour policy' and are shifting towards having a 'relationship policy' instead. These schools have usually done significant theorising about behaviour and have agreed on an approach that relies much more on a relational model, rather than conceptualising behaviour as something that requires 'managing'. One school that we have written about elsewhere (Sackville-Ford and Baggaley, 2020) is Barrowford Primary School, which has adopted a compassionate approach to behaviour, founded on notions of restorative approaches and a redistribution of power:

> We recognise that most children self-regulate their behaviour and never need reminding about how to behave appropriately … Our relationship policy is not primarily concerned with rule enforcement. It is a tool used to promote good relationships, so that people can work together with the common purpose of helping everyone learn. (Barrowford Primary School, 2019: 2)

It is interesting to note that it is more challenging to find secondary schools that subscribe to a rewards and punishment-free approach, particularly in the mainstream.

Theory: How is behaviour understood as a concept?

In this section of the chapter, we map out theories of behaviour in order to help you understand how these might align with each other and your own practice.

Figure 4.2 Framework for theories of behaviour

Figure 4.2 presents three broad categories of approaches to behaviour in schools, conceived as a broad spectrum. In this chapter, we want to focus on 'guiding' and 'controlling', as these act as the main structures for theorising behaviour in schools. We agree with Porter (2014) that the concept of 'indulging', whilst important for giving context here, is not an approach advocated in schools. However, it is included here to demonstrate that we are not wanting to create a binary system for the guidance and controlling approaches to behaviour. Instead, there is a spectrum of approaches that overlap and are nuanced rather than simplistic representations of opposite poles.

Controlling approaches

The main theory underpinning controlling approaches to behaviour management is that of behaviourism. This covers a range of theories that aim to control behaviours and maintain discipline in schools. The main assertion is that individuals' behaviour is governed by external consequences and therefore any disruptive behaviour is due to a lack of incentive to behave better. Behaviourism owes its genesis in 1914 to psychologists such as John Watson and was later popularised by B.F. Skinner, who supported the development of concepts such as operant and classical conditioning, as well as reinforcement. Famously, proponents of behaviourism experimented on animals to form theories of human behaviour, including Skinner (pigeons), Ivan Pavlov (dogs), and Edward Thorndike (cats). Where desirable behaviours were exhibited, these would be reinforced with positive rewards with the converse issued for undesirable behaviours. The most obvious connection to theories of behaviourism in schools is the prevalence of rewards and sanctions as the main basis for managing behaviour, and this pervades many schools in all phases to this day.

The word discipline, used in policy, has it links with behaviourism and the movement in the twentieth century to see mass schooling as part of the economic purpose of education. That is, a more educated population is able to participate in the labour market and contribute to the growth of the economy. It is historically associated with a time when many thought children 'should be seen and not heard', and as such children's bodies and minds were perceived as passive and docile. According to behaviourist approaches, the teacher is the expert who deposits knowledge into the obedient child, and any child who is not obedient is identified as defiant and a challenge to the authority of the teacher and the school.

Modern interpretations of behaviourism allow us to further subdivide this theory into **pragmatic behaviourism**, **radical behaviourism**, and **cognitive behaviourism**.

Pragmatic behaviourism. This is the most common approach used in schools and is associated with zero-tolerance approaches, as exemplified by the

Michaela Community School in Brent, north London (Birbalsingh, 2016). They strongly assert that rewards and punishments are all that is needed for compliance in schools and if these are not immediately successful, then we need to apply more of them. Porter (2014) suggests that such approaches can be considered 'pop' behaviourism.

One example of pragmatic behaviourism comes from the approach of *assertive discipline*, coined by Canter and Canter (2001). According to this, the teacher, as the authority, sets the rules and boundaries required and students are forced to comply with them. It is assumed that pupils will misbehave, and this undermines the teacher's needs, wants, and feelings, plus their right to teach without interruption. Appropriate behaviour is reinforced through rewards; otherwise it is punished. Teachers can build positive relationships and in this zero-tolerance approach we get concepts such as 'warm, strict' relationships.

Radical behaviourism. Radical behaviourism is built upon the idea that environmental and contextual factors are of critical value and should be taken into account when 'managing' behaviour. This approach relies on objective data to monitor interventions. Examples of radical behaviourism include:

- *Applied behaviour analysis*: understanding the relationship between behaviour and environment.
- *Positive behavioural support*: teaching behavioural expectations.
- *Functional behavioural analysis* – all behaviour serves a function; this is an individualised model.

Table 4.1 Examples of how schools implement controlling approaches

Primary schools (including Early Years)	Secondary schools
Rewards	Rewards
Verbal praise	Verbal praise
Non-verbal praise (thumbs up)	Badges
Team/house points	House points systems
Stickers	Praise postcards
Attendance awards	Raffles/prizes
Good work assemblies	Phone call home
Sanctions	Sanctions
Sad cloud/visual systems	Warnings
Thinking chair/cushion	Detentions
Withdrawal of break/lunch times	Loss of privileges
Time away from peers	Managed moves
Formal exclusions	Formal exclusions
Systems	Systems
ClassDojo	NUHOPE system
IRIS behaviour management system	Zero-tolerance approaches
Assertive discipline	

Whilst each of these are distinct approaches, they share an analytical approach that seeks to understand the contextual factors surrounding behaviour in a significant way.

Cognitive behaviourism. This model considers the role of cognitive processes at work in a child's behaviour, although it is underpinned by behaviourist methods. It suggested that students will feel better when their behaviour improves and by adjusting their thought processes, this will help them to be successful.

What do controlling approaches look like in schools?

In Table 4.1, we have tried to separate approaches into different phases of the education system, yet we recognise that in reality this may be more fluid.

Vignette: The water bottle incident

Whilst recently visiting a school in the Midlands, I observed a Year 9 pupil (aged 13–14) receive a punishment for an action that was viewed within the school as a serious misdemeanour and to the classroom teacher as a clear signifier that the pupil was not fully applied to his classwork.

Towards the end of a sixty-minute lesson and just before lunch, the pupil (who, throughout the lesson, had answered many questions voluntarily and showed a good level of effort) rested his chin on his water bottle, allowing his eyes to wander to the middle distance. The teacher issued a 'C1' penalty and explained that it was due to the pupil not 'tracking' the teacher and paying full attention according to the **SLANT** rules of the class (that is, 'Sit up, Lean forward, Ask and answers questions, Nod your head, and Track the speaker'. When I discussed this with the teacher afterwards, I was told that the pupil's action itself had not bothered her to begin with but having to enforce the SLANT expectation had caused her to feel irritated and reactive to pupils who could not remember to follow the rules for themselves all of the time. She explained that the expectation was simple enough and was there to ensure that pupils were mindful of how committed they were to learning at all times. She did not feel it was unreasonable to expect pupils to comply with a rule that was there for their own benefit.

In many ways, this seems to be a perfectly reasonable stance – to want pupils to learn, to make the most of lesson times, to have high expectations, and to encourage pupils to self-regulate their own engagement, behaviour, and learning. However, this struck me as peculiar in a number of ways. First, that the expectation itself seemed to obstruct rather than support the teacher's practice because it wasn't the pupil's 'misdemeanour' which irritated her, but that she had to remind the pupil to follow the rule. Second, the pupil's hard work and commitment to learning was marginalised by an act that was not intended to be disruptive. Third, a teacher feeling irritated in their classroom is rarely a good thing and especially when attributable to such an inconsequential action on the part of the child.

I'd like to say that this was a singular example of such a framing of pupil behaviour but throughout the rest of the day in the same school, I observed a number of teacher practices, expectations, and responses which enacted the school's 'zero-tolerance' policy on pupil behaviour. All of the teachers I spoke to cared greatly for the pupils in their care but many had come to accept zero tolerance as a legitimate approach even when they could not attest to its impact on pupils beyond orderly and silent spaces (corridors, the dining room), and using its effects as proxies for concentration, application, and learning.

In short, the teacher in the example above provides a good illustration of a situation where a rule that is based upon compliance is not followed. The teacher becomes distracted by the non-compliance of the pupil rather than with any fundamental objection or concern about the pupil's actual actions or behaviours. Whilst the above situation would not count as poor behaviour in most teachers' judgements, it still serves as a good illustration of how 'framing' behaviour can have a significant impact on how you react to situations. Sometimes you do things because you are supposed to, or because your emotions lead you there.

Guidance approaches

> There is a time to admire the power of an influential idea, and a time to fear its hold over us … At the point when objections are not answered anymore because they are no longer even raised, we are not in control: we do not have the idea; it has us. (Kohn, 1999: 3)

Guidance approaches offer an alternative to behaviourism and are theorised in fundamentally different ways. They are built upon humanist theories established by Carl Rogers in the 1980s and taken up by theorists such as Alfie Kohn, who assert that behaviour is related to needs rather than consequences. According to this theory, behaviour that is disruptive is associated with an unmet need and is therefore addressed in a different way. The learner is actively engaged and their emotional and social wellbeing is nurtured. Rather than education having a purpose to principally contribute to the economy, it is driven by a need for equity and personal development. Children are actively taught about behaviours and led to interact peacefully and solve problems as part of a community.

As the quotation at the start of this section outlines, behaviourism is so entrenched in our systems of schooling in the UK that it is very hard to think differently about behaviour and how it is managed. In fact, guidance approaches do not seek to manage behaviour, as this frames it in a different way. Instead, a whole new language and set of apparatus is needed to support children and young people learning to communicate, and problem-solve differently. For instance, humanism recognises that behaviours have natural outcomes, such as getting cold after swimming in the river, whereas consequences (behaviourism) are contrived by adults to make children suffer for their choices (Porter, 2014: 40).

Table 4.2 Comparison of guiding and controlling approaches to behaviour

	Controlling approaches	Guidance approaches
Language of...	Compliance and obedience Judgemental language Misbehaviour unacceptable, inappropriate	Consideration and compassion Responsive relationships
Disciplinary style	Psychological and behavioural control achieved through rules and consequences Surveillance of children	Using structures and relationships to teach the skills of behaviour Leadership skills
Adult status	Authoritarian approach Adult as authority holding all the power	Constructivist approach Adult as leader and guide with expert, referent, and connective power
Views on motivation	External locus of causality – motivation can be fostered externally	Internal locus of control – motivation is governed by internal needs
Views on behaviour	Challenging behaviour should not happen and should be punished Behavioural problems are due to faulty reward and punishment systems	Behavioural mistakes are natural and demand teaching of skilful behaviours. Behaviour is an attempt by children to meet needs (sometimes ineptly)
Internal causes of behaviours that challenge	Students displaying inappropriate behaviours are being reinforced for their disruptive and antisocial behaviour	Some students may have experienced trauma or have lacked nurturing approaches This approach also looks towards external causes, such as the context
Teacher as	Teacher as expert, delivering curriculum to empty vessels Subject-dominated curriculum, examinations, and rote learning	Teacher as guide and supporter, learning alongside children Child-centred curriculum; project-based approaches; enquiry approaches
Child as	Children as attention-seeking, taking advantage and requiring limits Children are inherently incompetent Children lack agency and do not think rationally like adults Children want to do well to impress adults	Children as rational and displays of behaviour relate to their needs (just like adults) Children are inherently competent Children and adults are equals and have similar rights Children want to do well to achieve something meaningful

What do guidance approaches look like in schools?

- Restorative approaches (see Sackville-Ford and Baggaley, 2020) – a relational and problem-solving approach used to underpin the culture of the school.
- Relationship policies replace behaviour policies – behaviour is seen as secondary to relationships and such approaches can be embedded in policy.
- No sticker/reward policies – schools that recognise that motivation should be conceived differently within guidance approaches have actively moved away from rewards and sanctions.

- Democratic schooling – schools that seek a leadership approach and share agency across all members of the school environment. They may use school councils to make decisions around behaviour.
- No-exclusion schools – schools that explicitly state that they will not use exclusions as a form of punishment. This promotes a sense of belonging and seeks alternative ways to repair any harm.

Some of the approaches above are used in the same setting and there is some indication that they are gaining traction. Through our reflections, it also seems that these have tended to be more common in the primary sector. We wonder what significance this has for the ways that child development influences behaviour management, or the ways that the size of the school might influence culture.

Prompt for reflection

Do you think there is any significance to the fact that guidance approaches may be more common in the primary sector? How might we account for the different approaches adopted in different settings?

Table 4.2 provides a comparison of controlling and guidance approaches.

Teacher: How your values, beliefs, and experiences have an impact at an individual level

The final domain in this model of reflecting upon behaviour is yourself, adding a final layer of complexity to be considered as you move towards understanding your own philosophy of education. In many ways, this could be the best place to begin your examination of your practice as well as your final consideration.

Arguably, who you are as a person influences who you are as a teacher. We contend that teachers should not be formed through an identikit model, teaching the same curriculum in the same way and presented as 'facilitators' of learning. In our view, teaching is so much more than this and the person inhabiting the role of the teacher is a human being with a dynamic role and purpose, which will and should change and evolve throughout your career. You are shaped by your own life experiences, which contribute to your own thoughts, feelings, and reactions (see Chapters 9 and 10 on 'The role of emotion' and 'Developing through reflection'). This then leads to a set of beliefs and values about the world; your own ideological outlook on life. As a person you have an identity, you have likes and dislikes, and these shift and change constantly throughout your lifetime. As a professional, these will emerge in your teacher persona; possibly, you are only partly conscious of these influences. Developing awareness of how you influence your praxis and becoming critically alert to how you shape events and behaviours in your classroom is extremely powerful.

> **Prompt for reflection**
>
> For a moment, consider the often-used criterion of respect. How does this mean different things to different teachers because of their own views, experiences, and beliefs?

A typical response to the question 'what kind of teacher do I want to be' elicits a response that refers to a significant teacher either from one's own education, or another teacher observed during your initial professional preparation. Considering what lies beneath these thoughts and feelings is useful not only in terms of developing your own teacher persona, but for realising which do or do not fit with you as a person. We often say to student teachers that in spite of their best efforts to be like another teacher and to adopt their ways, this is neither realistic nor sustainable: you will always emerge.

Conclusion

At the start of the chapter, we introduced the notion of congruency so that you can start to map the territory of yourself in relation to knowledge and what you do in your classroom. We have suggested that there is more than one way to think about and enact approaches to behaviour, and more than one way to be an effective teacher. Many of the policies and practices presented to early career teachers recommend a core set of 'high leverage' practices and approaches that are deemed to have universal applicability. Yet teaching is a profession that requires creativity, judgement, and autonomy. This chapter invites you to realise your autonomy in the fullest sense by questioning the philosophies that lie beneath behaviour policies and practices.

Through exploring the three domains of praxis (school), theory (context), and teacher (you), we hope that you are able to locate yourself within each of these and to conceive of this as an ongoing and dynamic process through which your own philosophy of education, schooling, and teaching evolves. We encourage you to locate this early in your career as a basis for developing confidence and to make informed choices as you navigate your behaviour journey.

Further reading and resources

Brooks, R. (2019) *The Trauma and Attachment-aware Classroom: A practical guide to supporting children who have encountered trauma and adverse childhood experiences.* London: Jessica Kingsley.

Dix, P. (2017) *When the Adults Change, Everything Changes: Seismic shifts in school behaviour.* London: Crown House.

Overland, E., Barber, J. and Sackville-Ford, M. (2020) *Behaviour Management: An essential guide for student and newly qualified teachers.* Abingdon: Routledge.

Porter, L. (2014) *Behaviour in Schools: Theory and practice for teachers,* 3rd edition. Maidenhead: Open University Press.

Rogers, B. (2015) *Classroom Behaviour: A practical guide to effective teaching, behaviour management and colleague support.* London: Sage.

5 Wellbeing of children and young people

Ben Wye, Aidan Brierley, and Moira Hulme

Introduction

When we ask prospective teachers why they want to teach, almost all speak of a desire to improve pupil wellbeing. Aspiring and early career teachers often talk about improving pupils' confidence, mental health, and enjoyment of life, both in and out of school. This chapter opens with an examination of how wellbeing is conceptualised and measured in education. This is followed by four examples – at national, school, and classroom level – to support your understanding of wellbeing as multi-faceted and malleable: (1) national policy approaches to promote wellbeing in schools; (2) school responses to protect pupil wellbeing in a crisis; (3) case studies of how individual schools strengthen wellbeing in response to locally decided priorities; and (4) classroom practices deployed by teachers to enhance the social and emotional wellbeing of their pupils. By the end of the chapter, you will have a better understanding of the multiple domains that comprise wellbeing, and the pastoral, curricular, and pedagogical strategies promoting wellbeing in schools.

Defining and measuring wellbeing

Personal and societal wellbeing has received increased attention within regional, national, and supra-national policy debates (European Commission, 2011; OECD, 2019a; UNICEF, 2007). Wellbeing metrics are expanding rapidly with the Organisation for Economic Cooperation and Development (OECD) playing a key role in knowledge brokerage and policy advice. The OECD wellbeing framework collects comparative data from 37 countries using over 80 wellbeing indicators in three areas: current wellbeing, inequalities in wellbeing outcomes, and resources for future wellbeing (OECD, 2020). Comparisons of national performance now draw on an emerging 'science of wellbeing' to supplement conventional economic indicators (Clark et al., 2018). From 2012, the annual World Happiness Report has published national rankings based on data from the Gallup World Poll in 115 countries (Helliwell et al., 2020). In the UK, from 2010 the Office for National Statistics (ONS) has collected data on societal and personal wellbeing across areas such as education and skills, employment, health, relationships, housing, finances, and the environment. Wellbeing in education, in common with pupil attainment and teacher quality, has become calculable and is increasingly subject to benchmarking.

In an applied policy field such as school education, it is important to understand how wellbeing is being defined and measured. This is not simply a technical question. What constitutes a good childhood and how the constituent elements of children's wellbeing are decided entails moral and evaluative judgement. Different definitions of wellbeing lead to different orientations within wellbeing-focused education policy and school-level programmes. Kempf notes that, 'Amid a larger discourse of accountability and demonstrable outcomes, the issues of what precisely constitutes wellbeing and how wellbeing will be measured, by whom, with what instruments, and to what ends are pressing and timely concerns' (2018: 5).

How should wellbeing in childhood and adolescence be defined? Selwyn et al. define wellbeing as, 'how children feel (for example, happiness, life satisfaction, life having meaning) and how they are functioning and flourishing (for example, relationships, self-efficacy and life getting better)' (2017: 4). This definition is helpful because it encompasses measures of wellbeing that are both objective (hard outcomes) and subjective (how people feel about aspects of their lives). Similarly, the Department for Education defines children and young people's subjective wellbeing as, 'their own sense of their quality of life and how well they feel their lives are going' (2019b: 59). Assessments of pupil wellbeing matter. By understanding the feelings and experiences of children and young people, we are better able to provide a 'good' education, tailor interventions to meet specific needs, and help prepare young people for wellbeing in their future lives.

The school curriculum and programmes to promote wellbeing reflect how wellbeing in education is conceptualised. It is widely acknowledged that the influences on wellbeing are multi-faceted. The OECD (2019b: 40) identifies five domains of pupil wellbeing:

1. *Cognitive wellbeing*: the knowledge, skills, and foundations pupils have to participate effectively as lifelong learners and engaged citizens.
2. *Psychological wellbeing*: pupils' views about their lives, engagement with school, and ambitions for the future.
3. *Physical wellbeing* or health status.
4. *Social wellbeing*: the quality of relationships with family, peers, and teachers.
5. *Material wellbeing*: the family and school resources available to meet children's learning and development needs.

Targeted interventions to improve pupil wellbeing at school typically focus on four dimensions: emotional wellbeing (including fears, anxiety, and mood), behavioural wellbeing (including attention problems), social wellbeing (including bullying and victimisation), and school wellbeing (including enjoyment and engagement) (Gutman and Vorhaus, 2012: 3).

There are a growing number of sources of evidence about children's wellbeing. These include the Department for Education (2019b) report State of the Nation 2019: Children and Young People's Wellbeing; the results of the OECD (2019b) Programme of International Student Assessment (PISA); the Children's Society (2020a) Good Childhood Report; and the World Health Organization's (2020) 'Spotlight on Adolescent Health and Wellbeing'. While analyses of PISA 2018 outcomes shows gains in pupil progress in reading, science, and maths, the

UK fares less well on international measures of children's wellbeing. Compared to 23 European countries, the sample of 15-years-olds in the UK who participated in PISA 2018 were the least satisfied with their lives, ranked lowest for having a sense of purpose in life, and second highest for sadness (The Children's Society, 2020a: 5). UK data indicates there has been a year-on-year decline in children's self-reported wellbeing from 2010, with a significant dip in happiness with school (2020a: 12).

We know that protective and risk factors associated with wellbeing vary between different groups of children and young people, and across life stages. For example, the State of the Nation Report indicates that, 'Females, older children, children with special educational needs, children from more deprived backgrounds, children reporting being attracted to children of the same or both genders, and children in need have been reported as more likely to experience low wellbeing and emotional difficulties than their peers' (DfE, 2019b: 6). Unsurprisingly, children who contend with multiple disadvantages experience lower wellbeing. Children experiencing disadvantages across multiple areas of their lives (school, family, neighbourhood, income) report lower average wellbeing than those experiencing more than one disadvantage in one area (2019b: 16). Self-report studies identify experiences of being bullied, difficult parent relationships, feeling unsafe in their neighbourhood, and economic inequality as risk factors for poor wellbeing, while a strong internal locus of control, positive peer relationships, feeling safe in your neighbourhood, sleeping well, physical exercise, and school engagement promote positive wellbeing (DfE, 2019b).

From the above, it is clear that wellbeing is a dynamic state. The risks and protective factors for individuals and groups changes over time. While methodologies for measuring individual and population wellbeing are evolving, trends suggest that policy attention to children and young people's social and emotional wellbeing in the UK is ever urgent, especially in the context of Covid-19 (The Children's Society, 2020b). The following section considers how wellbeing is embedded within policy for schools across the four nations of the UK.

Example 1: Wellbeing policy in the UK

Devolution has encouraged policy divergence between the four nations in how pupil wellbeing is instantiated in the school curriculum, Teachers' Standards, and school inspection frameworks. The English national curriculum provides guidance for teaching pupils about physical health and mental wellbeing (DfE, 2020). This guidance recommends that pupils be given the language, opportunities, and knowledge to understand and articulate how they are feeling. Primary pupils should 'know simple self-care techniques' and secondary pupils 'know how to talk about their emotions'. School staff should encourage a culture of openness, collaborate to develop age-appropriate curriculum content, recognise and refer the early signs of wellbeing concerns according to school safeguarding policy and procedures. The Teachers' Standards (DfE, 2011) reiterate that all teachers have a professional responsibility for pupils' wellbeing, as well as for their achievements. Arrangements for safeguarding are assessed under the Education Inspection Framework (Ofsted, 2019).

The Children's Services Co-Operation Act (Northern Ireland) 2015 set down eight characteristics for assessing the wellbeing of children and young people: physical and mental health; living in safety and with stability; learning and achievement; economic and environmental wellbeing; the enjoyment of play and leisure; living in a society in which equality opportunity and good relations are promoted; the making by children and young people of a positive contribution to society; and living in a society which respects their rights. The Children and Young People's Strategy, 2019–2029 addresses progress in each of these areas (DENI, 2019). The competences framework for teachers in Northern Ireland, Teaching: The Reflective Profession, emphasises the moral purposes of teaching and articulates 'an ethical and value-based approach to teacher professionalism and professional identity' (GTCNI, 2011). In addition, it states, 'education must contribute not just to the individual's well-being but also to the common good' or civic wellbeing (2011: 7).

The Wellbeing of Future Generations (Wales) Act 2015 requires public bodies to work to improve the economic, social, environmental, and cultural wellbeing of Wales. Progress towards the achievement of seven wellbeing goals is measured through 46 National Indicators, which include the development of education, health, and the social and material wellbeing of children and young people. The school inspectorate in Wales, Estyn, assesses the impact of school-level approaches designed to improve the achievement and wellbeing of vulnerable and disadvantaged pupils (Estyn, 2020). The Health and Well-being Area of Learning and Experience of the Curriculum for Wales promotes responsive practitioner-led curriculum design to address local needs. School-to-school collaboration is encouraged with regional consortia supporting the development of school cluster Wellbeing Plans. The Professional Standard for Pedagogy requires teachers undertaking induction in Wales to consider how they help all learners to cultivate 'habits of well-being' (Welsh Government, 2017: 41).

The National Performance Framework in Scotland incorporates a wide range of wellbeing measures (Scottish Government, 2019). Getting it Right for Every Child (GIRFEC), introduced across Scotland from 2006, provides a rights-based framework for the coordination of children's services to improve outcomes for all (Scottish Government, 2017). GIRFEC specifies eight interconnected wellbeing indicators (SHANARRI): every child or young person should be **S**afe, **H**ealthy, **A**chieving, **N**urtured, **A**ctive, **R**espected, **R**esponsible, and **I**ncluded (Scottish Government, 2018). The national curriculum in Scotland, Curriculum for Excellence, aims to ensure that 'children and young people develop the knowledge and understanding, skills, capabilities and attributes that they need for mental, emotional, social and physical wellbeing now and in the future' (Scottish Government, 2011a). Curriculum materials draw explicit attention to four dimensions that are the responsibility of all teachers irrespective of stage or subject:

1. *Mental wellbeing*: the health of the mind, the way we think, perceive, reflect on, and make sense of the world.
2. *Emotional wellbeing*: recognising, understanding, and effectively managing our feelings and emotions.

3. *Social wellbeing*: being and feeling secure in relationships with family, friends, and community, having a sense of belonging, and recognising and understanding our contribution in society.
4. *Physical wellbeing*: the knowledge, skills, and attitudes that we need to understand how physical factors affect our health (Scottish Government, 2011b: 7).

Prompt for reflection

Use the eight SHANARRI wellbeing indicators to consider how in your classroom practice, with your school community and with allied professionals, you work to ensure that your pupils are **S**afe, **H**ealthy, **A**chieving, **N**urtured, **A**ctive, **R**espected, **R**esponsible and **I**ncluded. Look at the aspects of practice you identify in each area and consider which are whole-school policies, embedded in the curriculum, everyday classroom practices, targeted interventions, or involve inter-agency partnership work. Have you identified strengths in some areas more than others? Which other stakeholders need to be involved?

Example 2: Wellbeing in a crisis event

On 23 March 2020, schools across the UK were closed for all pupils except priority groups (the children of critical workers and more vulnerable pupils) to slow the transmission of the coronavirus. Below are some of the ways schools continued to support pupil wellbeing in the short term during the period of school closures. The examples are drawn from interviews with headteachers of primary, secondary, and special schools in May and June 2020.

- Every child in a primary school received a welfare telephone call each week, with vulnerable pupils contacted every day by a designated key contact.
- A primary headteacher handwrote letters posted to individual pupils to maintain a connection with school and to motivate pupils to engage in learning activities.
- Distanced doorstep visits and outdoor conversations to drop off physical home learning packs tailored to individual needs, and in some cases stationery packs, hardware, and 4G routers (Wi-Fi).
- Being aware that families may have limited access to devices for online learning. Planning for students only using a mobile phone. Reducing pressure on limited resources by recording and not scheduling 'live' classes at the same time for multiple year groups and having realistic expectations about what can be achieved by home schooling. Setting timing guidance for task completion (how long to spend on activities) and allowing more flexible deadlines.
- Close monitoring through the development of a school-wide online system for reviewing and recording the welfare and engagement in home learning of every child on the school roll each week.

- Pastoral leaders at a primary school meeting a pupil of concern for regular short supervised cycle rides; arranging Forest School placements for pupils who would benefit from outdoor learning and family respite time.
- Regular online form group meetings by video conference at secondary schools to check-in, clarify expectations, set targets, and reassure pupils; plus two-to-one video conference meetings with individual pupils. Establishing and revisiting clear ground rules for online communication.
- Signposting all pupils and parents to resources to support good mental health. Directing staff to targeted online professional learning to enhance teacher skills.
- A secondary school set up a designated 24-hour pastoral telephone helpline that was available for pupils in need.
- Close liaison with allied professionals in children's social care, family liaison officers, and psychological services to support pupils and their families/carers, including looked-after and previously looked-after children. Continued multi-agency meetings, done remotely.
- Close liaison with carers, therapists, and clinicians to risk-assess and provide some continuity of support for pupils with education, health, and care (EHC) plans.
- Close liaison with local charities, including food banks, in regard to community volunteer support (with safeguarding checks).
- Continuation and extension of remote school counselling services.

Prompt for reflection

Which of the approaches and actions above are intended to address pupil wellbeing in general, and which are in response to the needs of particular individuals or different groups of pupils? How are 'at risk' and more 'vulnerable' pupils defined? How does this range of strategies indicate how schools and teachers were addressing the *social* determinants of wellbeing? How do social and economic factors influence pupil wellbeing? What are the possible implications of crisis events for pupil wellbeing for the longer term? If you have concerns about the wellbeing of pupil(s), how should you take this forward? When is it appropriate to disclose information given in confidence? If you are at all unsure about procedures, talk to the designated safeguarding lead at your school and read (again) the current school safeguarding and child protection policy.

Example 3: School wellbeing case studies

The four examples below illustrate how primary and secondary schools are working, in partnership with allied professionals, to place pupil wellbeing at the centre of their activity (Hulme et al., 2020). For each of these examples, think about the points that need to be considered by schools and teachers when introducing these interventions, and how their impact might be assessed. What are the hard and soft outcomes that might be used as indicators of wellbeing in each case?

Promoting positive family relationships. Foundation leaders at a primary school in an area of social disadvantage, with pupils for whom English is an additional language, developed family oracy packs. Each pack contains enjoyable and accessible activities linked to a story or a rhyme that can be done at home or outdoors with links to National Trust resources. Activities might focus on colour names or shape names, or involve searching the house, garden, or a local park to complete simple tasks. Parents can respond in any way they wish, without pressure. Completing activities should never feel like homework. With their parents/carers, children record their learning adventures to share with each other and school staff. Activities completed at home stimulate talk in school. Children are proud and excited to share their activities and talk about their adventures, such as going on a bear hunt in the park together at the weekend. Other forms of community engagement for wellbeing include an inter-generational walking group and beginners' running group for families; healthy eating 'adventures in food' cookery classes for parents with their children; partnership work with residential care settings to encourage inter-generational understanding and build community links. Community adult learning sessions make optimal use of the school estate and strengthen school–community links. A walking bus and breakfast club supports families and helps to improve punctuality and attendance.

Creating wellbeing spaces in school. A primary school has a multi-tiered approach to wellbeing with designated spaces for pastoral work. These include a school farm and two therapeutic spaces – a sunshine and rainbow room. The farm was created as an inclusion project to offer alternative lunchtime provision for those pupils who struggle in the playground. It provides outdoor nurture activities that help to keep some children in school by meeting their needs away from the bustle of the playground in an over-subscribed school. The farm has chickens, polytunnels, and raised beds of fruit and vegetables, a small orchard and daffodil farm. Start-up costs were covered by donations. Produce is sold to the school community. The farm also provides mainstream curriculum opportunities for pupils. The rainbow room is a therapeutic space where strategies are developed to build resilience around friendship (for example, falling out with friends) or family illness. Activities are led by a family and pastoral support leader with a higher degree in counselling and psychotherapy. The sunshine room is a space for one-to-one support for children experiencing trauma, parental physical and mental health issues, bereavement, family breakdown, or emotional dysregulation. Professional learning for wellbeing is open to all staff, including mindfulness training. Wellbeing themes, including the impact of adverse childhood experiences, are regular themes at whole-school meetings and training events. A sister primary school with limited space introduced a Monday lunchtime 'Happy Café' as a safe space for children who might need additional support at the start of the week. Wellbeing officers and volunteer staff take their lunch with pupils and organise activities.

Redesigning the curriculum to promote engagement. A Pupil Referral Service (PRS) supports young people who have severe adverse childhood experiences including, for example, family break-up, bereavement, substance misuse, or criminality in the home. Adverse childhood experiences leave young people traumatised to various degrees, often with significant attachment issues and a mistrust of adults, including those attempting to support them. They generally feel helpless in the face of their experiences and when they do try to exercise some control over their lives, this can often manifest in disruptive and violent behaviour in and out of school, vandalism and other anti-social behaviours such as petty theft, as well as substance misuse. Many have not been attending school regularly, have been excluded, or are at risk of exclusion. The PRS team recognised that these young people needed to rebuild trust and to regain a sense of control over their lives. They worked with a local high school to redesign the upper school curriculum to address wellbeing priorities. The first stage is an individual assessment of literacy, numeracy, digital skills, and social and emotional resilience. This assessment offers a profile of strengths and needs. The second stage is a revised curriculum offer with a bespoke high-status vocational pathway in addition to traditional courses, combined with sustained work on managing emotion. These learners need to feel a sense of investment in a curriculum that seems relevant to their lives, and their current and future plans. This is achieved through social-emotional support and by negotiating bespoke curriculum pathways that open doors to a positive post-16 future.

Professional collaboration. A high school serving an area of disadvantage with declining trends in attendance, engagement, and attainment put in place a suite of interventions that place wellbeing at the centre of operations. Stronger inter-professional and cross-sectoral collaboration was needed. Changes include additional programmes to support transition from primary to secondary school; regular Health & Wellbeing drop down weeks (when space is made in the timetable for wellbeing activities); designated days to support mental health involving health professionals and psychological services; the appointment of a school nurse with a background in mental health and a part-time school counsellor based on-site for 'time to talk' self-referrals; a 'chill out' zone and mediation sessions co-led by the school family engagement officer and a youth worker. School attendance and wellbeing officers liaise closely with children's services key workers and the school community police officer. External mentors and alumni networks are utilised to work with carefully matched target groups to raise aspirations. External consultants were commissioned to raise teachers' awareness of the challenges facing some pupils (including looked-after-children and young carers), and to develop a toolkit for person-centred planning to support more vulnerable pupils. Many pupils arrive at school with barriers to their learning. School staff felt these young people would not fulfil their potential until inclusion was prioritised, and the school supported the development of pupils' emotional wellbeing as much as their academic progress.

Discussion

The developments outlined above address priorities set down in the school development plan, and are subject to collective deliberation with school governing boards or Trusts, and other local groups including parent and community representatives and multi-agency working groups. When planning change, schools may use a **theory of change** and **logic model** (see Chapter 12 on 'Becoming research literate' for an example) to articulate shared aims (what is needed and why), and the inputs/actions needed to generate valued outcomes. Practical considerations include planning for effective communication (with families, teachers, and allied professionals), timescale, physical resources (rooms and equipment), team composition, skillset and leadership, volunteer training (including safeguarding) and screening, anticipated demand, staff capacity and investment in professional learning, with clear resource implications (budget, time, expertise). Assessment of short-/medium-/longer-term impact will depend on the complexity of the challenge being addressed. Remember that impact can be positive, neutral, or negative. Some outcomes will be visible quite quickly (for example, participation rates), others are less direct and may take several months or even years to appear (for example, positive destinations). Common indicators of impact include baseline data (numerical and descriptive), records of participation (take-up), the products of activities (work samples and artefacts), evaluation data from participants at early, mid- and end-points (structured feedback loops). Interventions often give rise to opportunities for professional dialogue, professional learning, and teacher leadership beyond the senior leadership team. The wellbeing interventions described above are multi-layered, grow from the school vision and values (ethos), and take a holistic approach to wellbeing, rather than a series of uncoordinated 'bolt on' activities.

Example 4: Wellbeing practices

In this section, we introduce pedagogical approaches deployed to support children's and young people's wellbeing with a specific focus on social and emotional skills. Social and emotional skills (or non-cognitive skills) include self-awareness, self-management, social awareness, relationship skills, and responsible decision-making (CASEL, 2015). The OECD (2017: 5) divide social and emotional skills into five categories: openness to experience (open-mindedness); conscientiousness (task performance); emotional stability (emotional regulation); extraversion (engaging with others); and agreeableness (collaboration). A growing body of research suggests that social and emotional skills are 'malleable' and 'learnable' in childhood and adolescence, and can yield significant benefits (2017: 28).

The development of social and emotional competence is associated with improvements in academic engagement and attainment (Banerjee et al., 2014; Clarke et al., 2015; Corcoran et al., 2018; Darling-Hammond et al., 2020). A meta-analysis conducted by the Education Endowment Foundation (EEF) of the findings of over 700 studies suggests that, on average, the teaching of social and emotional skills may have a positive impact on academic attainment that is equivalent to four additional months' progress (Wigelsworth et al., 2020). More specifically, high-quality programmes for teaching metacognition (that is, awareness and understanding of one's own thought processes) and self-regulation (controlling one's behaviour, emotions, and thoughts) may result in as much as seven months' additional learning progress. Effective programmes of social and emotional learning (SEL) have been associated with fewer negative behaviours, reduced emotional distress, and long-term benefits in terms of health and employment (Taylor et al., 2017).

In a review of 39 school-based Social and Emotional Learning (SEL) programmes used in the UK, Clarke et al. (2015: 5) found the strongest evidence of effectiveness for the following programmes (presented with the age of the pupils involved in the evaluation): Promoting Alternative Thinking Strategies (PATHS; EEF, 2015) (4–7-year-olds), Friends (7–11-year-olds), Zippy's Friends (5–8-year-olds), UK Resilience (11–12-year-olds), Lions Quest Skills for Adolescence (13–17-year-olds), and Positive Action (7–17 -year-olds). Interventions with an emerging evidence base included Circle Time (4–11-year-olds), Lessons for Living: Think Well, Do Well (9–10-year-olds), Strengths Gym (12–14-year-olds), Rtime (5–11-year-olds), and the .b (Stop-Breathe-Be) Mindfulness Programme (12–16-year-olds). The size of the effect and how long it lasts is influenced by the skill of the facilitator, the quality and duration of the programme, and the context of use.

Below are two contemplative wellbeing practices that are used regularly in the classroom by Aidan Brierley, an experienced primary teacher: kindness meditation and wellbeing journaling. These techniques draw on positive psychology.

Kindness meditation

Wellbeing is rarely unrelated to the social environment. Pupils learn that others tend to cause problems when they are stressed, confused, or cannot manage their own feelings. Kindness meditation in a safe space can be used with younger pupils to help break a cycle of negative attitudes, creating a classroom culture in which everyone works together to help each other. Meditation can provide a sense of calm, peace, and balance for pupils and their teachers (Graham and Truscott, 2020). Regular meditation has been associated with increased attention, empathy, and resilience to stress (Zenner et al., 2014). Kindness meditation helps pupils to visualise desired outcomes and rehearse and develop positive feelings and thoughts about themselves or others. Helpful words and phrases can be practised and used in structured visualisation as part of meditation (Rhodes and Long, 2019). Whether it be visualising a relaxing safe space, or a complex academic concept, the level of detail needed will vary according to the subject and pupils' experience. Younger pupils will need prompting and guidance to develop affirmations that generate emotions of kindness and positivity (e.g. *may I be happy/ healthy, I am kind, I am calm, I belong here*, etc.). Many schools use friendship tokens that primary pupils exchange with one another. Older or more experienced pupils can develop their own visualisation and affirmations, but the class teacher might introduce and explore some as a theme that could help at a particular stage or context.

Wellbeing journals

Journaling is a method of intentional reflecting that explores thoughts and feelings about events in daily life. Regular, timetabled journaling gives pupils structure for reflection, and can be adapted and developed according to circumstances

Kindness meditation protocol

Introduction and focusing
Ensuring that everyone is comfortable, take a few deep breaths and allow your bodies to become relaxed. Focus on your own breathing, and gently bringing attention back to the breath when the mind wanders. Older or more experienced pupils are asked to try to maintain focus for ten consecutive breaths.

Tip: It is important to explain that the mind will wander, and that pupils should not feel they are failing when this happens. The teacher will offer gentle guidance to support re-focusing.

Once focused and relaxed, you might suggest a theme for meditation, that reflects your school values, kindness for yourself and others. Try this in four subsequent phases:

Phase 1: Kindness for yourself
Bring to mind an image of being kind to yourself perhaps repeating a specific affirmation.

Phase 2: Kindness for a best friend
Think about a best friend or a person who is very important to you and repeat the same phrase you used in Phase 1 but with reference to them. Be aware of how you are feeling.

Phase 3: Kindness to others
This might be someone in another class, another teacher, or a neighbour that you have neutral feelings about. Use the same words to create kind thoughts towards them. Be aware of how your feelings change as you think about different people.

Phase 4: Kindness for someone you have difficulties with
Carefully choose someone you find it difficult to get on with (not one who elicits strong feelings) and repeat kind words about them. Be aware if your feelings and thoughts change about them.

Figure 5.1 Kindness meditation protocol

and need. Journaling should encourage freedom of expression, freedom to think, to explore, to be creative. The journal journey of exploration and expression is more important than the product. There is no performative pressure because journal entries are not assessed; there is no WAGOLL, or what a good one looks like. There is no right answer. Portman (2020) recommends starting with two minutes of writing and building up to twelve minutes, perusing (but not marking) journals weekly and, where appropriate, encouraging pupils to share carefully selected entries (pair-share, small group). Writing can be free writing or prompted with sentence stems or questions to scaffold reflection. Randomised controlled trials have found that writing about stressful events counters stress, negative feelings, and improves cognitive functioning (Scott, 2020). Confronting previously inhibited emotions, and the development of a coherent narrative, can help reorganise memories resulting in more adaptive internal schemas. Teachers of younger children might want to model the process at the end of each day in a class diary or Big Write session. For teachers in secondary schools, journaling can be a useful activity in form time, or in combination with mentoring. For an example, Outside the Box Learning Resources (Forman, 2020) have produced a free downloadable

Table 5.1 Wellbeing sources of support and resources

Barnardo's, emotional wellbeing	www.barnardos.org.uk/
Bounce Forward, resilience skills	https://bounceforward.com/
Center for Healthy Minds	https://centerhealthyminds.org/
Child Bereavement UK, loss	www.childbereavementuk.org/
ELSA Network, emotional literacy support assistants	www.elsanetwork.org/
Place2Be, improving children's mental health	www.place2be.org.uk/
SEAL Community	http://www.sealcommunity.org/
The Children's Society, mental and emotional wellbeing	www.childrenssociety.org.uk/
Thrive approach, social and emotional development	www.thriveapproach.com/
Wellbeing Journal, inclusive education example: Chadsgrove Teaching School	www.butterflyprint.co.uk/inquiring-minds/
Wellbeing Journal, primary example: Wynndale Primary School	www.wynndale-notts.co.uk/wellbeing-journals/
Wellbeing Journal, secondary example: Stokesley School & Sixth Form	www.stokesleyschool.org/key-information/the-wellbeing-journal/
Winston's wish, loss	www.winstonswish.org/
Young Carers in Schools programme	https://youngcarersinschools.com/
Young Minds, young people's mental health	https://youngminds.org.uk/

wellbeing journal for children aged 8–12 years. Links to open access journal templates from primary, secondary, and special schools are provided in the resources list in Table 5.1.

Conclusion

It is important for educators to engage critically with debates about what constitutes a good childhood and a good education. This chapter set out the domains of wellbeing and the challenges of measurement in these domains. In policy conversations, pupil wellbeing is frequently linked to school-based attainment and future productivity. The examples in this chapter illustrate the wider concerns of school professionals for wellbeing, including their awareness of the complex situational, structural, and equity-related factors that influence wellbeing. While there is a growing range of research-endorsed promising practices, a focus on pedagogical techniques may distract attention from whole-school or out-of-school factors. In your busy world, it may be tempting to 'deliver' packaged wellbeing solutions. In his critique of the mindfulness industry, 'McMindfulness', Purser (2019) cautions against the commodification of wellbeing and the commercialisation of pedagogy by edu-businesses. Interventions that link wellbeing with resilience – learning to 'keep calm and carry on' – do not address adverse contextual conditions. In this regard, there are clear connections between pupil wellbeing and teacher wellbeing (see Chapter 11 on 'Teacher wellbeing'). As Ott et al. note, 'schools cannot be settings that promote mental fitness for students if they are not psychologically healthy settings for educators' (2017: 13). In this chapter, we maintain that wellbeing policies and programmes are more likely to be successful when they grow from democratic deliberation on school priorities translated into integrated policies and practices that are supported over time and evaluated at whole-school and classroom level. An integrated approach to wellbeing takes seriously the perspective of children and young people, and utilises and values the knowledge of allied professionals, parent groups, and community partners.

Further reading and resources

Bethune, A. (2018) *Wellbeing in the Primary Classroom: A practical guide to teaching happiness*. London: Bloomsbury.

Collaborative for Academic, Social, and Emotional Learning (CASEL) (2015) *Effective social and emotional learning programs*. Chicago, IL: CASEL. Available at: http://secondaryguide.casel.org/casel-secondary-guide.pdf.

Education Endowment Foundation (2019c) *Improving social and emotional learning in primary schools*. London: EEF. Available at: https://educationendowmentfoundation.org.uk/tools/guidance-reports/social-and-emotional-learning/.

OECD (2017) *Social and emotional skills: Well-being, connectedness and success*. Paris: OECD. Available at: https://www.oecd.org/education/school/UPDATED%20Social%20and%20Emotional%20Skills%20-%20Well-being,%20connectedness%20and%20success.pdf%20(website).pdf.

Wigelsworth, M., Verity, L., Mason, C., Humphrey, N., Qualter, P. and Troncoso, P. (2020) *Primary social and emotional learning: Evidence review*. London: Education Endowment Foundation. Available at: https://educationendowmentfoundation.org.uk/public/files/Social_and_Emotional_Learning_Evidence_Review.pdf.

6 Digital classrooms: Pedagogy and practice

*Gary Beauchamp, Helen Borley,
and Nigel Pritchard*

Introduction

In this chapter, we will explore how digital technology can be used to promote effective learning within and beyond school (including remote learning and distance education). Although the case studies we use are from primary schools, the ideas and concepts discussed (for example, engaging with parents) apply to education at secondary level, and indeed beyond compulsory schooling. Digital technology plays a key role in enabling new learning opportunities, but also presents challenges, especially to newly qualified and early career teachers. The range of digital technologies available in schools continues to increase, but it is important to state from the outset that we are 'more concerned here with the thinking behind their use (the why?) rather than providing instructions on their use (the how?)' (Beauchamp, 2017: 88). All teachers use technology in many different ways in their professional lives, but in recent times this has moved from working within the boundaries of the school, largely with other members of the school community, to a wider global community. As the Digital Education Advisory Group in Australia asserted,

> The walls of the classroom and the home have been expanded by social media, the cloud, wikis, podcasts, video-conferencing etc. These are new learning environments and they are local, national and global and populated by whole communities in addition to family, teachers and friends. (DEAG, 2013: 4)

Since this was written, some of these rapid changes could have been predicted from inevitable advances in technology, but others are the result of totally unpredictable events, such as the Covid-19 pandemic. What has not changed, however, is that the primary purpose of technology use in the classroom and beyond is to help you to support and improve the academic, social, and emotional needs of those you teach.

Example: Engagement beyond the school

An early career teacher of a Key Stage 2 (age 7–11 years) class found that pupil engagement with a new topic was low and was keen to innovate and find new ways to engage the pupils. Having had success with a range of Science,

Technology, Engineering, and Mathematics (STEM) work online, the teacher decided to reach out to the global classroom. The teacher made connections through a science and maths scheme that connects scientists to schools through video conferencing. The pupils had a live linked video call with a park ranger in Yosemite National Park, as well as engineers who make robots for army tanks. This activity, impossible without technology, deepened understanding of maths and science, but the wider experience also informed the pupils of possibilities in the wider world of work, especially related to STEM careers. Pupils and the teacher were also given insight into the potential of the global classroom.

It is essential, therefore, to be clear that technology is there to *support* you in your teaching, not to *replace* you. It is very good at some things, but it remains a tool to be used only when it can do something better or faster than any other available resource. It has always been possible to teach very effective lessons with no technology, and this has not changed. When planning any lesson, your first decision is what you want the pupils to learn, in the context of your own existing knowledge of the content and your existing repertoire of teaching strategies. As Shulman suggests,

> The key to distinguishing the knowledge base of teaching lies at the intersection of content and pedagogy, and the capacity of a teacher to transform the content knowledge he or she possesses into forms that are pedagogically powerful and yet adaptive [to] students. (1987: 15)

In this context, technology represents a very powerful tool for transforming your own knowledge into different representations (analogies, metaphors, demonstrations, explanations), which can be adapted to the age and ability of your pupils. It might be, however, that another resource does it better. For instance, why show 3D shapes on an interactive whiteboard or iPad, when they can be handled and manipulated as solid shapes?

If you do decide to use technology, however, it is worth considering what it is good at. Although there is a large, and ever increasing, range of digital devices, they all have the following common and interrelated general features:

- *Speed*: things happen more quickly individually and collectively.
- *Automation*: processes are automated, such as moving between slides on a presentation or running an animation.
- *Capacity*: information can be stored and retrieved from local discs or from virtual storage systems.
- *Range*: materials can be presented in different formats (e.g. still images, a movie, through an electronic microscope or viewer), individually or in combination, using a range of devices, both fixed and mobile.
- *Provisionality*: the ability to 'play' with content to see the impact or change (e.g. undo and redo in text or change numbers in a spreadsheet and seeing difference in a graph).

- *Interactivity*: in this definition, a device responding to user input repeatedly – without getting bored like a person! – and providing (pre-programmed) feedback based on input from the user (adapted from Kennewell and Beauchamp, 2007).

Prompt for reflection

On your own, or with another teacher or mentor, consider how you have used, or could use, each of the features of ICT described above in your teaching. You should see how features could be used in combination, such as fast automation, or quick retrieval of data or presenting a range of ideas from different storage media. You could also consider which digital devices makes best use of these combinations.

When considering these strengths, it is essential to consider this from your own perspective, but also from the perspective of your pupils, who are themselves a great resource in a digital classroom! We need to consider the classroom as an ecology of resources (Beauchamp and Kennewell, 2010), defined by Luckin as 'a set of inter-related resource elements, including people and objects, the interactions between which provide a particular context' (2008: 451). Although technology is one of those resources, 'in reality, learning is always distributed in some form between the technology, the learner and the context and there is nothing inherent in technology that automatically guarantees learning' (John and Sutherland, 2005: 406). This is important to remember as you start your career and may feel overwhelmed by the sheer amount of technology available and expectations to use it. It is perhaps useful to remember that technology sits between you and the pupil (or between pupils) and, as such, mediates learning. However, it is 'only by being part of action do mediational means come into being and play their role. They have no magical power in and of themselves' (Wertsch, 1991: 119). In other words, the technology you choose has to serve a purpose, and not just be used because it is there. This can be challenging early in your career, as you may feel under pressure to use, for instance, a new set of iPads or digital touchscreen the school has just bought.

Prompt for reflection

Discuss the expectations of technology use with your mentor to clarify school priorities and how you can contribute, while also developing your generic teaching skills. Set small but achievable targets and monitor regularly, asking for support from colleagues (or pupils!) as necessary. Remember, it is a sign of strength to recognise you need support, and be prepared to seek and act on advice. Equally, if you feel your digital skills are strong, and you are confident in classroom technology, discuss with your mentor how you can help and support others.

An important advance in school technology in recent years has been better internet access (both cabled and wireless), with an associated advance in relatively affordable mobile devices that can connect wirelessly to remote devices (such as printers and network storage), to save work on shared school networks or to access programs remotely. This, in turn, has led to an increase in mobile learning, or **M-learning**. This can, however, be a slightly confusing concept in that 'does it relate to mobile technologies, or the more general notion of learner mobility?' (Kukulska-Hulme, 2009: 158). Kearney et al. conclude that all definitions 'consider the nexus between working with mobile devices and the occurrence of learning' (2012: 1) and provide a simple definition of M-learning as the 'process of learning mediated by a mobile device' (2012: 2).

Research suggests that M-learning can enhance, extend, and enrich the concept of learning in a number of ways and can take many forms, including (adapted from Haßler et al., 2015: 139):

- *Contingent mobile learning and teaching*: pupils can react to the environment wherever it is, as there are no predetermined learning and teaching opportunities.
- *Situated learning*: learning is made meaningful by the surroundings.
- *Authentic learning*: tasks have direct meaning to the learning goals and learners.
- *Context-aware learning*: physical surroundings help to inform the learning.
- *Personalised learning*: customised to the interests and capabilities of the learners.

In all these situations, however, echoing a theme we have seen throughout this chapter, Duncan-Howell and Lee point out,

> The use of M-Learning tools themselves does not guarantee their potential being realised. The key to success is the ability of educators to design and develop pedagogically sound opportunities and environments that enhance learning. (2007: 223)

Prompt for reflection

On your own, or with others, look at each of the forms of M-learning above and how they may apply to your teaching and what technologies you have that you could use and how.

One aspect of contingent learning, where 'learners can respond and react to their environment and changing experiences, and where learning and teaching opportunities are no longer predetermined' (Haßler et al., 2015: 139) that was perhaps not anticipated by the authors was a major global pandemic where learning took place in individual homes through distance learning – for those with access to technology at least. A key challenge for teachers at all stages of their career was to try and emulate the high-quality teaching and learning that took place in their classrooms. The example below shows the approach taken by one school in Wales.

Example: Maintaining quality teaching and learning online

Following analysis of pupils' engagement in online learning during the lockdown, it was clear that expectations needed to be set around good quality online learning. This needed to match the same expectations for class-based learning. Prior to lockdown, there had been considerable continuing professional development on literacy teaching and an approach to bring consistency to literacy teaching across the school.

The school literacy lead, working with the Digital Competence Framework (DCF) lead, drew up a list of 'non-negotiables' around online learning specifically for teachers. Those leaders then offered teachers training in how the expectations in classrooms could be matched to online learning, specifically matched to literacy learning. Part of this was that any work that was not up to normal expectations was returned to learners with video or audio-recorded verbal feedback for them to improve upon. It was made clear to teachers that if they would not accept the work in class, then they should not accept it online. As a result, engagement leapt in all the classes where this approach was taken. The feedback provided was acted upon and consequently the quality of the work returned was vastly improved. Teacher feedback was that the consistency of approach both aided planning and provided a structure.

What became apparent when working with technology remotely was that the engagement of parents was vital, both in 'normal' times and in more challenging situations, and led to improvements for all.

The example below shows how one school approached this and the resultant benefits.

Example: Digital leadership and building links with parents

In Wales, a new curriculum is being developed, in which digital competence is a core feature, with a non-statutory DCF available from the Wales Government website – see 'Further reading and resources' at the end of the chapter. As a result, school improvement planning had a strong element of building cross-curricular links, with the development of digital skills central to this. The class teacher who was DCF lead was placed in one of the reception classes to model practice with the youngest children and this would then permeate through the school as they moved classes. The DCF lead also trained a team of pupils (aged 7–11 years) who were adept at technology as DCF ambassadors. These pupils helped to train other pupils, teachers, and parents to use a range of devices and platforms. They also presented their work to the school governing body. As well as increasing their confidence, this allowed the school to celebrate skills in technology in the same way they did, for instance, in music and sport.

Innovation in teaching and learning was also a central tenet to the school improvement plan, supported through regular sessions, including work with the local authority to train staff on new technologies/platforms. This became more urgent as all schools were locked down due to the pandemic, and all teaching went online. The DCF lead surveyed parents early in lockdown about what their needs were and how successful the new home learning strategies were. Although the parents were broadly engaged and happy with the provision, they did offer suggestions. Many of the suggestions led to changes in approach, including a dedicated help email to address any technical issues, and video calls with teachers to whole classes.

Teachers were encouraged to try out new ideas in all areas of teaching and learning and given a safety net. If there were failures, then the teacher was expected to self-evaluate and, with support, find ways forward. Successes were celebrated and disseminated.

In all of these activities there are particular challenges for early career teachers, but it remains important that you are prepared (and feel supported in) taking risks. This does not mean risk as in something that may present danger, but risk as in trying something new, which may not always work out as well as expected, such as a new teaching strategy or using a new piece of technology. In a digital classroom, it is almost impossible not to take risks when first using new technology, but the considered decision to use it in the first place will be based on potential benefits for pupils, so has a positive intent. It can be very hard in the early years of your career, particularly in a probationary period, to try out new things, especially with new technology. However, Schenk et al. (2019) suggest that consequence, uncertainty, probability, and severity are key factors in teaching *through* risk. All of these can be alleviated within a supportive school culture. In an empathetic classroom, with pupils who can often help in mitigating the risk of technology not working, and a school management that regard trying new things out for the benefit of the pupils as a positive, do not be afraid to take a risk. Most 'risks' with technology can be mitigated by talking to colleagues and pupils in advance, but, even if things do not go as well as expected, through a process of evaluation you will learn something new.

In reality, many teachers lack confidence in using new technologies. However, trying new technologies can have many benefits for all members of the school community, as the example below shows.

Example: Benefits of 'risk' in trying new technologies

The school had identified low parental engagement with children's learning in school, poor digital skills amongst pupils, and low confidence amongst teachers.

To address these issues, teachers experimented with a range of packages for children to build digital portfolios of their work. Pupils were initially given free range on the platform to become familiar with the packages and what they would do. As time went on, the teachers began to add digital skills into planned activities, alongside numeracy and literacy skills. A range of strategies was then used to engage parents, who had an app to see their child's work in school in real time. Pupils became more selective about what they uploaded as they became more confident, knowing that their work could be seen.

The end result of taking a risk with new technology was a 100 per cent parental take-up of the app and positive feedback from parents. This opened up an easy line of communication with parents, pupil skills were improved, and they showed increased independence and risk-taking in other areas of learning.

As a result, the DCF lead led a series of online training sessions and follow-up tasks to address any issues, develop teacher confidence, and demonstrate the potential learning opportunities of digital platform use.

Another area where early career teachers may need to take a 'risk' in a digital classroom is in providing pupils with greater autonomy, as they become co-constructers of knowledge, making their own choices of when to use technology and what hardware or software best suits their own understanding of how they learn (metacognition). We have already discussed risk, and it can be hard to 'allow' pupils to work in a more symmetrical power relationship. Nonetheless, allowing pupils to demonstrate their own skills and knowledge can also provide a unique method of your own professional development. For instance, a study of iPad adoption in primary schools in Scotland and Wales found that 'in the classroom, teachers and pupils provided support to each other, and both were prepared to involve other family members and friends as "consultants" in solving problems' (Beauchamp et al., 2015: 173). Such an approach, and a willingness to empower and listen to pupils about using technology, can be very helpful in developing a repertoire of teaching strategies with technology.

Although discussing university teachers, Åkerlind (2007: 34) provides a useful overview of how the career of a teacher develops over time, which has been adapted below to consider how to teach in a digital classroom:

1. Building up a better knowledge of your content area(s): *becoming familiar with what to teach and how technology can help develop your ongoing understanding of the content.*
2. Building up practical experience as a teacher: *how to teach with technology – taking risks!*
3. Building up a repertoire of teaching strategies: *becoming skilful as a teacher with technology – taking even more risks!*
4. Finding out which teaching strategies do and do not work for you as a teacher: *becoming effective as a teacher with technology – learning from your mistakes!*

5. Continually increasing your understanding of what works and does not work for students: *becoming effective in facilitating student learning with technology with your pupils.*

Wherever you sit on that continuum, you will see that you never stop learning about teaching in general, and using technology in particular. In reality, even as you reach stage 5, as new technology emerges you may go back to stage 3 again as you build up new strategies to exploit the unique potential of new combinations of technology.

We have been very careful in this chapter to use the plural for technologies, as no individual piece of hardware or software will provide all the answers. It is much more likely that you will develop a pick-and-mix approach where you may only use one piece of technology once as part of a lesson, or several different pieces of technology on their own or in combination at different parts of another lesson. Part of this pick and mix will be choosing to use no technology at all, if it does not add anything of value to the lesson.

Conclusion

In this chapter, we have considered the unique features of technologies and how they should be used selectively when they can add something that you could not do better any other way. We have noted that technology continues to evolve and offer new features, which can be exploited based on the needs of individual pupils or a whole class. Part of this use may involve taking risks as you master new tools and techniques. We have also considered that learning can take place in person and virtually, anywhere in the world, with a wide range of partners, including parents and pupils in other schools. As technology continues to evolve, we must remember that 'there is a danger that teaching and learning can be driven by developments in technology (technological determinism), rather than being driven by effective pedagogy' (Beauchamp, 2017: 223). You have a role in making sure this does not happen, but that your digital classroom remains a 'partnership, where pupils take an active role in co-constructing knowledge and understanding, using a range of tools (including ICT) as appropriate' (2017: 224)

Further reading and resources

Beauchamp, G. (2017) *Computing and ICT in the Primary School: From pedagogy to practice*, 2nd edition. London: David Fulton/Routledge.

Digilearn Scotland – Digital Learning Community: https://blogs.glowscotland.org.uk/glowblogs/digilearn/.

Education Scotland (2020) *What digital learning might look like: Examples of digital literacy and computing science learning at early, first and second levels*. Available at: https://education.gov.scot/media/uh2jebbs/nih158-what-digital-learning-might-look-like.pdf.

Welsh Government (2008) *The digital competence framework* (Wales), including from Foundation Phase to KS4, and a curriculum mapping tool. Cardiff: Welsh Government. Available at: https://hwb.gov.wales/curriculum-for-wales-2008/digital-competence-framework-curriculum-for-wales-2008-version.

7 Inclusive pedagogy: Using Universal Design for Learning to teach beyond labels

Dominic Griffiths and Irene Leach

Introduction

As an early career teacher, the idea of developing an inclusive pedagogy may seem a little daunting. You find yourself faced with a new class with a number of children listed as having Special Educational Needs and Disabilities (SEND), some who are identified as 'gifted and talented' students, and others who have English as an additional language (EAL). How can you plan for all these learners? First, it is important to understand that inclusive pedagogy is not just about SEND (in fact, we believe that notions of 'SEND' are somewhat inadequate, as we will explain). Second, inclusive pedagogy does *not* mean thirty lesson plans for thirty class members! What inclusive pedagogy *is* about is recognising the diversity of your learners and making a positive commitment to gradually developing your practice to become more flexible and responsive to this diversity.

In this chapter, we aim to help you develop your inclusive pedagogy within a theoretical framework of **neurodiversity** and the practical framework of **Universal Design for Learning**. We will present examples of these ideas in action from within our own practice and will help you reflect upon your teaching and to begin taking the next small steps in making it more inclusive. We believe that in doing so, you will start to develop your confidence as a teacher and will soon see the fruits of your labour in your students' engagement with learning and progress towards their learning goals.

Defining inclusive pedagogy

Florian and Black-Hawkins make an important distinction between inclusive pedagogy and what might be termed 'bolted-on' differentiation, which requires a change in our thinking as teachers:

> It requires a shift in teaching and learning from an approach that works for most learners existing alongside something 'additional' or 'different' for those who experience difficulties, towards one that involves the development of a rich learning community characterised by learning opportunities made available for everyone. (2011: 826)

This approach is founded upon a rejection of traditional 'bell-curve thinking', which assumes notions of people ranged along a scale of inborn 'fixed ability' and rejects the idea that SEND labels can adequately describe individuals and their potentials as learners (Guðjónsdóttir and Óskarsdóttir, 2016). In order to reconceptualise the learners in our class, we feel that the concept of 'neurodiversity' can be not only helpful, but liberating.

Teaching for neurodiversity: Teaching beyond 'labels'

What is neurodiversity?

Various conceptions of neurodiversity currently exist. Originally it was used as a term to reframe the label 'autistic spectrum disorder' in less deficit-laden language (Singer, 1999). Others use 'neurodiversity' to refer to a range of SENDs (Baker, 2011), though some of these maintain focus just upon people's difficulties (DANDA, 2006). Armstrong (2012) suggests, instead, that the term neurodiverse should be used as part of a move away from deficit-focused discourses of SEND, to focus upon the individual strengths of different learners. However, there are problems with maintaining conceptions of neurodiversity within a traditional framework of categories of special educational needs (SEN). The problem is assumptions of levels of similarity within each labelled SEND 'category' that is not sustained by research evidence (Pernet et al., 2011). Much research also points away from the idea of 'pure' SEND categories. Many researchers note that those with one diagnosed 'SEND' seem also to have traits from other SEND categories. This has often been conceived as 'co-morbidity' of different SENDs. However, this co-morbidity model has also seen sustained criticism. Gilger and Kaplan (2001) found that, 'in developmental disorders comorbidity is the rule not the exception'. However, in later work considering 'comorbidity', Kaplan has moved away from the rather blunt-edged idea of co-occurring 'whole' SENDs. Instead, she proposes the rather more nuanced concept of *dimensions* of people's strengths and weaknesses, ranged across continua, with no clear cut-off points and consisting of 'multidimensional developmental pathways' (e.g. of skills in working memory, executive function, attention, fine motor skills etc., rather than simple categorical SEND labels; Kaplan et al., 2006). This move towards a more 'dimensional' account of individuals has been echoed in the field of reading disorders (Snowling and Hulme, 2012) and other areas of learning (Bishop, 2010).

These critiques are also finding support in neuroscience. For example, Cambridge University research in mapping brain connectivity has found that active brain networks of people 'diagnosed' with a range of SENDs do not show any regular patterns consistent with given SEND labels, and that there is significant individual variation in the brain network hubs and activity observed within these labelled groups (Siugzdaite et al., 2020). These results lend further support to those who argue that, if *everyone of us is neurodiverse*, then categories and labels and the cut-off points for their diagnosis seem increasingly arbitrary. This 'universal' conception of neurodiversity is where both of us would locate ourselves. We would also reject notions of 'neurodiverse' being defined against some non-existent idea of 'neurotypical'. We are *all* neurodiverse.

Teaching for neurodiversity

Given this evidence, it may come as no surprise to find that many educationalists are moving away from traditional 'SEN bolt-on differentiation' approaches to teaching. Summarising evidence about teaching in a variety of SEND categories, Lewis and Norwich conclude 'it is unlikely that "pure" group-specific pedagogical practices based upon the nature of the group could be sustained' (2005: 207). This is an important point, because many teachers' confidence in developing inclusive pedagogy is undermined by incorrect beliefs that many children require specialist pedagogies that they have not been trained in (Florian and Black-Hawkins, 2011). Masataka, adopting the analogy between neurodiversity and biodiversity, goes further in his critique.

> Rather than putting children into separate disability categories and using outmoded tools and language to work with them, teachers engaging in both special and regular education are able to use tools and language inspired by the ecology movement to diversify learning and assist children to succeed in the classroom. (2017: 86)

In the UK, this 'universal' understanding of neurodiversity has started to inform more dimensionally based approaches to inclusive pedagogy (Griffiths, 2020; Honeybourne, 2018). In the USA, a radical approach reconfiguring inclusive pedagogy is Universal Design for Learning (UDL), which advocates a move away from SEND/deficit accounts of learning and the somewhat arbitrary systems of labelling children and making assumptions about their limitations as learners. This is not the only pedagogical model that can inform inclusive pedagogy, but represents a useful framework to guide practice.

Universal Design for Learning

What is UDL?

The origins of Universal Design for Learning can be traced to the USA in the mid-1980s, when the Center for Applied Special Technology (CAST) was set up as an educational charity to focus on developing facilitative educational technology for students with disabilities. However, by the 1990s, CAST's research had revealed that the most effective way of developing inclusive pedagogy was not a *separate* focus upon certain learners identified as having 'disabilities', but on transforming the organisation of learning for all the students in a class. This approach, based upon inclusive whole-class lesson planning, rather than retro-fitted 'bolt-on' differentiation, is now known as Universal Design for Learning (UDL).

UDL owes much of its inspiration to the principles of Universal Design being adopted in architecture and town planning. For example, the dropped curb in pavements, originally designed for cars to access driveways, has also proved useful for wheelchair users, pushchair users, and cyclists (Hall et al., 2012). In the same way, in pedagogy, multisensory teaching, often traditionally seen as useful in supporting the particular needs of learners identified as 'dyslexic' (Pavey, 2007), is now widely regarded as effective for a much broader range of students (Taljaard, 2016).

UDL is based upon three Core Principles, drawing from neuroscientific research (Meyer et al., 2014), which correspond to involving three brain network systems. UDL's inclusive pedagogy aims to:

- Provide multiple means of engagement.
- Provide multiple means of representation.
- Provide multiple ways of action and expression.

Provide multiple means of engagement. This principle involves affective networks of the brain and is all about engaging learners' interest and keeping them motivated. It is about *why* students are learning. It addresses the 'What's the point of this, Miss?' question. This principle is primarily about making clear the relevance of the learning goals to students' lives, as well as empowering them to engage with learning at their own level of challenge. This means developing activities that will promote independent learning, backed up with assessment for learning to help them develop mastery level skills. This principle also draws upon collaborative learning techniques to help achieve learning goals. Teachers can encourage students to monitor their own learning through self-assessment, coupled with peer assessment.

Provide multiple means of representation. This principle involves recognition networks of the brain and is all about presenting information and content in different ways. It considers *what* is to be learned in a lesson or unit. This principle therefore focuses upon flexibility in using varied media to present new learning points. This means considering how a single modality of presentation can be adapted to be more multisensory. Thus, for example, a verbal/auditory presentation of new learning would be backed with visual stimuli such as symbols, pictures, images, or diagrams. In the same way, primarily visual presentation such as text would be backed with text-to-speech software and text read-back options. The same principle can be used in developing conceptual understanding through moving learners from concrete, through visual to more abstract levels of tasks. It could also involve highlighting to pick out key words and phrases in text or to show patterns, and to show how ideas relate to each other.

Provide multiple ways of action and expression. This principle involves the strategic networks of the brain and is about *how* learners plan and perform tasks and *how* they organise and express ideas. It considers *how* students can use different ways to express their new knowledge, skills, and understanding. This principle underlines the benefits of offering alternative recording strategies for students to choose. This principle challenges the traditional idea that the only way for students to show knowledge, skills, and understanding is in the form of extended writing. This could entail students developing posters, PowerPoint presentations with a recorded voice-over, news bulletins, acted out role-plays, or short film clips or animations. Where extended writing is the *necessary* final assessment medium, techniques such as mind-mapping, storyboards, or writing frames will help students organise their ideas in ways that are easier for they themselves (and teachers) to monitor. This principle encourages students to monitor their own learning and planning strategies. Teachers can support the setting of learning goals and can scaffold early stages of these tasks.

In the UDL framework these three Core Principles are each divided into sub-sets of three Guidelines, each expressed in a variety of numbered Checkpoints, which can provide an overview of options for lesson planning. The full 2018 table of UDL Principles, Guidelines, and Checkpoints is available on the CAST website: http://udlguidelines.cast.org/. In the specimen lesson plans outlined in the next section, where appropriate, these numbered checkpoints are cross-referenced in brackets.

Using UDL in lesson planning

It is important that this set of ideas is seen as your toolbox, to be used flexibly as you see fit, given the diversity of learners in your particular class in this particular lesson. As Meyer et al. stress:

> UDL is not a prescriptive checklist … with set methods and tools … applied in every situation … From the principles we derive guidelines for creating and choosing tools, methods, and practices, whose specifics depend upon context: learners' developmental levels, varied schools and communities, and the proclivities of teachers … among many other variables. (2014: 50)

The key to applying the UDL philosophy is considering your inclusive peda-gogy and making your adjustments *at the initial design stage*, not after planning a core lesson, but as *part* of that core lesson. This approach is not just 'something for the SEND students', but a menu of learning opportunities for everyone in the class. Here, UDL proposes four steps for lesson planning as part of a six-stage reflective cycle (Figure 7.1). (The pre-Step 1 US 'academic standard' would be the relevant curriculum level(s) in the UK context.)

In starting to adopt UDL into your pedagogy, teacher Libby Miles suggests keeping it simple: '… just think, how am I going to present this lesson in a

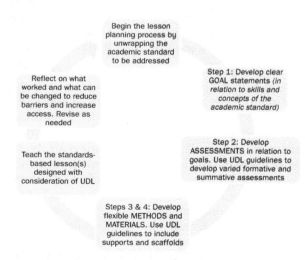

Figure 7.1 UDL cycle of instructional planning

Adapted from Rao and Mao (2016: 5)

variety of modalities and how am I going to keep my students engaged in a variety of modalities, and how am I going to assess in a variety of modalities?' (in Meyer et al., 2014: 56).

We endorse this and further suggest that you need to be realistic. You are not suddenly going to be using every idea in the UDL Guidelines in your lesson planning. We agree with Novak (2016), who recommends taking an incremental approach to developing inclusive pedagogy.

Prompt for reflection

Consider the Checkpoints in Guideline 6 (https://udlguidelines.cast.org/). Which of these are you already using? You may be pleasantly surprised to find that you have already embarked upon the inclusive pedagogy journey!

Novak suggests that you might try a focus upon one Guideline in a week's lesson planning. Alternatively, you may just start with adding an idea from one Checkpoint. You may well find that implementing just one in your planning soon improves student engagement in your lessons! You can then build from there.

Do not be scared of offering choices to learners. Evidence from our own experience and the research (Novak, 2016) suggests that most students don't just tend to opt for the seemingly 'easiest' option. Most like the satisfaction of a challenging but achievable task. Where your pedagogical skills are needed is in helping to scaffold those tasks, especially for learners lacking in confidence

Inclusive approaches in practice

The example below is a primary-level integrated learning lesson that employs some inclusive UDL approaches both in its planning and delivery. The accommodation of diverse learning preferences together with the quality of pupil–teacher relationships underpin the success of the learning experience and engender a positive climate within the learning environment. This, in turn, promotes a sense of community learning gained through mutual respect, tolerance, and collaborative working – individuals' strengths can be drawn on to enrich the learning experience and to celebrate diversity.

Example 1: An integrated learning lesson (Geography, Year 3, age 7–8 years)

A number of UDL checkpoints are applied in the following lesson with references given in brackets.

Task: *Which of the UDL checkpoints could you apply to a lesson you will teach soon?*

A 45-minute lesson was the first in a series on the theme of 'Our Active Planet' – a predominantly geography-based topic. Integrated cross-curricular elements were drawn from other subject areas to add a broader dimension, which enabled learners to make connections between subjects. With pupil voice being integral to curriculum planning, learners had previously voted on which topic they wished to engage with from a choice of several options, the preceding topic having been history-based (7.1).

To introduce the new topic, a short discussion was had with all learners about the importance of learning about our planet and particularly about how our planet undergoes physical changes that are beyond our control and impact on human activity (7.2). Ascertaining individuals' previous knowledge was necessary to make future learning relevant to individuals. Verbal responses were recorded to support future planning. Following this, a brief pre-teach vocabulary session took place, which established the language for learning, enabled an opportunity to gauge levels of understanding, and addressed any misconceptions or difficulties in accessing the material (2.1). Learners are always given the opportunity to share in the lesson planning by contributing ideas for content by selecting materials, learning roles, and by conducting research in collaboration with peers (8.3).

Key words, which included the specific geographical terms the learners were encouraged to learn, understand, and use, were presented in various ways. These included: the use of text, text and image, text and symbols (**widgets**) presented in a range of fonts, colours, and sizes that accommodated individual preferences and expanded access to supporting materials (6.3). The use of gesture and Makaton, for learners with speech and language needs, as well as those with auditory needs, clarified meaning and video clips were additionally used to illustrate key terms, for example 'eruption' and 'earthquake' (2.1, 5.1).

A learning wall was prepared that was used throughout the topic and upon which learners' work was displayed in addition to any specific language for learning. Setting up the learning wall was a collaborative effort and learners could add to this wall in any way they chose throughout the topic's duration, perhaps a drawing of a volcano, a piece of illustrated text such as a news report on an earthquake, or adding a QR code, which gave access to a voice recording or sound effect (1.1). This wall also served as part of an exhibition space. Coupled with a display table, all the work presented by learners was enjoyed by all stakeholders through an end-of-topic celebration of learning event. At the start of the topic, parents and carers were asked for their support in discussing and sharing their knowledge of the topic with their children and wherever possible, asking their children to share what they had learnt in lessons throughout the duration of the topic (3.4, 8.1, 8.3).

In preparation for the topic, a simulation of the aftermath of an earthquake was set up with the help of the teaching assistants in an empty mobile classroom. This was staged as a 'disaster zone' and was duly cordoned off with clear signage signalling the entry point. The whole school was informed of this to allow other groups to visit if they wished (7.1, 9.2). The start of this lesson involved a discussion in class of the term *natural disaster*, starting with a two-minute chat with their talking partners. Having completed the pre-teach lesson, the learners were able to refer to their learning wall for the key words, images, and symbols to assist them. All learners were pre-warned of the change to their usual routine and were given the changes to their lesson plan the day before, in order to prepare them for these changes and to ask any questions (to support the needs of students who find managing changes to routines difficult). On the day of the entry point to the topic, learners were guided to the 'disaster zone', the aim being to enable them to be immersed in a multisensory experience, which included taking a slow walk around the site, which was further enhanced by making use of a smoke machine, flashing blue lights, and sound effects (1.2, 1.3, 3.3).

Learners could walk through alone or in pairs. One learner decided they would prefer to watch from outside – this was accommodated and they were provided with a microphone and asked to record their thoughts on what they could see (9.2). Ear defenders and face masks were provided for those who wished to use them (7.3, 9.2). This embodied experience made an immediate impact on learners on many levels and resulted in positive engagement and responses (7.2). What followed was a reflective discussion in a group 'debrief' session, which gave individuals the opportunity to share their experiences and to talk about how they might want to present their feedback. Everyone was encouraged to contribute to the discussion and supported wherever necessary to communicate their thoughts and feelings (8.3). This provided them with an opportunity to share, be heard, and also to reflect on what it might be like to experience such a disaster in real life. A mini question time followed to gather more information for the topic learning wall for all to use as a reference point and to determine the next steps for subsequent lessons.

Learners were given the choice to work alone, with a partner, or in a small group of up to three individuals to report on their 'disaster zone' experience (7.1). Teamwork was encouraged.

Students were given the opportunity to set up their workstation in the classroom to work away from distractions and could also use the space and opportunity for self-regulation if they wanted to move around or even to work standing

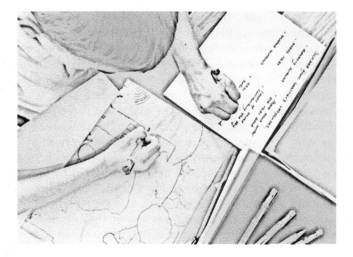

Figure 7.2 Teaching assistant scribes a learner's verbal responses

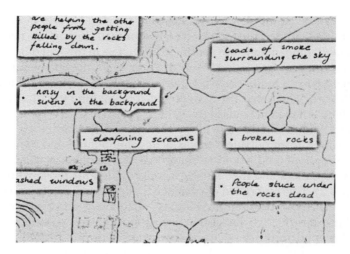

Figure 7.3 Verbal responses added to a pupil's work

up. Quickly setting up an individual learning zone enabled one learner to be directed there who felt that they needed to desensitize from the group experience and regain focus. Learners were also provided with a wide choice of formats for carrying out their work (4.2). Some began to work on written reports – either handwritten or typed on an iPad or laptop. To support literacy access, some asked for and were given opportunities to use the speech-to-text facility on their device, or have their words scribed; some produced a PowerPoint presentation; some chose to simply write key words on card/paper with accompanying drawings. Others preferred to create storyboards together and were provided with a choice of writing frames created then and there under learner instruction. Some chose to undertake and record reflective discussions with their group members using the iPad, recording microphones, or voice buttons (the teaching assistant supported individuals with communication skills and asked **targeted questions** to probe understanding further) (5.1, 5.2). Key words and photographs of the disaster zone (taken before the lesson) were provided as supporting material and references to spellings for written work (2.1, 2.4). For two learners using a laptop, a demonstration of the use of the spellchecker was given and they were encouraged to practise this skill and share it with others (8.3).

Work in progress was shared with the class and there was a choice of doing this either directly or through the teacher or teaching assistant. Completed examples were promptly displayed. A real-time film and photographs of the walk around the disaster site was recorded by two volunteers and subsequently used as reference and prompting material at the beginning of the follow-up lesson. Learners could feedback on the lesson via a graded feedback sheet, with reflective questions and illustrated with emoticons (6.4, 9.3). The start of the next lesson would always begin with a pupil review of the previous lesson's learning, with reference to their feedback and a collaborative plan drawn up for that lesson in terms of personal and subject goals and, most importantly, their areas of interest (6.1, 8.3).

Example 2: A secondary level GCSE art lesson

Task: Decide *which of the UDL Guidelines and Checkpoints have been applied in the following lesson*

A 60-minute Year 10 GCSE art lesson (age 14–15 years) focused on collaboratively preparing supporting material to enable learners to develop analysis of artists' work. This is one of the assessment objectives of GCSE Art & Design and is often one aspect of the course which many learners find particularly challenging. It can often be excessively focused on extended writing.

This lesson was the fifth in a series of twelve which began with an introduction to the theme of 'Structures'; a broad enough theme to encompass the interests of all learners and to offer opportunity for varied responses. Learners had spent five lessons gathering visual and other relevant information on the topic as a starting point and had produced mind-maps and other visual responses and worked on recording skills. Drawing offered a choice of media and a choice of subject matter relating to the theme.

It must be noted that a typical characteristic of inclusive lesson planning is providing a level of flexibility and, in the context of GCSE Art, learners typically work towards achieving their own personal and subject goals with one-to-one guidance where necessary. Individual learning journals offer a level of independence with respect to self-reflection, review, and target-setting. A lesson such as this is often a highly focused workshop used to develop specific skills to arm all learners with confidence to tackle the course requirements independently. Towards the end of the previous lesson, when asked, most of the learners indicated that 'analysis' was a skill they could develop further.

Responding to this immediately, a focused ten-minute group discussion on the meaning of 'analysis' in relation to works of art was undertaken. This served as a pre-teach session in preparation for the workshop – a decision was made to video record this via iPad to serve as a reminder to the group of the discussion at the start of the next lesson. The workshop group consisted of twelve learners, four of whom stated that they were happy to work independently in pairs on this task. Several examples of successful critical analyses were provided for reference, including a video clip of an art historian giving a short review of an artist's work and also three examples of writing frames to support recording. Students were given choices in how they wanted to record this work. Writing frames were also available digitally so that they could be customised (see Figure 7.4). There is always a set of relevant key words available for all to use, with a glossary of terms accompanied by a visual reference/example. Learners are encouraged to add to the glossary and the general key words list as they come across unfamiliar terms. These could be shared to aid concept, language, and vocabulary development and also as an *aide-mémoire* for written tasks.

The art room offers more space, which provides learners a little more flexibility in terms of choosing their own designated spaces to work alone or in pairs/ small groups of three or four (it is worthwhile planning for lessons to happen in spaces other than classrooms to offer variety). All learners are encouraged to engage in 'talk' and peer collaboration, taking questions from their peers, which fosters a sense of community learning. The eight learners who elected to join the

Analysis of Artist's Work

Upload an image of your chosen artwork here

What was your initial reaction to the work?

What materials have been used?

How have the materials been applied?

What is the meaning of the work? What do you make of it?

Why do you say this?

How has the artist used the following visual elements

and what effect does this have on the viewer?

Colour

Shape

Space   **Name of the artist?**

Pattern   **Title of the work?**

Form   **Year it was made?**

Tone/value   **Where was it made?**

Figure 7.4 Example of a writing frame

workshop were involved in a review of the pre-teach session from the last lesson and a question-time followed, as in the primary lesson (above), to gauge and clarify any ambiguities and misunderstandings.

To make the task more engaging, one learner was asked to select, from a range of postcard images, one to be used for this activity. The question, *'What questions do we need to ask to analyse this piece of art so we can talk about it effectively?'* acted as the prompt and was written on a small A4 dry-wipe board for reference. A version with widgets (a picture symbols system for vocabulary) was also available to support understanding in a visual way. Learners were given the opportunity to devise their own questions, which were subsequently recorded by a volunteer in the group. The questions were reviewed, with guidance and scaffolded questions from the teacher, that were levelled at individuals' conceptual understanding (this built on current knowledge to support development of higher-level thinking skills). Finally, a group decision was made on whether any modifications needed to be made or whether there were specific kinds of questions missing that might generate a more in-depth analysis.

Having made modifications, one member suggested they challenge their peers who had been working independently, to answer some of their questions to ascertain if this group had indeed considered a range of questions in their analyses. The rule is always to make feedback constructive and to give learners the opportunity to develop reflective skills and become more confident at self-assessment in light of peer feedback, particularly if they are paired with a more confident 'study buddy'. The final list of questions was later prepared for the next lesson as a checklist, with a selection of supporting writing frames.

Learners were prompted to select one of the postcard images to use in undertaking their analysis. Learners completed learning journals in the last ten minutes of the lesson. A choice of checklists, key words to circle, and sentence starters provided support for those struggling with independent sentence writing to record their reflections. Journals were shared with the teacher who could then give immediate feedback, either verbally, with a symbol, a colour code, in writing, or a combination of these according to individuals' access needs.

Conclusion

The aim of inclusive pedagogy is to offer learning experiences that are accessible to all. Teachers need to be responsive to the range of levels in pupil communication access needs, knowledge, skills, and understanding, in order to provide fair learning challenges that support progress towards personal and subject learning goals. If pupils feel that there are equal opportunities to participate in group or individual learning as needed, that they are fully involved in the learning experience through access to choices in learning tasks and expression, and that their contributions are valued, increased levels of learner motivation and engagement invariably follow. We believe that considering the neurodiversity of *all* your pupils, rather than just the labels some attract, and gradually building UDL into your lesson planning can offer you a pathway towards achieving this aim in your teaching.

Further reading and resources

British Dyslexia Association website is a useful source of ideas and training opportunities for working with people with literacy difficulties: https://www.bdadyslexia.org.uk/

CAST is the umbrella organisation for Universal Design for Learning, offering further information on UDL and its implementation in the classroom, as well as links to UDL's underlying research base: http://www.cast.org/

The Communications Trust is a coalition of over fifty not-for-profit organisations offering training and resources for children and young people with speech, language, and communication needs: https://www.thecommunicationtrust.org.uk/

The Dyspraxia Foundation website offers advice, resources, and training for those working with people with cognitively based motor coordination needs: https://dyspraxiafoundation.org.uk/

Elkan offers short training courses and resources for the teachers and families of people with speech, language, and communication needs: https://www.elklan.co.uk/

The Learning Development Aids website is a really useful online store for resources to support inclusive pedagogy: https://www.ldalearning.com/

8 | Setting ambitious expectations

Majella Dalton-Bartley and Tony Brittain

Introduction

In this chapter, we will review research on the crucial impact of teachers' **ambitious expectations** on pupil learning and progress. You will explore what is meant by ambitious expectations and what this looks like in the classroom. You will unpack the relationships within the classroom and the potential impact of these as an accelerator to learner progress. Attention is afforded to the importance of relationship building, benchmarking, visualisation, modelling behaviour for learning, empathy, and positive behaviour management. You will explore practical ideas to assist and develop your classroom practice, with prompts for reflection and activities to guide your learning.

What are ambitious expectations?

For an early career teacher, the thought of considering, enacting, and embedding ambitious expectations within your practice can be daunting, yet it is vitally important to do so. Once in place, high expectations will have a significant impact on your practice leading to a strong culture of expectation, aspiration, and success within your class or classes for all pupils. In 1968, Rosenthal and Jacobson explored teacher expectation and the impact this had on pupils; their conclusions resonate today. The effect of teacher labelling and the subsequent development of a self-fulling prophecy can be highly significant. Rosenthal and Jacobson concluded that pupil progress and outcomes were affected by the expectation of the class teacher (this can be both positive and negative). Your effective teaching practice can influence greatly the pupils you teach, particularly those from disadvantaged backgrounds. The Early Career Framework in England explores this and recognises that, 'teachers have the ability to affect and improve the well-being, motivation and the behaviour of pupils' (DfE, 2019a: 8).

Prompt for reflection

Considering either your teaching or your own learning journey, what was the impact of high or low levels of expectation on subjective wellbeing and outcome? In less than one hundred words, state what 'ambitious expectations' means to you. What does this look like in your classroom? You may wish to revisit this in the future.

Ambitious expectations involve the teacher consistently setting and insisting upon high standards for each pupil to work towards fulfilling and achieving their potential regardless of ability. Ambitious expectations should permeate *every* aspect of your teaching, from lesson planning through to setting learning outcomes and behaviour management. As an early career teacher, considering how you will achieve this is crucial. This chapter sets down a number of strategies to help you.

Getting the climate right

Hattie states, 'A positive, caring, respectful climate in the classroom is a prior condition to learning' (2012: 5). Whilst there are many variables in the classroom and you cannot control all of these, you, the teacher, have the opportunity and responsibility to work towards a safe and meaningful learning environment so each of your pupils can make strong progress and have positive outcomes.

Prompt for reflection

Describe how you convey ambitious expectations in your classroom practice. What would this look and feel like? What language is used? Where do you position yourself in the classroom? What do the display boards look like?

A positive learning environment does not happen by accident. The climate of your classroom is influenced by many variables. A climate of ambitious expectations, rooted in mutual respect and trust, takes time to build but the results are overwhelmingly positive and your hard work will bear fruit.

Within this *right climate*, you will consistently and fairly apply ambitious expectations to all pupils in all aspects of the learning environment from setting appropriate work to behaviour. Prior to your lesson, effective planning is crucial to ensure you have identified student differences and needs, planning accordingly for these so each pupil can access the curriculum with the clear expectation for them to reach their potential. The Early Career Framework stipulates the importance of communicating a belief in the academic potential of pupils by,

> [s]etting appropriate tasks that stretch but are achievable in a challenging curriculum. Creating a positive environment where making mistakes and learning from them and the need for effort and perseverance are part of the daily routine. (DfE, 2019a: 8)

The right climate for learning involves a culture shift that aims to empower and invigorate each pupil to have belief in themselves and their abilities. In this ambitious and meaningful classroom culture, there will be mutual respect, engagement, and appropriate tasks will not limit pupils but open them to the possibility that they can achieve and be proud of themselves. If this culture permeates your classroom, you are more likely to have engaged, well-behaved pupils who make good progress. As an early career teacher, it is important that you not only have ambitious expectations for your pupils, but that you consistently share these with them. When the pupils know you believe in them, they will start to believe in themselves!

Research

A *growth mindset* influences teacher and pupil expectations. Carol Dweck identifies two different mindsets: fixed and growth. With a fixed mindset, there is a belief that this is what you can do and that will not really change; conversely, a growth mindset sees the potential and opportunities to develop without limiting oneself. Dweck poses the question, 'What are the consequences of thinking that your intelligence or personality is something you can develop, as opposed to something that is a fixed, deep-seated trait?' (2007: 68). As an early career teacher, this is a valuable question to reflect upon. Having a growth mindset goes hand in hand with ambitious expectations.

Dweck's theory is applicable both to you and your pupils. Her work suggests the power of a growth mindset and continuous effort. This entails not giving up when mistakes are made, learning from these and moving forward as a positive endeavour, and trying different strategies and ideas in the classroom. The strategies that work for one class will not necessarily work for another. You need to be flexible and draw on a repertoire of strategies, whilst not negotiating on standards or expectations at any point. If you, as an early career teacher, can embrace this and endeavour to *live* and *model* it in your daily teaching, then the impact could be significant. If each pupil in your class believes they can develop, learn more, and achieve highly, their progress and outcomes will be positively affected. A *growth mindset*, a belief in one's abilities and possibilities, for both you and your pupils is essential for ambitious expectations to be lived in your classroom.

Ruby-Davies recognises the significance of having, sharing, and consistently applying high expectations to the pupils you teach. She found that,

> in contrast to the average progress of low-expectation teachers, high-expectation teachers spent more time providing a framework for students learning, provided their students with more feedback, questioned their students using higher order questions, and managed their students' behaviour more positively. (Ruby-Davies, 2010: 289)

The strategies presented later in this chapter will unpack this further.

Prompt for reflection

We have established that the teacher is crucial in enabling each pupil to reach his or her potential by the setting of appropriate and challenging work with a clear framework for pupil success. Can you think of ways in which you could be a high-expectation teacher? How will you set appropriate and challenging work for your pupils?

As an early career teacher, having, demonstrating, and consistently sharing high expectations is essential for your future teaching. The impact on children's future outcomes cannot be underestimated. Pantaleo argues that every 'school needs competent, caring and high expectation teachers who are knowledgeable about and confident in their pedagogy, who understand the multifaceted nature of their responsibility for student learning and who expect the best of and for their students' (2016: 92). This remains a challenge for all teachers, yet is an essential component of successful teaching.

The strategies below, supported by research and practitioner experience, will enable you to consider how you can effectively set ambitious expectations for all pupils. Each of the strategies is accompanied by a suggested activity designed to support the development of your practice.

Benchmarking for ambitious expectations

It is sometimes assumed that new teachers are innately programmed with a clear understanding of what good practice in the classroom looks like. This is not necessarily true and the practice of effective *benchmarking* can be of significant help. As an early career teacher, it is easy to be consumed by the intense demands and pressures that teaching can bring. Indeed, Middlehurst states, 'the purpose of education can be quickly subsumed by the difficulties of our daily practice', and worse still, 'our hopes and passions can be quickly squeezed by our workload pressures' (2013: 2). Despite the demands of the teacher's role, deliberately designing opportunities for your professional development is crucial (see Chapter 10 on 'Developing through reflection and collaborative enquiry') and none more so than benchmarking. Berger writes passionately about fostering a culture of excellence in the classroom. Using the metaphor of carpentry, he writes, 'If you're going to do something, I believe, you should do it well. You should sweat over it and make sure it's strong, and accurate and beautiful and you should be proud of it' (2003: 1). The philosophy of artisanship can be applied to how early career teachers develop their understanding of what excellence looks like, what ambitious expectations look like, and, crucially, what pupils are capable of achieving. Teacher practice, like pupils' work, should be crafted, shaped, honed, and cherished. As Berger states, 'They need to build a new culture and a new ethic. I do not believe there is a shortcut to building a new culture. It is a long-term commitment. It's a way of life' (2003: 4). Teaching is a highly personal and bespoke craft. Any teaching approach must be nuanced to suit each teacher and be right for that individual and the pupils they are supporting. Finding a way to identify what works doesn't happen by accident; it must be forged, developed, shaped, and as Berger would argue, 'crafted' until we are proud of it.

As an early career teacher, it is important to observe a range of lessons across diverse curriculum areas, stages, and phases. For this to be helpful and effective, it helps to know what to look for. Consideration should be given to establishing a basic framework for effective observation. It may help to consider both pedagogical elements and behaviour management elements of teacher practice (see Chapters 4 and 7 on 'The complexities of behaviour management' and 'Inclusive pedagogy'). The suggested activity provides a template that may offer a helpful framework.

Suggested activity

Observe the lesson of a more experienced colleague, or ask a colleague to observe one of your lessons, with the aim of generating a better understanding of excellent practice when setting ambitious expectations in the classroom. The template in Figure 8.1 provides a framework to support lesson observation and benchmarking. It is structured around the five themed modules of the Early Career Framework (DfE, 2019a). For each theme, prompts are provided to focus your attention when observing. Try using these prompts in a lesson to benchmark ambitious expectations and consider what strategies you might use in your lessons.

Visualisation

Having established a better understanding of the nature and feel of ambitious expectations, we now direct attention to visualising these expectations in action, and encourage deliberate practise using intentional and consistent language to promote challenge and aspiration. **Deliberate practice** means devoting time and resources to engage in two key elements of professional development. First, *visualisation* of the classroom when ambitious expectations are being met. Second, the development and deliberate practice of consistent and intentional *language* to tackle a range of scenarios. Berger's 'craftsmanship' resonates through the professional development described here; this will take time and effort, but enables effective habits to be established from the outset.

Berger states, 'Students may have different potentials but, in general, the attitudes and achievements of students are shaped by the culture around them: Students adjust their attitudes and efforts in order to fit into the culture' (2003: 34). It can be argued that successful sportspeople visualise success in order to develop a positive mindset. It is common practice for a golfer, for example, to visualise their next shot several times in their head before it is taken, considering all possible variables. In this way, the muscles implement what the head has already decided is going to happen. The same can apply to teaching. A useful exercise is to consider the minutiae of the classroom in terms of the *sound*, the *look*, and the *feel* when ambitious expectations are being met. By committing these mental images, sounds, and feelings to long-term memory, you will be better equipped to consistently set and command ambitious expectations in the classroom.

The second element in effective visualisation is to develop and plan specific language that may be used to promote a culture of positivity and trust, tackling scenarios where pupil behaviour falls short of your expectations. Devote time to plan a range of potential scenarios and, subsequently, develop a well-scripted response for each. The use of **assumed compliance** in your deliberate language illustrates how a planned and well-rehearsed instruction can be delivered in an assertive and positive manner. For example, 'thank you for correcting your shirt' is far more powerful than 'please tuck your shirt in'. Whilst it is impossible to plan for every eventuality in the classroom, it helps to be ready for as many

Benchmarking of Teaching and Learning through Observation			
Teacher		**Class**	
Year		**Key Stage**	
Subject		**No. of Students**	
Date		**Support**	
Context of Lesson			
Notes:			

Engaging Pupils in Learning	• How does the teacher motivate pupils from the outset to be interested in the lesson? • How does the teacher relate the lesson to previous learning? • How does the teacher allow pupils to attend to prior attainment? • How does the teacher ensure and maintain enthusiasm and engagement? • How does the teacher motivate and engage pupils beyond the specification? • How does the teacher challenge and inspire the pupils? • How do the pupils respond to the teacher?
Enabling Pupil in Learning	• How does the teacher ensure that pupils are ready for learning? • How are students made to feel comfortable and safe within the lesson? • What clear routines, habits and social norms exist in the classroom? • How are ambitious, high standards set and enforced within the classroom? • How does the teacher use praise and rewards to reinforce positive behaviour? • How does the teacher use sanctions to reinforce positive behaviour? • How is mutual trust and respect fostered and developed within the lesson? • How are students encouraged to make mistakes and be inquisitive in their learning?
Developing Quality Pedagogy	• How are instructions delivered to the pupils? • How are learning activities chunked and sequenced? • What forms of teacher modelling take place? • How are pupils of all abilities supported in their learning? • What is the balance of teacher talk and pupil deliberate practice? • What different types of learning activities are employed within the lesson?
Making Productive Use of Assessment	• How do the classroom displays and resources support learning? • How do pupils work with each other during the different phases of the lesson? • How are questions asked within the lesson? • How are pupils assessed both within the lesson and outside the lesson? • How are pupils learning targets shared with them? • How does the teacher check pupils understanding?
Fulfilling Professional Responsibilities	• How are relationships within the classroom managed? • How does the teacher ensure that the lesson is challenging, and pace is engaging? • How does the teacher inspire the pupils to develop a curiosity and a love of learning? • How much reflection time takes place within the lesson?

Figure 8.1 Lesson observation template

as is possible. This provides you with confidence and security internally, and outwardly leads to a more calm, positive, and consistent approach, which will accentuate trust and respect between teacher and pupils.

Suggested activity

For each of the scenarios below, write a script detailing the intentional and consistent language that could be used to best tackle the pupil behaviour for learning and reinforce ambitious expectations. Consideration should be given to the use of **positive recognition** and positive, assertive language.

Scenario One: As a classroom teacher, you are delivering an exposition to your class of students. Your expectation is that all students will be listening to your instruction. The vast majority of the students are meeting this expectation; however, a small group of three students is engaged in what appears to be an off-task discussion.

Scenario Two: You are delivering an exposition to your class, modelling and questioning your students on their understanding. Your instruction is for students to keep their hands down, whilst you target questions; however, one student shouts out without being asked to contribute.

Reflection on the suggested activity

Rather than 'zooming-in' on the small group of students who are not meeting expectations, try to 'zoom out' and recognise and praise the vast majority of students who are.

In Scenario One, a typical challenge in any classroom, try to develop a series of planned scripts that positively recognise compliant behaviour. For example, 'thank you to all those students who are sat up straight, with eyes on me, and listening in silence' is non-confrontational and far more positive than any criticism of the off-task students. Similarly, consider asking a student to repeat your instruction back to the class (**positive repetition**) rather than confronting the minority as follows: 'Student A, why don't you tell the class what my instruction was', or 'Student A, why do you think I've said well done and thank you to you?'

In Scenario Two, similar scripted language, if used consistently, will become habitual and will allow you to tackle this common issue with positivity; however, you may also consider scripted body language and non-verbal signals too. Proximity can be a powerful tool for any teacher; simply approaching an off-task student, whilst continuing with the class, works wonderfully in modifying behaviour without the need for negative language. Similarly, a well-rehearsed and positively delivered visual sign or cue allows the teacher to maintain flow in the lesson without the need for negative language and a confrontation.

Modelling behaviour for learning

The first two strategies provide the early career teacher with support in both understanding ambitious expectations and recognising and describing what they look, sound, and feel like in the classroom. We now turn our attention to the importance of 'living' out these expectations. A useful starting point is to consider the language that you may use to model three typical classroom discussions, listed in the suggested activity below. Having tackled the activity, read through the strategy and then revisit the activity again. Is your response different?

Suggested activity

Consider the instructions to pupils below. In each case, consider how you would effectively model this instruction. What language would you use? What does each instruction *look*, *sound*, and *feel* like?

1. You have asked pupils in your class to engage in a task that requires a written response. You instruct your pupils to carry out this task in silence.
2. You have given your pupils a reading stimulus, which you would then like them to discuss in pairs. Your instruction is for the pupils to read the stimulus together and then discuss.
3. You have given your pupils an extract to read on their own. Your instruction is for them to read this individually and you have allowed five minutes for this task.

Whether demonstrating or unpicking the nuances of a practical experiment, or perhaps making clear the structure of a topic sentence, teacher modelling is crucial. Rosenshine (2012) describes improving instruction by identifying and dealing with misconceptions. How else would we expect pupils to know what to do? How else would pupils understand what excellence in a learning outcome looks like? The application of modelling to clarify and instruct is crucial in establishing ambitious expectations in pupil behaviour. A common misconception for an early career teacher is to assume knowledge in relation to behaviour. Consider one of the most common instructions a classroom teacher can make: to state that work must be completed in silence. Consider now what silence actually sounds like! Often classroom teachers instruct silence but do not model or reinforce the instruction and expectation, and this goes to the very heart of ambitious expectations. The term 'silence' needs unpicking and delimiting with pupils. Pupils must be left in no doubt what is expected when you use this word. If we instruct 'silence', we must demand it; if we do not, and we are willing to concede on this one word, where else will we concede ground – homework deadlines, effort and application? Silence means silence; no words, noises, just thought and hard work. Silence does not mean a slight buzz and chatter; this goes to the very heart of 'living' ambitious expectations. What does a 'healthy buzz' around the classroom sound like? What is an appropriate volume for a pair-share activity? Both need explaining and sharing with pupils so that from the outset ambitious expectations are set clearly.

Consistent use and application of language is key to developing mutual trust and respect, and supporting effective learning. Cognitive science recognises that to commit new knowledge to long-term memory, pupils must be asked to consider what they already know, their current schema, before engaging in deliberate practice (see Chapter 3 on 'Understanding memory'). This cannot happen in an environment that is not positive and conducive to learning. Shimamura emphasises the importance of establishing an effective framework for learning, stating: 'Inside the classroom, it is critical at the outset to be engaged and attuned to the topic at hand' (2018: 9). Pupils must be ready for learning and motivated to learn and understand your ambitious expectations. Shimamura argues, 'There is one critical time for focussing attention, which is the settling in period – the first four or five minutes of a lesson … Student engagement is essential at the start' (2018: 16).

Prompt for reflection

Having read the explanation of the strategy, tackle the suggested activity again. Consider how you would articulate the instructions to your pupils. What descriptive language would you use to model exactly your expectations in response to each instruction?

Empathy

Having mastered the first three strategies, you should now feel positive about identifying and demanding ambitious expectations within the classroom. However, despite the best efforts of the most diligent and positive early career teacher, pupils may still fall short. The final strategy examines how best to modify pupil behaviour should this happen.

Empathy is crucial when setting ambitious expectations and managing pupil behaviour to ensure expectations are met. Csikszentmihalyi's (2008) 'flow theory' allows teachers to consider the relationships that exist between the challenge of the task, and the attitudes and skills of the pupil. Where pupils' attitudes and skills match the challenge of the assigned task, pupils will be fully engaged and happy in the task, and in full 'flow'. Conversely, off-task behaviour for learning may be caused by a mismatch in both the challenge of the task, and attitudes and skills of the pupils. Where this occurs, it may be that the off-task behaviour is caused by an underlying anxiety in the pupil(s) due to their lack of understanding. Similarly, it may be that a pupil has completed the task quickly, finding little challenge in the activity. In both cases, you should unpick the reason behind the behaviour; if an empathetic, objective standpoint is adopted from the outset, this will lead to the outcome being positive. Understanding this concept de-personalises pupil behaviour and allows you to better deal with classroom behaviour positively and constructively.

Suggested activity

Consider a scenario presented earlier in this chapter. Your pupils are engaged in an activity that requires peer-to-peer discussion before responses are written down. You are happy with the volume of discussion in the class. However, two students seem to have stopped working – one is looking out of the window, the other daydreaming. What reasons might there be for the behaviour displayed by the two students? How might your answer to this first question shape your response as a classroom teacher?

Reflection on the suggested activity

A common occurrence in any classroom, it is far too easy for the early career teacher to judge the off-task behaviour outlined in this activity as a deliberate, negative response. Viewing the behaviour in this way may lead to less effective interaction with the two students, and may not tackle the issue at the heart of their behaviour. Could it be that the students find the task too simplistic? Have they completed the task? Conversely, perhaps the task is too challenging and the off-task behaviour is a manifestation of their anxiety. The starting point here is to unpick the students' understanding of the task through positive questioning, always trying to assume the best.

Positive behaviour management

Classroom management can be a stressful element in the professional life of a teacher. If classroom management can be undertaken positively, objectively, and empathetically, it will be beneficial for both the teacher and pupils, and will create a positive learning culture of mutual respect and trust. Earlier, we examined the importance of modelling language leading to positive behaviour. However, there will be times when you must intervene to modify pupil behaviour. In these moments, one of the most powerful strategies in establishing and maintaining ambitious expectations is to employ positive recognition to modify pupil behaviour in a meaningful and effective manner, avoiding confrontation and conflict. Canter and Canter state, 'The best way to build responsible student behaviour is to continually provide frequent positive recognition to those students who are on task' (2001: 146). Positive recognition is extremely powerful, providing a sound foundation for you to set the tone for the management of your class. As Canter and Canter explain, 'Positive recognition and support results in students feeling good about themselves. When students feel good about themselves, when they feel confident about what they are doing, their self-esteem rises and they are motivated to behave better and achieve academically' (2001: 158).

Consider a typical classroom scenario used earlier in this chapter – you are delivering an exposition to your class, modelling and questioning your students on their understanding. Your instruction is for students to keep their hands down, whilst you target questions; however, one student shouts out without being asked to contribute.

Rather than direct any intervention to the individual, stop the class taking the time to praise every other student, thanking them for following the instruction. Consider targeting a question to another student to ask him or her to reiterate the instruction. Consider asking another question, targeting a different student and thanking everyone again for following the instruction. With praise, positive recognition, and repetition, students in the class will understand and learn what is required without the need for any confrontation with an individual pupil. Where further individual modification is required, this should always be done 'privately' rather than in front of the class, and can again be done through positive interrogation rather than accusation: 'Why do you think I thanked Student A for their contribution earlier?', or 'What was it about the way they answered the question that I would have liked?' In developing a positive culture within the classroom, the early career teacher must embed and instil habits and this is better served through positive recognition.

Insights from practice: Early career reflection

The ascent of any peak will involve moments of challenge, exertion, and perhaps, moments so demanding it may not seem possible. When standing at the top and admiring the view it is, of course, all worthwhile, and easy to forget the trials involved in getting to that point. The completion of the first years in teaching can feel just like this.

This section draws on the early career experiences of Lesley, who has successfully completed her first year of teaching and is now stood on top of her own personal mountain, admiring the view below. Reflecting on the ascent, there were indeed trials and challenges, but also those shining 'light-bulb' moments that illuminate the darkness, that pervade the uncertainty, and pave a way to the summit. There were three key milestones or moments for Lesley.

Effective benchmarking, Lesley reflects, is crucial. Enthusiastic, determined and driven, early career teachers are often directed by their mentors or proactively request to observe colleagues teach. However, knowing what to focus on during observations is vital or this can be confusing at best and redundant at worst. Lesley's advice is to go in with a plan. One approach is to focus on one key element of classroom practice in each observation. For example, focus on classroom climate and management in one observation, and questioning in the next. This affords the early career teacher clarity and efficiency and makes optimal use of valuable time spent benchmarking.

In Lesley's experience, consistency in both setting and demanding ambitious expectations is important. A common mistake made by teachers is to allow the idiosyncrasies of different classes to shape our standards and expectations. We become guided by pupils' understanding of what is acceptable, not our own.

Should an older year group, for example, be afforded greater trust to work independently with a healthy buzz in the classroom? Surely, that is okay? Similarly, it is surely acceptable to allow pupils to shout out in a certain class because they are more vibrant, dynamic, and excitable? It is fine, surely. They are just being enthusiastic, aren't they? For Lesley, understanding that her ambitious standards must be maintained in every lesson, for every class, regardless of their differences was a key moment, and one that ensured success in the end.

Finally, and perhaps the simplest principle of all, Lesley states that persistence in all forms is necessary. Resilience, grit, and absolute persistence in demanding students follow our ambitious expectations is the key to making it to the summit. This is not easy, yet ultimately the effort and skill required is worth it. Just think of the view from the top!

Conclusion

As an early career teacher, you already have experience and will be continually learning and developing your practice. As you develop, you will recognise that you have your own style and will apply various strategies that feel comfortable for you and work! You will vary your strategies to address specific needs and circumstances. However, while your strategies and practice may change, one consistent feature will be setting, sharing, and insisting upon ambitious expectations for all pupils, without negotiation. Consistency is key. Developing a belief and a growth mindset yourself will help you to facilitate this for your pupils. Setting ambitious expectations for *all* your pupils will make a significant impact upon the progress, outcomes, and ultimate life chances of the pupils you teach.

Further reading and resources

Griffith, A. and Burns, M. (2012) *Engaging Learners*. London: Crown House.

Hattie, J. (2012) *Visible Learning for Teachers: Maximizing impact on learning*. London: Routledge.

Lemov, D. (2010) *Teach Like a Champion: 49 techniques that put students on the path to college*. San Francisco, CA: Jossey-Bass.

Pantaleo, S. (2016) Teacher expectations and student literacy engagement and achievement. *Literacy*, 50 (2): 83–92.

Rosenshine, B. (2012) Principles of instruction: Research-based strategies that all teachers should know. *American Educator*, 36 (1): 12–19.

Ruby-Davies, C. (2010) Classroom interactions: Exploring the practices of high- and low-expectation teachers. *British Journal of Educational Psychology*, 77 (2): 289–306.

The role of emotion in relationships with parents and carers

9

Charlotte Booth and Geraldine Carter

Introduction

This chapter focuses on the role of emotion in the development of effective working relationships between pupils' parents and carers and their teachers. Parents and carers play a crucial role in children's education. Research documents the advantageous impact of effective working relationships, including increased attendance, improved behaviour and social skills and, significantly, better academic attainment (Goodall, 2015, 2018; Iver et al., 2015; Lendrum et al., 2015; Tobin, 2017; Wilder, 2014). In examining how emotion influences relationships between parents/carers and early career teachers, we draw on three key concepts: autobiographical experience, **unconscious bias**, and cultural myths that exist within education.

We advocate an effective working relationship as one where both parties are considered co-constructors of knowledge about the child (Goodall, 2018). They each become one-who-teaches and one-who-learns, in a fluid dialogic relationship, eventually a partnership, in which knowledge about how to support the learning of the child is created (Fretwell et al., 2018; Jeynes, 2018; Pushor, 2012; Vincent, 2017). Quite often, early career teachers are expected to 'direct' or 'manage' relationships with parents through established school policies and practices. In many school contexts, emphasis is placed on the giving and receiving of information to/from parents and carers (Goodall, 2016b; Ofsted, 2015). This is an approach advocated in official documentation across the four national school systems of the United Kingdom (Office of the First Minister and Deputy First Minister, 2016; Ofsted, 2015; Scottish Executive, 2006; Welsh Government 2016). The influence of emotion in education is potentially an uncomfortable construction for policy-makers (Clarke and Phelan, 2015). Policy documents present an image of the 'good' parent/carer working collaboratively with the teacher, to ensure the child achieves the best possible outcome from their education (Vincent and Maxwell, 2016).

The involvement of parents and carers typically orientates around approaches such as school reports and parent consultation meetings. School reports containing a high level of jargon can be considered inconsequential or even incomprehensible to some parents and carers (Pearson, 2014), and discussions at parents' evenings may take place in an adversarial atmosphere, across a table, in a rushed timescale (Goodall, 2016a). Often, such approaches 'tick a box', satisfying the requirement of parental involvement in their child's education, yet can create ambiguous situations and unhelpful responses from both parties. This leads to attempts to disguise feelings, with either party concerned that their emotional reaction may appear as either inappropriate and/or unprofessional. Both parties must take responsibility for conveying their emotions towards each other but also to the child, who may internalise them (Whitehead et al., 2013). It is our belief that to flourish as an early career teacher, contemplation of emotionality, and its role in developing effective working relationships with parents and carers, is a priority.

Key concepts

Educational autobiographical experiences

Both parties bring to the relationship **educational autobiographical experiences**, which influence their expectations of what constitutes an effective working relationship, including both parties' perception of the other in their role in the home and/or school context. For either party, uncertainty may stem from childhood experiences or from relationships that are more recent. Either or both parties may have had a positive experience or they may feel compelled to right what was lacking in their own education and, in some cases, a barrier of disengagement is evident. For example, many early career teachers speak fondly of teachers in their educational autobiography, often trying (whether consciously or unconsciously) to relive and replicate relationships, environments, and experiences with pupils in their own classes. Memories of their own education may have influenced their decision to become a teacher. In contrast, early career teachers who have memories of their parents/carers being disinterested in their education, seek to compensate when in role, in some cases becoming too emotionally invested in relationships. Awareness of the impact of educational autobiographical experiences, particularly past unresolved conflicts, should be of fundamental importance, particularly to teachers, as their familiarity with the context makes them susceptible to the re-enactment of childhood memories (Freud, 1930). Whether the teacher and/or parent/carer considers any conflicts resolved/unresolved is irrelevant – anxiety is nevertheless generated. The reliving of associated emotions does not equate to the same as the event previously experienced; yet it has a significant influence over expectations. In all instances, these past experiences fuel present-day expectations.

Unconscious bias

Unconscious bias is an unintentional and immediate processing of external stimuli in an individual's subconscious, producing an outcome via the conscious mind (Agarwal, 2020). Personal to the individual, biases can result in an altered interpretation that influences outward behaviours. Our unconscious biases can influence engagements positively; however, negative influences can lead to inaccurate judgements and irrationality. Consequently, tensions and anxieties can be provoked by both parties. For example, a teacher provides detail when explaining phonics to one parent but brushes over it with another, suggesting an unconscious decision that one parent needed more detail than another. Research has shown that unconscious biases are not always explicitly recognisable or easily measured (Hahn, 2019). The challenge faced by any teacher is generating a conscious awareness of the barriers we incite. By understanding our reactions to such barriers, we can understand our unconscious bias to a greater degree (Agarwal, 2020).

Cultural myths

Early career teachers should develop an awareness of **cultural myths**, allowing them to approach future familiar situations with a more grounded perception. Socially constructed cultural myths serve as temporal anchors that taint reality and subsequent representations on offer, influencing expectations of relationships between teachers and parents/carers, maintaining established policies and practices. Cultural myths provide a set of justifications and measures of thought and feelings that make 'certain' the reality they seek to produce (Britzman, 2003). They provide a semblance of order, structure, and control in the emotional world of education. For example, expectations and a societal need for teachers to fulfil a vast array of other roles, such as social controller, disciplinarian, pastoral carer, contravene the commonly held belief that a teacher's primary role is to educate children.

Prompt for reflection

Contemplate the following:

- What memories do you have of teacher/parent relations from your educational autobiography?
- How did interactions between teachers/parents make you feel?
- How have these experiences influenced your expectations of a parent's role in their child's education?
- What aspects of parent–teacher relations are uncertain? What strategies do you/might you use in uncertain situations?
- Identify how unconscious bias might influence your existing teacher–parent relations.
- What impact do other stakeholders' unconscious bias have upon your self-perception?
- Identify cultural myths that surround your role as a teacher.
- Identify cultural myths that influence your perception of a parent.

Stories from practice

Three vignettes containing early career teachers' stories from practice are now presented. They capture atypical, potentially emotive scenarios involving early career teachers and parents/carers. Consider your responses to the reflection prompts before moving on to the analysis. The analysis illustrates how the key concepts explored within the chapter may influence either or both parties' perceptions. It provides examples of how you can develop your practice and considerations for professional conversations with your mentor.

Vignette 1

About four weeks into the autumn term, a man and woman approach me at the cloakroom door, asking for a chat about their child's homework. The child in question is working towards age-related expectations in mathematics and it is widely known that Mum has additional learning needs also. The homework set for the past three weeks has been a consolidation of concepts taught in class. I invite them into the classroom and begin to explain the homework to the child again, modelling the activities. The child successfully completes a couple of examples. I mention to the child that Mum and Grandad would be able to help them if they were stuck. 'Grandad' angrily states he is 'Dad'. I apologise for my mistake, but he excuses himself from the room. Trying to regain control of the situation, I praise the child for successfully getting the answer to the last question correct, at which point Mum breaks down in tears, explaining she does not understand what I modelled to the child and has 'no idea how to help [her child] when I do not know myself'. She explains she sits down to support her son but confuses him in the process; he then becomes frustrated and refuses to engage any further. Mum confesses that she Googles answers to the questions, recording them on the homework sheet. She alludes to the impact this is having on her relationship with Dad, believing him to have low expectations of the child due to her learning difficulties. She admits, 'he blames me', and confesses this causes a lot of conflict in front of the child. Mum then asks if I can teach her how to do the homework set each week, as 'teachers know everything ... you are an expert!' Mum explains how guilty she feels, and I empathise, explaining that her child has the capability to complete the homework independently and that I will address any misconceptions when the homework is returned. I feel guilty that I cannot help more and that I have unintentionally eroded my relationship with Dad before it has even started!

Prompt for reflection

- Do you think Mum's actions surrounding homework completion are commonplace amongst parents?
- How might the early career teacher's perception of Mum influence her future relations with Mum and Dad?
- How will this affect their relationship with the child?
- How do you think the child's perception of a teacher's relationship with their parent/carer influences their own relationship with either party?

Analysis

Both parties feel pressure to know and the corresponding guilt in not knowing. Mum does not know how to support her child, and the teacher does not know how to support Mum. The perception that either party lacks what they are required to know affects both parties' perception of the experience, creating anxiety. Dad appears to affirm Mum's guilt by endorsing her concerns that her past educational autobiographical experiences are having an influence on their son's education. The potential blame accorded by Dad and the guilt felt by Mum infiltrate the child's home context. The teacher confirms this when she too assumes that 'Mum and Grandad' will support the child with his homework, even though she admits she had an awareness of Mum's potential insecurities. In your future practice, you cannot assume that parents/carers will be able to support their child with homework. Therefore, you may wish to provide modelled examples using various methods, if appropriate. You may also wish to consider signposting the child and/ or the parent to other support in place, such as a homework club, specific websites, or contacting a homework buddy from the same group.

Knowledge is conceptualised as a possession: for Mum, a possession she struggled to obtain in her educational autobiography; and for the teacher, a possession she has obtained through initial teacher education and on achieving **qualified teacher status**. Mum perceives her lack of knowledge as having an impact on her relationship with her son. This perception of lack of knowledge is fuelled by cultural myths surrounding a parent's role in their child's education and the potential advantageous impact it can have. The teacher is anxious that her not knowing how to best support Mum disrupts the cultural myth that 'teachers are experts'. Unconscious biases from both parties may be present in these perceptions and influence their reactions. When appropriate, it is important to draw attention to the productive collaborative partnership between teachers and parents/carers – after all, each parent/carer is an 'expert' about their child within the home context, even if they experience different emotions within educational contexts.

The early career teacher's perception of 'Dad' as 'Grandad' may be influenced by his age and/or appearance, although this is not expressed within the narrative, thus demonstrating an unconscious bias surrounding the construct of the image of a Dad. The teacher recognises this error in judgement has the potential to influence their future relationship and his involvement in future learning. The child witnessing this incident may inadvertently influence his future relations with his teacher and parent/carer in the future. In your future practice, inviting the child to introduce whoever they are with, before introducing yourself, followed by what they would like to be known as, gives the parent/carer the opportunity to set the parameters of the relationship, including how they would like to be referred to going forward.

Mentor considerations

- Ensure the early career teacher understands the homework policy.
- Share examples of different approaches to homework activities.
- Discuss and challenge assumptions made by the teacher about parental involvement in learning.

- Discuss how an early career teacher might approach similar scenarios in their future practice.
- Create opportunities for the teacher to observe you and other teachers communicating with parents and carers.

Vignette 2

Parents' evening is held in the school hall at ten-minute intervals. Throughout the previous appointments, I, and all those around me, had witnessed a parent becoming increasingly agitated with their child's behaviour. Whilst I continued with the appointments, I was distracted by the behaviour of both the parent and child – she was becoming increasingly agitated at his behaviour, which from my experience of him, was out of character. As the parent's appointment time arrived and she sat down, she was visibly flustered with the child still. So as not to appear judgemental to the parent, I continued with my pre-planned structure for the discussion. Towards the end of the appointment, I spoke about the exemplary behaviour of the child in the classroom – all true. The parent's facial expression changed instantly. She spoke at length about his 'naughty' and 'bad' behaviour at home and demanded to know what I was going to do about it. How was I going to 'fix' her child? What 'magic' did I possess to make him behave? What 'top tips' could I give her? I explained that we could arrange a further meeting to discuss in depth the strategies we might both use in school and at home to support the child. Unsatisfied with my response, she stood up, accusing me of lying about the child's behaviour at school. The parent then questioned my ability to 'cope with a class of thirty' when she 'struggled to control one'. The parent then walked off, with the child trailing behind her. As I move on to the next appointment, with a parent who has just witnessed the outburst, the previous parent chats loudly to a cluster of parents waiting in the seating area. Whilst mustering my most professional composure, I overhear the parent making comments such as, 'How would she know, she's only a child herself!' and 'How long is it since she left the classroom?' If I could hear her, so had the parent in front of me, those teachers and parents sat beside me, and many of the children who attended parents' evening.

Prompt for reflection

- Map the early career teacher's emotions throughout the vignette. Compare these to the emotions you would feel, or have felt, during a similar scenario.
- What does the use of the parent's language suggest about her perception of education and a teacher's role? Consider each of the key concepts – autobiographical experiences, unconscious bias, and cultural myths.

- How do these considerations help us to understand the behaviour presented by the parent?
- How might the environment have influenced all parties' behaviour towards each other?
- Why might the teacher have such concerns about other people's perceptions of her on the periphery?

Analysis

The parent expresses a desire to obtain practical knowledge for immediate application. Her demands for the early career teacher to know 'top tips' or 'magic' further these assumptions, adding to the anxiety fuelling her reaction. When the teacher does not immediately address how to 'fix' or 'make' the child behave, the avalanche of uncertainty leads the parent to conceptualise the teacher as lacking in some way. The parent's perspective is that 'top tips' and 'magic' enable the teacher to adapt within an unpredictable environment centred on structure, routine, rules, and rationale – what the parent perceives as lacking in the home environment. These feelings intensify because of the context in which the conversation occurs – one in which many stakeholders are observing it unfold. Having control over oneself and the environment is considered desirable, whereas spontaneity serves as a temporary solution for a lack of preparation. This pursuit for 'certainty' – a cultural myth – by both parties is established within their educational autobiography, specifically familiarity with a teacher's role as a social controller. As both parties appear to judge themselves and others on their ability to manage behaviour, as an individualised struggle, the cultural myth of creating and maintaining certainty within contexts prevails. In preparation for your future practice, it may be helpful to anticipate and consider common concerns parents may raise at parents' evenings. Write down example strategies you can suggest.

It is entirely appropriate for early career teachers to prepare pre-planned structures for parents' evening events – many do. Preparation can help early career teachers to make conscious choices about the language they use to convey information to parents. Unfortunately, in the above vignette, the teacher's comments on the child's 'exemplary behaviour' are interpreted by the parent as questioning their ability to manage, meaning that on this occasion the teacher is left feeling anxious and potentially vulnerable when facing future similar situations. In your future practice, it is advisable to invite the parent to share anything they have concerns about with you first. This enables you to judge the 'feel' of the conversation and how much time you have left prior to offering your pre-planned information to the parent. It enables you to anticipate how your potential use of language may trigger reactions in future consultations.

For the parent, the early career teacher's proximity to initial teacher education and assumed lack of experience in school contexts, equates to an assumed lack of competency – an unconscious bias. The teacher is anxious that other stakeholders will be influenced by the parent's perception of her, potentially influencing her emotive response in future parents' evenings. This is a completely understandable reaction as an early career teacher. Ultimately, it does not matter what other parents' perceptions of you are in similar situations – your focus should remain on the situation unfolding in the moment and on how to move forward, building your relationship with the parent after the event.

Mentor considerations

- Considering the above prompts and analysis, how would you support an early career teacher following such an incident so that they can move forward in a positive way with the parent?
- How would you support this early career teacher's emotional response?
- What prompts and strategies could you help her to develop for her next encounter with this parent and/or in anticipation of any future situations?
- Model how you structure parents' evening discussions with the teacher.
- Create opportunities for the teacher to be present in more formal discussions with parents and carers.

Vignette 3

The night before my first day with my first class, I lay awake for hours feeling anxious. I knew my class's names, I had prepared the classroom, I had planned all the activities, and I had contingencies for every eventuality. I had read every policy, I knew where everything was, and I knew the timetable for the school day. What I had not considered were the parents.

Dressed in my most professional attire, I made my way to the cloakroom door to let the children in. Most parents gathered around the door eager to usher their child in, locate their peg, and usher themselves back out again, preferably as quickly as possible. I stood back and allowed them to undertake their well-practised routine – smiling on the outside and crumbling on the inside. It was at that moment the realisation hit me – it was all on me!

As the rush died down, I approached a few parents who lingered behind, suspecting they wanted to mention a few things to me before their departure. I hurried my answers to their questions. It was the usual concerns about PE kits, homework, medication, who was collecting their child. One parent caught my eye, a Dad who was unsure where to put his child's lunch box. I had not met this parent before, so popped the lunch box onto the trolley and politely guided him out of the door. As I walked back through the cloakroom, I felt compelled to check the lunch box. Inside was a can of fizzy pop and a chocolate bar. These items are against school policy, so I quickly swapped them for a carton of milk and some fruit, and returned to the classroom.

When I finally shut the classroom door and turned to see the children smiling up at me, I felt a sense of relief. This is what I had been waiting for – my own class – the children to myself at last!

Prompt for reflection

- Is the early career teacher's realisation of 'it was all on me' one you shared? If so, where does it derive from?
- Was it the teacher's place to make a judgement on the contents of the lunch box? Where might any unconscious bias come from?
- What indications are there about how the teacher feels in relation to parent/carer relationships?
- What implications might there be for an early career teacher who is unable to 'disguise' emotion?

Analysis

It is evident both parties are aware of each other's anxieties by the way in which they behave. The early career teacher acknowledges all she has done to control uncertainties, through her avid preparation prior to the first day, in other aspects of her role. She takes several measures to ease these anxieties and disguise how she feels inside. The parents' usual approach in waiting behind demonstrates adherence to cultural norms through their 'well-practiced routines'. This suggests the influence both parties' educational autobiographies have had upon their expectations and behaviour towards each other. When anticipating your future practice, taking time to consider if such measures are effective or a placebo is helpful in ensuring your time and energies are productive.

The incident with the lunch box may reveal something of the early career teacher's unconscious bias towards this Dad, perhaps in his appearance or behaviourally in how he lingers. In your future practice, noting that you behave differently towards different people, in this case parents/carers, is an important step towards recognising how your unconscious biases operate, allowing you to reconsider interactions as a result. The teacher admits she has not previously engaged with this parent, yet she appears to doubt this Dad's capabilities to pack a suitably healthy lunch box. The teacher chooses to swap the unhealthy items for alternatives provided by the school. She does not allude to whether she intends to speak to Dad about the contents on his return. Interestingly, she does not check the other children's lunch boxes. In your future practice, being clear about a school's policy surrounding healthy eating and acceptable lunch box items may influence how you would react. It may be that you will need to have an appropriate conversation with the parent or carer, or send a pre-written letter home in the lunch box. In some school contexts, this may not be your responsibility, so be clear about who to pass this information onto if required.

Whilst teaching is individually experienced, in actuality it is a socially negotiated construct. The pressure for individual control over all aspects of education obscures its social origins. This inevitably has an impact on both parties' expectations of teacher and parent/carer relations, and how an effective working relationship develops. Policies and practices advocate the cultural myth of individualisation through their inherent positioning of the early career teacher as *solely* accountable for a child's development. This is a cultural myth the teacher affirms when she says, 'I finally shut the classroom door and turned to see the children smiling up at me, I felt a sense of relief. This is what I had been waiting for – my own class – the children to myself at last!'

Mentor considerations

- Prior to an early career teacher's first day with their class, discuss strategies with them as to how to initiate and develop effective working relations with parents and carers in the first few days of term. It is vital that the early career teacher appreciates the importance of early morning transition periods between home and school contexts.
- Reflect upon your first day with your class, what was similar/different? Invite the early career teacher to discuss first days with other colleagues.
- If you could go back to that day and give yourself advise, would you suggest any changes? Would the same things still have priority?
- Share and discuss the school's healthy eating policy with the teacher, ensuring they understand the protocols and procedures.
- Does it matter that the early career teacher affirms a cultural myth? Will this affect them in the future?

Activity: Choose one of the cultural myths you can relate to: *teachers are experts*, *certainty*, or *individualisation*. Summarise a 'story from practice' that affirms the cultural myth you have chosen (100–200 words).

Prompt for reflection

Contemplate the following:

- What expectations might each party have bought to the experience?
- What happened within the experience that may have caused either or both parties' anxiety?
- Which reactions (verbal/physical) may suggest either/both parties experienced anxiety?
- How did emotions contribute to the experience (positive and negative)?
- How have these derived from your educational autobiography?
- Do you think unconscious biases may be a part of either/both parties' reactions?
- With this awareness, what biases can now be made explicit and therefore responsibility be taken for?
- Can any new habits be formed in relation to these biases?
- What impact has the experience had upon subsequent teacher–parent relations?
- Have you thought/spoken about the experience since it happened and why?

Conclusion

The vignettes described above offer insight and practical considerations into three key concepts that influence relationships with parents and carers: autobiographical experiences, unconscious bias, and cultural myths. The development of effective working relationships evokes an emotional awareness of expectations, anticipations, and judgements towards the self and others. Understandably, early career teachers are keen to present themselves as 'fitting in', thereby reaffirming cultural myths associated with the role. The idea that education pivots around an early career teacher's emotional world, simultaneously with an array of other sometimes unconscious influential factors, is difficult to prioritise, for it means that in teaching every aspect of the self, including its most unknown parts, is called upon. Stakeholders are increasingly perceiving education as a site for individual growth, encapsulating the personal alongside the practical, recognising how emotion is required to enable teachers to become analytically reflexive (Ecclestone and Rawdin, 2016; Gilmore and Anderson, 2016; Storrs, 2012).

This chapter makes the following key points:

- An effective working teacher and parent/carer relationship is one that is dialogic, where both parties are co-constructors of knowledge about the child.
- Both parties bring to the relationship educational autobiographical experiences, which influence their expectations and perception of the other party.
- Our subconscious mind constructs bias, which can manifest in outward action and cause tension, hindering the development of effective working relationships.
- Cultural myths are socially constructed and serve as temporal anchors that taint reality and subsequent representations on offer. Cultural myths maintain established policies and practices and inhibit change.

Further reading and resources

Britzman, D.P. (2003) *After-education: Anna Freud, Melanie Klein and psychoanalytic histories of learning*. Albany, NY: State University of New York Press.

Gilmore, S. and Anderson, V. (2016) The emotional turn in higher education: A psychoanalytic contribution. *Teaching in Higher Education*, 21 (6): 686–699.

Jeynes, W. (2018) A practical model for school leaders to encourage parental involvement and parental engagement. *School Leadership and Management*, 38 (2): 147–163.

Moody, C. and Moody, R. (2020) *Unconscious Bias Journal: Change the way you live and work with positive reflection and action*. London: JCRM Journals.

Tobin, B. (2017) Understanding the direct involvement of parents in policy development and school activities in a primary school. *International Journal for Transformative Research*, 4 (1): 25–33.

10 Developing through reflection and collaborative enquiry

*Corinne Woodfine, Karen Meanwell,
Helen Ryan-Atkin, Moira Hulme, with
Reihana Aitken and Rachael Rivers*

Introduction

Professionalism in teaching is not a status ascribed on qualifying to teach, but a dynamic process of action, reflection, enquiry, and experimentation. This chapter identifies critical reflection and collaborative enquiry as core tenets of professionalism in teaching. We acknowledge that professional learning is most effective when it addresses the specific needs of teachers and the pupils they teach (that is, grows from locally identified priorities), is undertaken *in situ* (within the context of practice), and is sustained over time (at least two terms for bespoke continuing professional development). The frameworks and strategies outlined in this chapter are intended to support your development as a learning professional in school. The chapter is structured in two sections. First, we revisit the crucial role of reflection for professional learning drawing on examples from primary teachers at different stages of their professional learning journey. **Cycles of reflection** are used to illustrate the process of iterative professional learning. Second, we address the importance of collaboration using four examples of collaborative professional learning used in primary and secondary schools, and across clusters of schools: guided viewing of video, **Lesson Study**, **learning rounds**, and **collaborative curriculum enquiry**. The chapter concludes by drawing key themes together to help you plan for professional growth through the early career stage.

Reflective practice: Learning to notice

Building on the work of Dewey (1933), reflection was advocated by Schon (1983) as a method to question taken-for-granted assumptions and teaching practices formed in the early stages of a teacher's career. Reflective practice is important in developing professional knowledge. Reflective activities, conducted individually and collaboratively, provide a mechanism for critical thinking that potentially supports career-long professional learning and the development of adaptive expertise (Bransford et al., 2000; Vrikki et al., 2017). Reflective practice promotes heightened self-awareness, learning from experience, and a capacity to contest prevailing practice and act and think professionally (Smith and Trede, 2013).

Teaching does not follow predictable patterns ('do this and that will happen') and there is no technical quick-fix to the complex problems of practice. Schon distinguished between **reflection-in-action** and **reflection-on-action**. Reflection-in-action relates to decisions made by teachers in the classroom as events occur, tacitly drawing on professional knowledge accumulated over time. Reflection-on-action is thinking about actions after the moment has passed, considering reasons for what happened. To ensure you do not become complacent and accepting of the status quo in terms of your own professional actions, we advocate an intentional process of 'teacher noticing', or self-reflective questioning (Goldman and Grimbeek, 2014; Mason, 2001; van Es and Sherin, 2002).

Reflective task 1

Think back to a recent lesson and use the questions below to guide your self-reflection. Select a few of these questions to concentrate on for a few weeks so that you can refine your skills in specific areas and give yourself time to experiment in your teaching. Choose different questions when you feel ready to move on.

• What factors influenced your plan for this lesson?
• What went well in the lesson? Which aspects would you probably repeat in the future?
• Would you change the amount of time devoted to each part of the lesson or was it about right? How do you know?
• Would you change the sequence of the activities or keep it the same?
• On reflection, could you have added anything to the lesson?
• Was the pitch of the lesson about right? Was the work too easy or was there the right amount of challenge? How did you plan to meet the varied needs of pupils?
• Did you deploy additional adults effectively? How do you know their deployment was effective?
• Were you effectively deployed in the session or should you have directed your energies elsewhere?
• Were the most appropriate resources available for pupils to use during the lesson?
• Do you need to adapt your lesson plan for subsequent lessons?
• How will you review the learning from this lesson so that the knowledge 'sticks'?

It is important that teachers engage in *technical, practical,* and *critical* reflection to assess the efficacy and appropriateness of the interventions they make in their daily practice (Valli, 1997). For example, rather than implement universal 'one-size-fits-all' pedagogies, teachers should engage in thoughtful reflection to consider the appropriateness of transferring promising techniques to their own settings (see Chapter 12 on 'Becoming research literate'). Below, Amy, a primary teacher in her sixth year of teaching, describes how she uses intentional noticing to appraise new practices. Technical reflection includes assessment of potential learning gains; practical reflection addresses the process through which such gains are sought; while socially critical reflection concerns how far the practice is defensible in terms of professional values.

I've done Year 6 [10–11-year olds] for a few years and you can get into a way of doing it … You get in your little zone and you know what works and what doesn't. I'm very keen to try new things. I've found that beneficial. It gives you that refresh. For example, it might be a special educational needs strategy that has been shared at a staff meeting or CPD [continuing professional development] that you've been advised to use with a particular child. Use it and reflect, look at what's working. You might take elements of it and make it work. It's got to work for you as well and the rest of your class. I am quite mindful of the rest of the class. You've got to have that wider span of what's going on and that takes a lot of reflection and jiggling to make that work for everybody. (Amy, primary teacher)

Reflection-on-practice can be supported using reflective writing/journals, portfolios and reflection cycles, either through self-reflection or within professional communities (Bolton and Delderfield, 2018). Reflective cycles, such as those of Kolb (1984) and Gibbs (1988), provide useful prompts for early career teachers and their mentors. Cycles of reflection typically involve describing an experience; recording how you feel; making sense of the experience; identifying what you have learned; and using the new knowledge generated to adapt practice in the future. Rachael, an experienced primary teacher and mentor, uses these frameworks to support reflection in Figures 10.1 and 10.2.

Self-reflection can be distorted by biography and social context. Life experiences can create unconscious bias and prejudices, but as a professional, you need

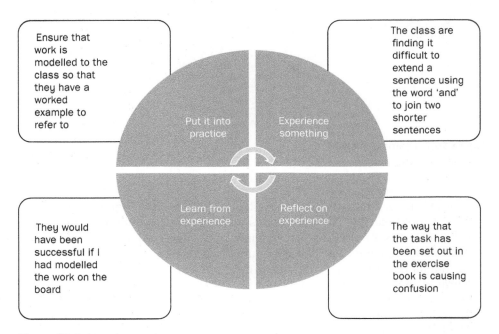

Figure 10.1 Learning cycle
Adapted from Kolb (1984)

Figure 10.2 Learning cycle
Adapted from Gibbs (1988)

to be able to recognise them and adjust your actions based on your own self-aware-ness. Brookfield (2017) refers to this process as 'assumption hunting'. As criti-cally reflective practitioners, it is important to interrogate the assumptions we have about teaching and the communities we serve. Darling-Hammond (2013) maintains that teacher professional development must be interwoven with the learning and wellbeing of pupils (see also Chapters 5 and 11 on 'Wellbeing of chil-dren and young people' and 'Teacher wellbeing and resilience'). Self-awareness and cultural competency are important attributes for teachers. Critical reflection can help to support the development of culturally responsive pedagogy where you engage with identities and identity issues across groups and communities: gender, ability/disability, religion, sexual orientation, socio-economic status, race, ethnicity, language, and nationality. Critically reflective and culturally responsive teachers avoid privileging or labelling pupils based on identity, and challenge unfairness and stereotypes.

Reflective task 2

Use the cycles (above) to reflect on your own practice and consider future developments. Discuss your notes with a peer or mentor. What assumptions do you have about 'effective' education and 'quality' in teaching, or about ability and 'vulnerable' groups? How far is your practice responsive and inclusive (in terms of classroom organisation, curriculum, pedagogy, and assessment practices)? How do you use visual supports and symbols of inclusion and safety in your classroom? To what extent do you provide a culturally responsive and supportive environment for all?

Collaborative professional learning in school

Traditional tools for profiling teacher development, such as professional development portfolios or participation on award bearing courses, offer individualised routes to recognition. Consequently, teachers may regard their career path as an individual trajectory, where 'good practice' is seen as a personal commodity rather than a shared community resource. In contrast, collaborative professional enquiry creates public spaces for sustained dialogue, reducing professional isolation and building professional self-confidence. In this way, collaborative enquiry contributes to the desirable development of the *teaching community* rather than enhancing an individual teacher's (or school's) repertoire of strategies and techniques.

Below, we introduce four examples of collaborative professional learning that are applicable across curriculum areas and phases of education: guided viewing of recorded lessons, Lesson Study, learning rounds, and collaborative curriculum enquiry.

Using video for guided professional learning

Recording part of a lesson on video can help support self-reflection and peer collaboration. Peer observation promotes learning for both the observed and observer (Coe et al., 2014). The ability to observe what is happening in a classroom – the intentional art of noticing – is an acquired skill. Research indicates that experienced and early career teachers exhibit 'selective attention' (Fadde and Sullivan, 2013) when viewing video of classrooms. Less experienced teachers are more likely to notice teacher and pupil characteristics and fleeting classroom management issues. In contrast, more experienced teachers tend to focus on pupils' learning rather than teacher behaviour. Providing opportunities for teachers to view videos together is not about providing exemplary teaching practices, but opportunities to observe, analyse, and interpret classroom interaction from multiple perspectives. In addition to a disposition to notice and a capacity to reason, social practices of seeing involve social skills and sensitivity

(Lefstein and Snell, 2011). Guided viewing with critical friends creates a third space bringing early career teachers and their more experienced peers together in a supportive environment. Video vignettes can be used to provide a structure for early career teachers to think and talk about their work and enter into dialogue with their mentors. The generation of this new space away from the busyness and pace of school work helps to address the enduring problem of induction – teaching while also still learning to teach well (Wang and Hartley, 2003). The overall aim is to cultivate cultures of observation that produce reflective practitioners who are willing to participate in communities of enquiry (Fadde and Sullivan, 2013; Patton and Parker, 2017). Do remember that the filming of practice should always comply with the school policy on recording, which may include verbal assent and explicit written permission from pupils and parents. If you are unsure whether the school policy on digital video covers professional learning, ask your mentor and consult the school senior leadership team before making any recordings. Agree ground rules in advance and always delete recordings after guided viewing.

In the extract below, Rachael explains how she uses video to reflect on teaching:

I agreed to take part in a project that involved a camera being installed in my classroom for the filming of my lessons. On a regular basis, my mentor and I analysed the footage to follow a chosen line of enquiry. From the start, the footage was my property and it was agreed that only the lessons that I selected would be shared and scrutinised. On some occasions, I deliberately planned a lesson with a view to sharing the footage with my mentor. However, there were times when I wanted to share a part of a lesson because of something that had happened spontaneously whilst I was teaching. Whilst in the moment, there are many events taking place in the lesson that I missed but I could focus on the details when watching the video footage later.

Having the opportunity to discuss the lesson with a remote mentor resulted in bespoke CPD and a personal plan for my development. At no point in the project did we discuss whether the lesson was good or outstanding, instead we took the opportunity to be curious about what we were seeing in the classroom. Our curiosity led us to experiment with different ideas and then observe the impact of our actions on learners. For example, I tried out different approaches to extracting prior learning from the children and then experimented with gathering evidence of understanding throughout a lesson. I was also able to identify children with short-term memory problems and put appropriate interventions in place. In retrospect, this CPD was among the best I have experienced. My skills as a practitioner were honed through the project. (Rachael, primary teacher)

Lesson Study

Lesson Study has been critically acclaimed as providing peer support during the planning of a lesson. Lesson Study originated in Japan and was promoted widely in the US and UK from the late 1990s (Elliot, 2019). There are three stages: the collaborative planning of a research lesson (development phase), live lesson observation (enactment) followed by reflective discussion and revision of the lesson plan (professional learning). Lesson Study should be conducted in iterative cycles to obtain optimal benefit. The process of professional learning through Lesson Study is incremental and cumulative. It may involve collaboration with a mentor or in a triad of teachers from your own school or a cluster of schools. Godfrey et al. (2019) suggest that for this approach to have an impact on pupil outcomes, teachers should identify an 'object of learning' that would be the focus of the shared aims for the Lesson Study. This helps to clarify the distinct contribution of the activity to the learning of teachers and pupils. The purpose of Lesson Study is to gain new knowledge and learning, rather than create the perfect lesson. The focus should be on teaching and learning rather than an evaluation of individual teacher performance. Observation should be collegial, non-judgemental, and non-threatening. Where possible, it is helpful if post-lesson discussion is mediated by a 'knowledgeable other' from outside the immediate teaching team. Takahashi and McDougal (2016) note that the role of the knowledgeable other is to help teachers connect larger issues in pedagogy and the lesson content. Coenders and Verhoef (2019) found that the pedagogical content knowledge (that is, subject knowledge for teaching; for further information, see Chapter 1 on 'The professional knowledge of teachers') of both early career teachers and experienced teachers developed through their participation in Lesson Study.

Learning rounds

Learning rounds (also called instructional or teacher rounds) is a professional learning technique conducted by groups of teachers to explore an authentic problem of practice at department, school, or school cluster level (City et al., 2009). The focus is on supporting improvement in locally decided priority areas and *not* making a pass/fail, success/failure judgement about the professional practice of individual teachers. The problem or priority for change needs to be observable and controllable at school level. Learning rounds involve groups of teachers observing a number of classrooms before engaging in collective deliberation on what they have seen, looking for patterns, and identifying next steps. During scheduled observations, small teams of observers make descriptive notes. They may talk to pupils but do not confer with each other. During de-brief, the group share observations without judgement and analyses all the evidence gathered. Deliberation leads to evidence-informed recommendations that may be reviewed in subsequent rounds. Learning rounds do not seek to implement and evaluate off-the-shelf solutions, or audit and appraise current practice. Rounds aim to identify local priorities and develop deeper understandings of what is happening in classrooms so that barriers to learning can be reduced. As Roberts explains, 'rounds is a practice' rather than a time-limited project or 'drive-by' form of CPD (2012: 34); this approach to professional development represents a 'shift from triage to learning' (2012: 53). Practising rounds regularly in a supportive setting can help to strengthen a sense of community, openness, and trust.

Reflective task 3

What is your experience of observation? How do you feel about being observed by your peers, induction mentor, and line manager? How do the techniques outlined above – video, Lesson Study, learning rounds – challenge norms of privacy and traditions of teacher autonomy? How do learning rounds differ from learning walks or coaching? What are some of the organisational challenges in arranging Lesson Study or learning rounds in school(s)? How do learning rounds challenge top-down, hierarchical approaches to school leadership and 'drive-by' CPD? In what sense might collegiality among teachers be 'contrived' (Hargreaves and Dawe, 1990) rather than authentic and deliberative? In what ways does your school improvement plan focus on the learning of adults? What are the resource implications of valuing adult experiential learning in school?

Discussion

Professional learning that involves observation should be followed by an open discussion to agree a focus for improvement. Effective professional conversations develop in a culture where teachers are willing to look deeply and critically at their own practice (Timperley, 2015). Importantly, the purpose of professional relationships must shift from 'feel good' into supporting and working through challenge and difference. Post-observation discussions are an opportunity for teachers to explain the rationale for the choices they make, discuss what happened, build on others' ideas, and share responsibility for improvement. In the early days of teaching, early career teachers will work closely with an induction tutor/supporter/mentor. The mentor will be a more experienced teacher, who is used to guiding the early stages of development of newly qualified teachers. This is an important relationship and both parties need to agree expectations and develop a shared sense of purpose. Discussion protocols can help to facilitate discussion. For example, Del Prete recommends that during post-round reflection, participants 'describe rather than evaluate', 'clarify' rather than 'judge', and 'reflect rather than react or prescribe' (2013: 143). Meetings should support professional dialogue and not feel adversarial.

Reflective task 4

You have just been observed teaching a lesson, and have had some fairly critical feedback. You spent a long time preparing the lesson, making resources, and thinking how all students could be engaged and given opportunities to succeed. However, your mentor noted that whilst the pupils were enjoying themselves, their learning was limited. You disagree with your mentor, and think the criticism overly negative. You are now quite upset, finding it hard to focus on any of the constructive comments that were made and you are dreading the next observation.

How could you work with your mentor to try to ensure that observation and feedback sessions are more positive and productive? What could you do in advance of the observation/at the de-briefing? How would you work with the feedback? How could you agree a joint plan of action? What other sources of support are available to you? What other professionals in school can broker dialogue around development.

Reflective task 5

Your school has a focus on improving children's writing, as results have traditionally been low. When you were training to teach you were shown an approach to supporting children as writers, which research indicates is extremely successful. You tried it out during teaching practice and are now keen to adopt this method as a newly qualified teacher with your own class. However, your mentor and the other class teachers are not familiar with the approach. The school has a commercial scheme that all teachers are advised to follow, causing reluctance amongst staff to introduce any changes. You have noticed that not all the children have responded well to the existing scheme.

What might you do? What should you avoid? How can you find a way forward? How would you initiate a professional dialogue around writing strategies? What do you need before you can make a case for change? What are the procedures for periodically reviewing the curriculum at school and school cluster level? What would a trial of new approaches look like?

Discussion

A school is a professional learning community, and ideally, presents a forum for discussion of new ideas to support pupil learning, achievement, and wellbeing (Timperley, 2011). School leadership plays a central role in creating spaces for professional discussion to occur and where such spaces exist, early career teachers should embrace opportunities to be involved in collaborative debate. Hargreaves suggests that sustainable professional learning communities are characterised by strong cultures of trusted colleagues 'who value each other personally and professionally, who are committed to their students, who are willing to discuss and disagree about evidence and data' (2007: 188). He stresses the importance of being willing to challenge one another's practice. It is important to have transparency in decision-making, and an acceptance that risk-taking is part of the journey of professional development. With interdependence comes vulnerability, as colleagues are exposed to the judgement of others (Tschannen-Moran and Gareis, 2015). However, if the conditions are right, collaboration can provide the opportunity for institutional learning and professional feedback in a 'mutual, non-judgemental environment' (Tinker, 2015: 10). New opportunities for teacher agency are evident in the UK, especially in Scotland and Wales, with a re-emergence of interest in school-based curriculum development.

Collaborative curriculum enquiry

Collaborative curriculum enquiry is a process of school-led curriculum-making. School-based curriculum development is not new (see Chapter 12 on 'Becoming research literate') but is less well supported in contexts where control over the curriculum is centralised rather than devolved. Recent policy discussions have acknowledged the limits of top-down mandated change that constrains the creativity of school professionals and the capacity of schools to respond well to local curriculum needs. In contrast, attention has turned once more towards building the capacity of 'schools as learning organisations' (OECD, 2016, 2018). Through collaborative enquiry teachers engage in deliberation on the how and what of the school curriculum. Collective deliberation is guided through cycles of collaborative enquiry, often with the support of independent external advisers. The example below describes a systematic approach to curriculum enquiry in eight linked phases. This approach has been used to support clusters of schools engaged in re-designing curricula in response to specific local needs.

1. Analysis of context – *Focusing inquiry* – what matters most?
2. Agreeing questions
3. Agreeing purposes – *Teaching inquiry* – what strategies will be tried?
4. Making use of the available expertise
5. Collecting and making sense of the evidence
6. Deciding on actions to be taken
7. Monitoring outcomes – *Learning inquiry* – what have we learned? How do we know?
8. Sharing learning.

Phase 1: Analysis of context. This initial phase of activity involves generating an overview of the current situation and defining a shared focus for enquiry. Working together teaching teams think about what is going on for pupils and what teachers already know about the situation (*reflective practice*). What are their 'hunches' and what evidence is readily available? What further evidence is required to enable them to develop a set of enquiry questions? (*effective use of data*).

Phase 2: Agreeing enquiry questions. In adopting an enquiry-based approach, strategic questions are crucial in determining what information is needed and how it should be collected. In the context of curriculum change, teachers need to decide where they are going to concentrate their energies so they can change the experiences and outcomes for pupils in line with their aspirations of the revised curriculum.

Phase 3: Agreeing purposes. At this stage, it is important to clarify shared understanding of the questions and issues in hand and check them out with a broader group. This will involve reflecting on initial 'hunches' and considering what the collected evidence suggests, discussing the priorities for action and thinking about who needs to be involved in taking action.

Phase 4: Making use of the existing knowledge base and available expertise. What sources of external support are available? How might gaps in knowledge and expertise be filled? How can the enquiry make use of the resources of school–university partnerships, subject associations, local authority officers, Research Schools, allied professionals in health and community work?

Phase 5: Collecting and making sense of evidence. Schools are rich in data, including attendance and performance data. This will give a general picture of what is happening for pupils. What is often then needed is a more specific analysis of the situation, using **qualitative** information and focused **quantitative data**, including evidence provided by pupils. Such data can be gathered via learning walks, class observations, interviews, focus groups, surveys, arts-based methodologies, etc. This type of evidence can provide a powerful means of moving schools forward, not least because it may provide 'surprises' that challenge the assumptions of staff.

Phase 6: Taking action. Having established agreed areas for curriculum development, designated leads will take plans forward that are sensitive to existing ways of working while providing clear challenge and innovation. This allows promising practices to be identified and shared whilst, at the same time, drawing attention to ways of working that may be creating barriers to pupil learning. It is widely acknowledged that school improvement is technically simple but socially complex. In other words, planning the actions that are needed is likely to be relatively straightforward; the challenge is to find ways of getting everybody involved.

Phase 7: Monitoring impact. Throughout the enquiry cycle, the process of implementation will need to be carefully monitored. Evidence gathering will be needed of what is happening as developments progress. This is to determine the impact on the experiences of pupils and other associated outcomes. This phase is supported by the collection of a diverse range of evidence of impact to offer a fuller picture than can be provided by self-report or statistics alone.

Phase 8: Sharing learning. Having collected and considered multiple sources of data, the enquiry team can then plan ways of sharing what they have learned. This might involve placing the matter on the agenda of senior leadership team meetings, training days, the pupil council, meetings of governors and parent groups. Where this is led well, it is a means of drawing people together around a common sense of purpose.

The final activity of the chapter draws on the key competences of a learning professional – critical reflection, collaboration, and enquiry – to help you make decisions about what is most relevant and important for your own development. Every teacher has a professional responsibility to review his or her development needs at least annually and engage in appropriate formal and informal professional learning. In Scotland, in addition to the annual professional review and development cycle, teachers are required to engage in re-accreditation via Professional Update every five years to maintain their registration. Northern Ireland's Strategy for Teacher Professional Learning (DENI, 2016) also reflects the objective for career-long learning with a distinctive focus on building teachers' capacity for leadership. In Wales, the five Professional Standards for Teaching and Leadership provide a focus for career-long professional learning in pedagogy, collaboration, leadership, innovation, and professional learning (Welsh Government, 2019). Teachers in Wales are encouraged to continue to use the e-portfolio generated in induction, the 'Professional Learning Passport', as they progress in their careers. In England, early career support is provided by within-school coaching following the introduction of the Early Career Framework (DfE, 2019a). In some contexts, professional development and review processes are linked with pay progression.

Reflective task 6

Try plotting your professional development path for the next two years. In addition to consulting the relevant Teachers' Standards, you might want to consider:

- What are your key strengths? Where are the gaps in your knowledge and skills?
- What are the main areas where you need to focus your attention? How do these priorities reflect your professional values and identity?

- What do you need to *stop*, *continue*, or *start* doing to achieve your goals?
- What sources of expertise could you draw on to further your development?
- How could collaborating with colleagues support your (and their) development?
- What is a feasible timeline for the achievement of your targets? Can you identify short- and medium-term targets? Can you set termly milestones to maintain and review progress?
- Can you identify a critical friend, formal or informal mentor (inside or outside your school) who might support you, or join you in joint work?
- What outcomes are most important and why? Who decides?
- How might you involve pupils in helping to identify priorities?
- How do your personal development goals align with the development priorities of your school or department?
- How will you know that you are achieving your development targets (using hard and soft indicators)?
- What sources of evidence, both numerical and descriptive, could you provide to show the impact of professional learning – lesson plans, pupil work samples, learning materials, observation records, video, curriculum development, new ways of working? Try to include varied types of evidence and have a clear rationale for their selection and inclusion. Impact can refer to actions, understanding, relationships, or outcomes for pupils.
- How will you maintain a record of your professional development activity that can be shared? What multimodal digital resources (e.g. e-portfolio platforms) are available to support you?
- How will you share what you have learned with colleagues? What are the most effective ways of communicating key learning to others (e.g. through co-teaching, modelling, workshops, network meetings, newsletters, briefing reports, posters)?

Conclusion

This chapter has revisited the value of critical reflection as a core tenet of teacher professionalism. Of course, what constitutes professionalism in teaching is contested. There is much debate about what constitutes high quality, good or good enough teaching, and where the authority lies to make such judgements (Biesta, 2010). Contrasting models of professionalism range from those that depict the teacher as skilled technician implementing high-leverage research-based strategies (Goldacre, 2013), through to the justice-oriented 'activist' professional (Sachs, 2003) who adopts an explicit 'inquiry stance' to their work (Cochran-Smith and Lytle, 2009). In considering your future development and aspirations, it is useful to draw on the four models of teacher professionalism articulated by Menter et al. (2010) and ordered in terms of increasing degrees of agency: the effective teacher (lower autonomy and agency), the reflective teacher, the enquiring teacher, and the transformative teacher (higher degree of autonomy and agency). Priestley et al. remind us that professional agency, 'is not to be understood as something that people can *have*; it is something that people *do*' (2013: 189). The agentic teacher exercises choice within professional and regulatory frameworks that both enable and constrain. While the effective teacher may execute highly efficient routinised practice, prospects for the development of adaptive expertise are constrained where there are few opportunities for creativity, critical reflection, and collaborative enquiry. Sustaining professional learning through the early career phase and across the career course should not be a solo pursuit. In this chapter, we have outlined a range of *collaborative* strategies that teachers and school leaders use to promote professional *and* organisational learning. We encouraged you to develop an action plan to identify and address your development needs. In doing so, we acknowledge that the self-directed efforts of learning professionals need to be matched by 'learning organisations' that direct resources and build relationships that enable professional growth.

Further reading and resources

The following textbooks and online resources provide further guidance and exemplification to support your professional development.

Bolton, G. and Delderfield, R. (2018) *Reflective Practice: Writing and professional development*, 5th edition. London: Sage.

Brookfield, S. (2017) *Becoming a Critically Reflective Teacher*, 2nd edition. San Francisco, CA: Jossey-Bass.

Del Prete, T. (2013) *Teacher Rounds*. London: Sage.

Forde, C., McMahon, M. and Reeves, J. (2009). *Putting Together Professional Portfolios*. London: Sage.

Hargreaves, A. and O'Connor, M.T. (2018) *Collaborative Professionalism: When teaching together means learning for all*. Thousand Oaks, CA: Corwin/Sage.

Tarrant, P. (2013) *Reflective Practice and Professional Development*. Thousand Oaks, CA: Sage.

Education accounts on Twitter	MOOC platforms	Blogs
• Teach Primary @TeachPrimary • #WeAreTeachers @WeAreTeachers • RubyTuesdayBooks @RubyTuesdayBks • Martin Burrett @ICTmagic • Vicki Davis @coolcatteacher • That Boy Can Teach @thatboycanteach • #PrimaryRocks @PrimaryRocks1 NB: due to the restrictive nature of the platform, legitimacy and accuracy of content will always need to be determined	• EdX: courses are interesting and challenging • Coursera: offers over 500 courses from more than 100 universities. • Khan Academy: courses are very simple yet rigorous • Udemy: practical but quality can vary • Canvas: more accessible and a good starting point • FutureLearn: good quality courses • Open University: easy to understand platform and the courses are accessible	• @TeacherToolkit: interesting discussion and useful resources • Teacherhead: shares contemporary educational ideas • The Learning Spy: shares constraints and irritations of the ordinary teacher • Learning with 'e's: covers technological changes • @LeadingLearner: learning, leadership, and the curriculum

11 Teacher wellbeing and resilience: A social ecological perspective

Steph Ainsworth and Nansi Ellis

Teaching is an incredibly rewarding and fulfilling profession. It is not, however, without its challenges. This chapter explores the concept of teacher resilience, which often frames accounts of how we might support teachers in coping with the demands of the profession. We provide a review of recent literature around teacher resilience and then connect the key ideas emerging from this research with vignettes based on teachers' everyday experiences of the job. The aim of the chapter is to support you in reflecting on which factors might help you to thrive within the profession, including practical strategies to support teacher wellbeing that you might want to try out within your school.

Factors influencing the resilience process

Within the current recruitment and retention crisis, people often emphasise the need to support teachers in 'building their resilience' so that they are able to cope with the challenges of the profession. However, researchers and teachers have expressed concerns about the way that this notion of resilience puts too much responsibility on individual teachers to develop the capacity to withstand whatever the education system throws at them (Johnson and Down, 2013). Contemporary conceptualisations of resilience have moved away from such an individualised approach towards a social ecological perspective, where resilience is not seen as a characteristic of the individual, but rather as a complex interaction between factors within the individual and their environment with positive adaptation as the outcome (Ungar et al., 2013). Within the context of teacher resilience, positive adaptation may be reflected in high levels of wellbeing and job satisfaction, alongside a low risk of burnout (Ainsworth and Oldfield, 2019). Over the last couple of decades, there has been a surge of interest in the identification of protective and risk factors associated with teacher resilience – the idea being that if we can understand the factors that affect teachers the most, we might then be able to manipulate some of these factors to promote teacher wellbeing. Figure 11.1 shows some of the most commonly cited factors grouped under three ecological levels of influence: the individual (white), the school (light grey), and the broader policy context (mid grey). While some of these factors have a protective effect on teachers (for example, high levels of self-efficacy and support from management), others tend to put teachers at increased risk (for example, disruptive pupil

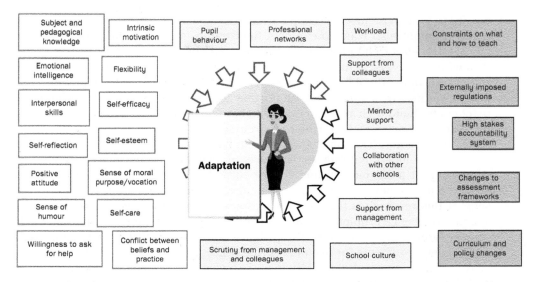

Figure 11.1 Influences on the resilience process operating at individual, school, and policy levels
Clipart image from: https://pixabay.com/illustrations/girl-skirt-smile-cute-point-1600991/

behaviour and heavy workloads) (Beltman et al., 2011). The figure provides the most commonly cited factors in Beltman and colleagues' review together with some additional factors we have found to be particularly salient in our own work with teachers.

Prompt for reflection

Which of the factors in Figure 11.1 do you feel have had the most influence on your experiences of being a teacher, and why? Are they mainly from one ecological level or all three?

Interactions between individuals and their social ecologies

A recent study (Ainsworth and Oldfield, 2019) found that five factors at the individual level were particularly important for teacher resilience: self-esteem, life orientation (how optimistic you are as a person), emotional intelligence, self-care, and conflict between beliefs and practice (the extent to which you feel you are expected to teach in a way that you disagree with). Taken at face value, this study suggests that by engaging in self-esteem boosting behaviours (more on this later), adopting a positive outlook, developing strategies to become more emotionally aware, and taking care of themselves (for example, eating a healthy diet, getting enough exercise, and sleeping well), teachers might be able (at least partly) to protect themselves from the stresses of the job. This work suggests that teachers might also want to examine their values about teaching and learning closely and either choose to work in a school whose ethos and practice aligns well with these values (more on this in the online companion resources), or learn to adopt a more flexible perspective. However, while these strategies may all have benefits for teachers, it is important to note that individual attempts by teachers to 'build their resilience' are likely to have only a limited impact unless the teacher's social ecology (their environment and their interactions with it) is taken into account. The same study noted that contextual factors were at least as important as individual factors, with school level influences such as workload, support from management, and school culture explaining just as much of the variance in teacher resilience as personal characteristics. The take home message of this research is that context matters. If we are to address the so-called 'teacher resilience problem', we need to address both sides of the individual/environment equation and think carefully about how we might foster more supportive working environments for teachers (Price et al., 2012).

A recent follow-up study (Oldfield and Ainsworth, unpublished data) suggests that the impact of contextual factors is likely to be greater still once we take into account the interactions that take place between ecological levels, rather than just examining the direct effects that a factor might have on a teacher's ability to cope within the profession. When teachers were asked to rank order some of the factors included within Figure 11.1 in terms of importance, they commented that it was difficult to arrange the factors hierarchically as they all had an influence on one another. Figure 11.2 provides an example of how some of these factors might be interrelated, based on teachers' accounts of the resilience process. The boxes within the diagram are colour-coded to indicate whether the factor operates predominantly within the individual (white), the school (light grey), or wider

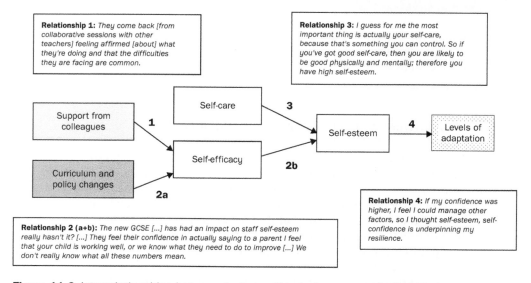

Figure 11.2 Interrelationships between factors within and across ecological levels

policy context (mid grey). The arrows, which represent the interrelationships between factors described by teachers, are accompanied by quotes from teachers (taken from Oldfield and Ainsworth, unpublished data) which reflect the nature of each pathway. The stippled box on the far right of the figure represents the outcome of the resilience process – the ability to adapt to the everyday challenges which teachers face (Luthar et al., 2000).

Figure 11.2 demonstrates the complexity of teacher resilience and the potential for interdependencies between factors operating across ecological levels. It is important to note that the way in which different factors interact with one another to influence the resilience process will vary between individuals and change over time (Ungar et al., 2013). The figure represents an amalgam of different teachers' experiences at different times and is therefore not meant to provide an impression of what the teacher resilience process looks like in all teachers at all times; rather, it provides an example of the kinds of complex interdependencies that we might expect at any given time for an individual. When considering the relationship that an individual level factor such as self-esteem might have on a teacher's ability to cope with the demands of their role, we also need to recognise that self-esteem is itself likely to be influenced by other factors within the school context and broader environment (Oldfield and Ainsworth, unpublished data). Once we take into account these interrelationships, it becomes apparent that the environment does not just have a direct impact on teachers' ability to cope, it also has an indirect effect, mediated by individual characteristics, which, in some sense, can no longer be considered truly individual after all. What this implies is that rather than talking about how we can 'make teachers more resilient', it might be more helpful to consider how to make our schools and our education system more conducive to resilience. Or indeed we might reframe the question to consider why teachers need to be so resilient in the first place (Price et al., 2012).

Equifinality and multifinality – multiple pathways to resilience

One important concept from resilience theory that is relevant to teacher wellbeing is **equifinality** (Martinez and Hinshaw, 2016): the idea that similar levels of resilience can result from very different processes of interaction between risk and protective factors. In other words, two teachers could be coping equally well with the demands of the profession, despite experiencing different challenges within their school context and drawing upon different resources to promote their resilience. A related concept, which also has important implications for how we conceptualise resilience, is **multifinality**: a term used to describe the process through which the same risk factor can lead to very different outcomes across individuals (Martinez and Hinshaw, 2016). In the context of teacher resilience, this might be observed in the form of two teachers working with a class who exhibit very challenging behaviour: while one teacher thrives, the other struggles.

So what does all this complexity mean for you as a teacher trying to find your way through the many challenges that come with the first few years of teaching? Taken together, the principles of equifinality and multifinality suggest that a search for a 'one-size-fits-all' intervention to support teacher wellbeing is likely to be fruitless (Oldfield and Ainsworth, unpublished data). Instead, the research suggests that there are multiple pathways to resilience, which might be supported by teachers, schools, and policy-makers developing a strong aware-ness of the range of factors that can influence teachers' ability to thrive within the profession. This awareness, in turn, can then be used to develop flexible approaches to promoting teacher wellbeing, which involve teachers working together with their colleagues and school leaders to create a more resilient and healthy workplace. Given the unpredictability that is inherent in the social-ecological nature of resilience (Ungar et al., 2013), an ongoing process of experi-mentation and review of practices at the individual and school level is likely to be needed to generate the most meaningful impact on teacher wellbeing.

Promoting wellbeing through experimentation across ecological levels

We will now consider what such a process of experimentation might look like by presenting a series of semi-fictional vignettes, which aggregate our experiences of working with teachers, student teachers, and leaders over many years.

Vignette 1: Managing feelings of self-doubt

Laura is a newly qualified teacher working in a large primary school in a socially disadvantaged area. She is excited about having her own class and feels well supported by her new school. There are some days, though, when Laura feels overwhelmed by the number of things on her 'to do' list. Sometimes Laura doubts her ability to be a good teacher, especially when a lesson doesn't go to plan or when she is struggling to manage behaviour effectively within her class-room. On days like these Laura tends to feel stressed and, on some days, even begins to question whether she has what it takes. When she is caught up in the moment of a lesson gone wrong, she blames herself for not being good enough and letting the pupils down. Her new school is very different to her previous placement schools and there are some pupils in her class who exhibit very chal-lenging behaviour. She sometimes feels out of her depth and doubts her choice of career.

Prompt for reflection

What risk factors can you identify within this vignette at the individual level and school level? What strategies might Laura use to support her in coping with the demands of the job?

When we analyse Laura's situation through a social ecological lens, we can see that there are various factors within Laura's environment acting to put her at risk of feeling overwhelmed: challenging pupil behaviour; high workload; and working in an unfamiliar context. These risk factors seem to be leading to low levels of self-esteem and self-efficacy, which are themselves risk factors, at the individual level.

Laura could try out strategies aimed at boosting her self-esteem, for example, by challenging negative thoughts about herself, writing a list of all the things she likes about herself, and avoiding comparing herself to others (Mind, 2019). Similarly, to boost her self-efficacy, Laura might find it useful to shift her thinking away from the one lesson that she believes went terribly wrong to three or four lessons that she taught that day that actually went quite well, focusing on evidence for how she made a real difference (however small) to the pupils throughout the day. Further strategies for boosting self-esteem are included in the online companion materials.

Laura might also want to think about the contextual factors that are influencing her experience of teaching, noting that it is normal to feel overwhelmed when dealing with a high workload and trying to manage challenging behaviour. Sometimes normalising the feelings that you are having and understanding where they have come from can go a long way towards managing them (Mind, 2019). This is one of the reasons why seeking support from other colleagues within school and from broader social networks (for example, your fellow newly qualified teachers who you trained with) can have a powerful protective effect. Research shows that teachers who seek out support from their peers are much more likely to thrive within the profession (Keogh et al., 2012). This support might lead to sharing of practical ideas around how to manage contextual factors such as workload and challenging behaviour, as well as fostering a general sense of belonging and the opportunity to hear about other people's mistakes and worries. As well as seeking informal support from her peers, Laura might also have benefited from discussing her concerns with her in-school mentor, who could have provided targeted support, for example, through facilitating observations of more experienced colleagues and providing suggestions in terms of strategies that Laura might want to try out to address specific areas for development.

Vignette 2: Working with workload

Claire is a newly qualified teacher in a large primary school. She struggled at school herself, and is keen to support her pupils as much as she can. She knows it is important to be a 'team player', so she has found herself agreeing to every request and suggestion from her colleagues. She seems to be helping with activities and catch up groups almost every lunchtime, and she often works late, writing very detailed lesson plans and creating her own resources. She hardly sees her friends outside work from one week to the next. Although she still enjoys working with the children, her increasing tiredness is making her less patient, and she is having more difficulties managing the children's behaviour. She feels like she is letting the children down.

Prompt for reflection

When do you find it difficult to say 'no' to requests from colleagues, parents, or pupils? How far is being 'available' to people part of your view of a 'good' teacher? How do these beliefs affect your resilience?

As a newly qualified teacher, it can feel hard to say 'no', but too many commitments detract from your core purpose as a class teacher, and can lead to burnout. It can be hard to find the balance in relationships with parents, too. Claire has also not yet moved from the detailed lesson planning which may have been required at the start of her training to a more manageable way of planning. These are all issues which an early career teacher should raise with her mentor, phase leader, or head of department in order to be supported to find ways through.

It can be hard to admit to colleagues that you are struggling. Too often, teachers only seek support when the pressure has become too much, and at that point they are often asking for help to leave teaching. This is hugely detrimental to the individual, but also to the profession as a whole. Mentors and others have a responsibility to look out for new teachers, even those who seem to be on top of everything. Resilience is not just about an individual's ability to cope; the culture of a school can be the thing that means that an individual succeeds or goes under. One exercise that you might find useful to undertake with a mentor is an audit of all the activities you are undertaking and the amount of time things take to finish. Even if you don't discuss this with your mentor, it can help you to understand where the time goes, which is the first step towards working out how to manage it.

Expecting each individual to find their own way through the workload probably means that high workload becomes the norm. Instead, colleagues working together can challenge a high workload culture, by asking fundamental questions about the purpose of the activities being undertaken, and then using research to find ways to address those purposes more effectively, or indeed to stop doing them altogether. In the long run, this benefits both the individual early career teacher and the school community as a whole, ensuring that teachers thrive rather than just survive.

Vignette 3: Developing a sense of community and self-efficacy through collaboration

Akira is in her second year of teaching. She is a reception teacher in a one-form-entry primary school, where she is the only Early Years Foundation Stage (EYFS) teacher (teaching children aged three to five). She loves her class, and has a lot of ideas for how to facilitate and assess children's learning through play. The school development plan is focused on reading, and she feels under pressure to fit with a rigid sequence of teaching, which she feels is led by the needs at Key Stage 2 (children aged five to eleven). All the staff meetings and continuing professional development (CPD) she attends are focused on the national curriculum, and she struggles to explain the principles of the EYFS to her more experienced colleagues. She feels she is losing her confidence in her abilities as an EYFS teacher.

Prompt for reflection

How is Akira's self-efficacy and integrity as a professional affected by the school environment? What strategies could she use to support her sense of identity as an EYFS teacher, and her sense of belonging?

The key issue for Akira is her sense of isolation within her school. EYFS principles and practice are only discussed if she raises them, and she feels as if her colleagues believe that it is not relevant to them. Her Key Stage 2 colleagues are under pressure from the high-stakes accountability system in England, and that stress is trickling down through the school, making her feel as if she and her children are being forced onto a narrow pathway. Her lack of experience makes it very hard for her to challenge her colleagues. She feels as if being an EYFS teacher is unimportant, and worries that she has chosen the wrong phase to work in, and yet this conflicts with her belief that her work with the youngest children is building the foundations for the rest of their learning. This is damaging her self-esteem and her self-efficacy.

A strategy that Akira could try is to seek out other EYFS teachers, whether by getting back in touch with teachers she trained with, engaging with EYFS discussion groups on social media, or by reaching out to nearby schools. Her local authority might have an established network with opportunities for more formal CPD; her union may have local or virtual forums for conversations about policy and practice; or her mentor, phase leader, or headteacher may be able to help. Conversations with others within her phase will remind her why she chose to teach this age group, and she is likely to find others with similar concerns who may have strategies she can use to bolster her self-esteem, or ideas for gently challenging her own and others' ideas.

She may like to take this further, and seek opportunities to develop her practice within this new network. She could identify with her mentor an aspect of her practice that links with the school development plan, find colleagues within the EYFS network to work with, seek out research and develop a plan together. This could involve observing others' practice and being observed by more experienced EYFS colleagues. Working with her mentor, she may decide to find a coach or an experienced leader who can help to structure this into a research project. This collaboration builds her confidence, her identity as an EYFS teacher, and her skills. Her increased confidence may enable her to share her learning with colleagues within her own school, and improve her sense of belonging with her immediate colleagues as well.

Finding time to engage in professional development is a key protection factor for wellbeing (Anderson and Olsen, 2006). Resilience is not about individuals 'knuckling under' and getting through. Teaching is hard work, but sometimes polices are introduced at national or local level that make things unnecessarily difficult. Networks of practice help both to foster self-confidence and to challenge poor policy.

Vignette 4: Developing collective agency through the unions

Niall is a history teacher in a large secondary school. He has found the history department very supportive and helpful; he has been able to share resources from more experienced colleagues and adapt them to his own ways of working. There is a collaborative culture within the department: he has always been welcome to drop in and observe colleagues and has welcomed feedback on his own practice. The school recently received a poor Ofsted judgement, with a number of subjects (though not history) singled out as particularly poorly performing. A new head has been appointed who has brought in a raft of new practices, including standardised planning processes across all departments, an expectation that lesson plans and marking will be monitored by the head of department, and a structured lesson observation process to monitor developmental needs and progress. This new way of working takes a lot more time, and Niall and his colleagues have much less time to work together. Niall suddenly feels very exposed, his lesson observations have identified a number of weaknesses in his teaching, and his pupil progress data is in decline. He feels under pressure to improve but he feels as if much of the work he is now required to do is more about proving what he is doing rather than supporting effective teaching. Niall feels as if he has suddenly become a poor teacher, while others around him seem to be doing okay.

Prompt for reflection

How is the pressure to perform, and to prove performance, affecting Niall's understanding of his role? How far can Niall realistically change practice in his school, and how far should he focus on his own practice?

Niall's concerns lead him to approach his union rep for advice. She talks him through his options, but also tells him that a number of his colleagues have expressed similar concerns and she is planning a meeting to discuss what they can do. Niall is nervous about attending because he thinks he should be focusing on his own weaknesses. At the meeting, there is a lot of heated discussion about the problems, with blame being attached to the new head and to the departments which were deemed to be at fault in the poor Ofsted judgement. However, the rep draws out a list of issues that members have identified, and then invites them to choose the top five. Niall decides that his top priority is the standardised lesson planning, which doesn't seem to work for him, and he's pleased to see a number of his history colleagues agree. They decide to form a working group to identify more clearly the reasons why the planning format doesn't work for them, and to suggest ways of improving it. Niall is still nervous of confronting the head with ideas for change, but instead the rep suggests that the group meets with the head of the history department first. They find that the head of department is very sympathetic to their concerns and their ideas, and helps them to think about how best to present them to the head. Niall begins to understand that the head is under pressure to bring about swift improvements across the school, and so they reframe their arguments to demonstrate how their suggestions would help to improve teaching and learning.

Prompt for reflection

What sources of support might Niall have drawn upon within his school before (or alongside) seeking support from his union? What are the benefits of working collectively with colleagues to overcome tensions within the workplace?

Developing collective agency gives a sense of professional ownership of practice and policies in a school, leading to higher levels of teacher efficacy, engagement, and 'emotional resilience' (Wilcox and Lawson, 2018: 184). As an early career teacher, you will be very aware of your inexperience, but you are also bringing fresh insight and creative thinking from your training and other experiences. Becoming a school leader does not mean that you have all the answers; ethical leadership means being open to listening and learning from others, and working out how to take people with you to create a successful school (Metwally et al., 2019). By working with his colleagues in this way, Niall has learnt important lessons in leadership, while also enhancing both his own and his colleagues' wellbeing.

Conclusion

Hopefully, this chapter has supported you in thinking about the complex nature of teacher resilience and to explore some of the factors that might influence your ability to thrive within the profession. The key message within this chapter is that it is not solely your responsibility to 'be more resilient'. We have tried to show that there are a number of strategies that you can experiment with at the individual level (for example, engaging in self-esteem enhancing exercises and auditing your current workload practice); however, it is important to note that school leaders and policy-makers also have a responsibility to protect teacher wellbeing. We would encourage teachers to work with their colleagues, leaders, and unions to develop a sense of collective agency, which works towards cultivating healthier environments for teachers, for example, through challenging unnecessary workloads and considering the potentially harmful impact of high stakes accountability frameworks. To support teachers and their colleagues with this process, we have provided a suite of companion online resources, including a list of strategies, which teachers and leaders might want to experiment with at both the individual and school level.

Further reading and resources

Day, C. (2013) *Resilient Teachers, Resilient Schools.* Abingdon: Routledge. A key text which explores the conditions needed for teachers to thrive within schools.

Ellis, N. (ed.) (2016) *Managing Teacher Workload.* Woodbridge: John Catt Educational. This book explores practical ways of managing workload with a specific chapter aimed at those just starting teaching. It also includes guidance on how to address key issues that contribute to increased workload and stress:

Smith, J. (2017) *The Lazy Teacher's Handbook: How your students learn more when you teach less.* Carmarthen: Independent Thinking Press. This book explores ways for managing workload while also promoting independent learning within the classroom.

The Education Support Network provides a range of resources to support teacher wellbeing, including a free and confidential helpline: https://www.educationsupport.org.uk/

The BRiTE program is a free online resilience program for teachers and student teachers: https://www.brite.edu.au/

The mental health charity Mind provides a range of quick guides for how to look after your wellbeing: https://www.mind.org.uk/

12 Becoming research literate

Moira Hulme and Rachel Marsden

Introduction

This chapter introduces the concept of research literacy and makes the case for teaching as a research literate profession. It is argued that all teachers should be supported to engage in professional enquiry as knowledge *producers* and discerning *consumers* of pedagogical research. The chapter offers a brief review of the progress and features of the evidence movement(s) in education. We consider the debate around what constitutes good evidence and its application to school settings, and appropriate quality criteria for appraising research. By the end of the chapter, you will be aware of the pluralistic nature of educational research, diverse approaches informing research use in schools, and the importance of knowledge translation before adoption in practice. The chapter demonstrates how defensible professional judgement can be supported by systematic collaborative enquiry. We show how your engagement with research as an early career teacher is nested within an evidence ecosystem that offers different degrees of involvement and multiple sources of support.

Why does research literacy matter?

The BERA-RSA Inquiry into Research and Teacher Education made a case for a research-rich, self-improving education system. The authors of the Inquiry Final Report argue that, 'To be research literate is to "get" research – to understand why it is important and what might be learnt from it, and to maintain a sense of critical appreciation and healthy scepticism throughout' (BERA/RSA, 2014: 40). It is important to remember that what constitutes 'best evidence' and 'best practice' is contested and can be approached from a variety of different positions in the evidence debate. As Cochran-Smith and Lytle point out, 'what it means to generate knowledge, who generates it, what counts as knowledge and to whom, and how knowledge is used and evaluated in particular contexts – are always open to question' (2001: 48). It is important to be aware of the debates around the role of 'research' and 'evidence' in deliberation on policy, pedagogy, and practice so that you can exercise informed professional judgement.

Teachers are subject to a flow of information about practice enhancement from marketing emails, Twitter feeds, edu-blogs, staffroom conversations, professional reading, professional learning events and courses, subject association and union communications, as well as contributions from education charities, think tanks, and advocacy groups. Information overload and initiative fatigue are troublesome attributes of a life in education. Becoming research literate is one strategy to help you discern the trustworthiness of claims made by an expanding number of edu-businesses selling teaching materials and continuing professional development (CPD) services. Research literacy matters in filtering out the snake oil remedies, silver bullets, and quick fixes from credible knowledge about teaching, generated for the enhancement of teaching as an ethical practice. Research literacy is far from sufficient in learning to teach well, but may equip the early career teacher with the confidence and skills to ask more of those who seek to shape their practice.

A short history of the long debate on research for teaching

The relationship between research and teaching is framed in three ways in policy discourse. First, the benefits of research for practice tend to be presented in purely pragmatic, taken-for-granted, apolitical, and ahistorical terms. Second, where tensions are acknowledged, the research/practice interface is caricatured pejoratively as a battle between opposing forces: esoteric academic knowledge and professional practice knowledge, theory and craft, 'ivory towers' and the 'chalk face'. Third, the advancement of evidence-based teaching is depicted as an onward march of progress towards more efficient and effective education. In the following, we disturb this narrative by outlining the pluralistic nature of educational research, the range of questions it seeks to address, and struggles for influence by different stakeholders over time, before moving on to consider how research is currently positioned in a dynamic education ecosystem.

While we hear a lot about 'what works' now, experimental pedagogy developed in the late nineteenth century. A set of practical principles for teachers, *Education as a Science*, was published by Alexander Bain in 1879. As national systems of schooling developed, experimental pedagogy was linked with school reform movements and the establishment of laboratory schools. The coupling of educational sciences and teaching has been characterised as a 'tumultuous' relationship (Hofstetter and Schneuwly, 2006: 1) of 'reluctant allies' (Lagemann, 2000: 23). For example, from 1904 John Dewey advocated collaboration in laboratory schools and *Democracy in Education* (1916), while his contemporary at Columbia University, New York, Edward L. Thorndike, advanced specialisation and the primacy of scientific knowledge generated beyond schools. Similarly, at the University of Glasgow, William Boyd championed teacher enquiry, Child Study, and the progressive ideals of the New Education Fellowship (Brett et al., 2010; Humes, 2015), while his colleague at the city's Teachers College, Robert R. Rusk, sought to secure legitimacy within the academy through controlled *Experimental Education* (1929). By the 1920s, the attractions of scientific status had drawn educational scholarship in North America and the UK closer towards empirical research and the 'hard science' of applied educational psychology. Experimental psychology and the mental measurement/school testing movement dominated research in education until the 1950s.

By the mid twentieth century, the 'scientific-experimental paradigm' (Nisbet, 2005: 34) was being challenged by an acceptance of the socially complex nature of school settings and the unpredictability of classrooms. The philosophical legacy of Dewey (and Boyd's commitment to teacher action) found expression in the teacher research movement pioneered by Lawrence Stenhouse in the 1960s, and John Elliot and others in the 1970s. This perspective challenged the notion of teachers as compliant technicians implementing teacher-proof curricula designed by experts outside the classroom. In contrast, proponents of teacher-led action research argued for the generation of local knowledge within communities committed to collaborative enquiry. The Collaborative Action Research Network (CARN) then, and now, promotes closer school–university partnership work.

The model of the teacher-as-researcher continues to appeal to those who seek to democratise research relations, reducing barriers between researchers and researched, and promoting more 'democratic' forms of professionalism (Sachs, 2001). Practitioner enquiry as an expression of professional agency remains evident today in the grassroots movement *Research Ed*, and amid calls to 'flip the system' (Rycroft and Dutaut, 2018). Intervention research traditions have developed that embed practitioner perspectives. These include 'design research' focused on the development and iterative testing of new educational materials and learning environments (Bakker, 2018), 'formative interventions' (Engeström, 2011), and 'change laboratories' (Sannino et al., 2016) that are founded on the notion of collective design by participants and researcher-interventionists. In addition, there is growing interest in the 'co-production' of service design and development involving citizens and professionals (Honingh et al., 2020).

In addition to new modes of enquiry, the first decades of the twenty-first century saw the promotion of outcomes-based or effectiveness research. Sahlberg (2016) has noted the spread of a pervasive Global Education Reform Movement (GERM) that promotes test-based accountability policies for schools. Policy incentives have directed researchers' attention to examining 'what works' in public policy and professional practice. The UK What Works Network, launched in 2013, is committed to 'generating evidence, translating that evidence into relevant and actionable guidance, and helping decision-makers act on that guidance' (Cabinet Office, 2018: 5). The Education Endowment Foundation (EEF) aims to: (1) raise attainment by identifying, funding, and evaluating promising educational innovations; (2) secure evidence on what works, and can be made to work on a larger scale; and (3) encourage schools to apply evidence and adopt innovations that are found to be effective. Since 2011, the EEF has commissioned over 150 experimental trials in England involving over three-quarters of a million children and young people. Across the UK, and elsewhere, targeted funding for schools from central government is increasingly contingent on demonstration of investment in 'effective', high impact interventions.

So, how is pedagogical effectiveness measured? Within formal hierarchies of evidence that have their origins in evidence-based medicine, the outcomes of **randomised controlled trials** (RCTs) are regarded to be the 'gold standard'.

In an RCT, two or more groups are randomly assigned (at individual or cluster level) to an intervention/treatment group or a non-treatment/control group; or groups access different versions of a programme tackling a common problem. Alongside RCTs, systematic reviews and **meta-analyses** (pooling of all available results from research in a particular area and the use of statistical methods to summarise findings) are regarded as providing the strongest evidence. Cross-sectional surveys (of a target population at a single point in time) and descriptive case studies (with no comparison group) are deemed to provide weaker but none the less valuable forms of evidence. For educators, it is important to remember that the type of question research is seeking to address will always guide the choice of method. Outcomes measurement is a common focus of teaching and learning research. However, other studies may focus on the critical analysis of schools policy or the wider purposes of education. Poorly conducted studies of any design do not provide a firm foundation for decisions. A well-conducted study will produce more compelling evidence. 'Lower' level evidence should not be disregarded if findings are consistent and highly relevant to the context of use.

In the opening chapter to this book, we emphasised that a commitment to critical reflection, collaboration, and an 'inquiry stance' (Cochran-Smith and Lytle, 2009) are essential attributes of professionalism in teaching. Research-based knowledge is not a substitute for informed professional judgement. Knowledge of context (including, for example, school intake, teacher experience, expertise and turnover, school policies and improvement priorities) is important when considering the introduction of any change. RCTs can establish if there is a change in intended outcomes between an experimental and control group, but are not intended to illuminate other important features. These include the details of the implementation process, the perceptions and behaviour of participants, the organisational climate (school culture), readiness for change, or the quality of working conditions and the learning environment. In the socially complex and dynamic settings of schools and classrooms, it is difficult to establish which elements of an intervention can be attributed with producing change. Equivalent control groups are very difficult to obtain. Withholding a promising intervention from a high-needs group may be unethical, even with a wait-list control group (for ethical issues in conducting research in education, see the Appendix). Therefore, when making decisions about practice it is important to assess not only whether the proposed intervention has been shown to be *effective*, but also whether it is *appropriate* (the likely take-up, impact, and acceptability), *feasible* in the context of use (adequate resources are available to fully support implementation and monitoring), and *defensible* in relation to professional ethics.

We maintain that while it is, of course, important to have knowledge about *what has worked well*, it is imperative for the professional to ask other questions as well. Professional knowledge for teaching also involves *know-how* (how to implement promising strategies); *know-who* (who to involve in building alliances between stakeholders); *know-why* (the values base behind a recommended action); and *know-whether* (how far estimates of impact actually transfer to new settings) (Morton and Wright, 2015: 3). In other words, the translation and mobilisation of evidence is as important as the generation of evidence.

Researchers working within the intervention research tradition do not seek to supplant the professional judgement of educators. Recent attention has focused on bridging the research–practice divide through, for example, multiple teacher-led RCTs (Churches et al., 2020). From this stance, research engagement is a recursive process, rather than the one-directional transfer of best practices. In this re-conceptualisation, the focus is less about replication and high fidelity delivery, and more about learning through collaborative enquiry. Just as quality in teaching is associated with the development of 'adaptive expertise' (that is, the capacity to adapt professional practice to the needs of new settings and emergent circumstances) (see Chapter 10 on 'Developing through reflection and collaborative enquiry'), then the relationship between research and practice can be assessed in terms of its responsiveness to context and commitment to practitioner dialogue.

Because context is so important, it is helpful to use a logic model at the planning stage and throughout the implementation and evaluation of school-level educational change. Logic models encourage professionals to think deeply about the specific goals, required resources, processes, and intended – as well as any possible *unin*tended – outcomes that may result from a change to established ways of working. Logic models are context sensitive and support the articulation of shared goals and purposes, as well as mediating expectations of what may be possible within finite resources (for example, time, budgets, and expertise). Many school project funders (for example, charities and local authorities) require applicants to develop a logic model to illustrate rigour in their planning. Logic models are underpinned by a theory of change (TOC). This is the 'big picture' that explores all the possible activities that might be undertaken to realise a desired change, and shows how and why the desired change is expected to come about. A logic model reduces a TOC to programme level decisions focused on specific inputs (going in), outputs (coming out), and outcomes (short-/medium-term results from the initiative) – see Figure 12.1 for a logic model template for evaluating school-level change.

From the above discussion, it should be clear that the educational research community is diverse and dynamic. The history sketched in the timeline in Figure 12.2 shows a field of activity under constant development, with new interdisciplinary research emerging in educational neuroscience and artificial intelligence. There are familiar debates between quantitative and qualitative approaches, 'learning sciences' and 'learning collaboratives', and between evidence-based practice (outside-in) and practice-based evidence (inside-out) (summarised in the continuum in Table 12.1). The pendulum swings back and forth between different movements as various stakeholders jostle for resources, influence, and authority. The range of designs and methods reflects the many normative questions – including but certainly not limited to attainment measures – that arise when a good education is subject to systematic critical examination.

Figure 12.3 shows the various levels of engagement a teacher may encounter when engaging with research. This ranges from the most marginal as a co-opted participant through to deep engagement as a legitimate co-producer of knowledge claims with other teachers and/or external partners.

	OBJECTIVES What exactly are you trying to accomplish?	INDICATOR MEASURES How will you know that a change is an improvement? *Quantitative and qualitative measures to monitor progress*	DATA COLLECTION TOOLS & SOURCES *The source of data and the methods to be used*	ASSUMPTIONS & RISKS *Factors that could impact on success*
INPUTS *(process evaluation)* *INPUTS are used in order to carry out activities* *Financial, technical & human resources*	For example: Budget Staff time External supporters	Grant agreement Target-setting Success monitoring	For example: Peer-reviewed improvement plan/success monitoring with targets	For example: Changes in staffing, workload, timetabling, curriculum funding
ACTIVITIES *(process evaluation)* *What will you do to achieve your aims?* *Number & nature of activities to be carried out* *ACTIVITIES lead to services or products delivered (outputs)*	For example: Levels of participation and nature of engagement Activities: 1. 2. 3.	Process measures of whether an activity has been accomplished		
OUTPUTS *(process evaluation)* *What exactly has the intervention produced?* *Short-term measurable results (First-level results)* *The OUTPUTS start to bring about change (OUTCOMES)*	For example: x number of staff over x period trained Take-up of exemplars Revised materials/strategies Participation in x networks by x number of staff	Process measures of whether an activity has been accomplished	For example: Records of staff attendance Minutes of meetings Curriculum materials	
OUTCOMES *Short-/medium-/long-term goals* *What is the impact of the change on the target group?* *(Second-level results)*	Specify the changes that will result from the intervention Improved outcomes in: x, y, z Short term/medium term/longer term	Evidence that changes have had an impact For example: Outcomes of assessments (in relation to prior achievement if appropriate)	For example: Baseline measures for target groups	

Figure 12.1 Measurement and evaluation plan

Figure 12.2 A timeline of professional enquiry and research for teaching

Table 12.1 Practice-based evidence and evidence-based practice: a continuum

Research in practice Practice-based evidence	Research into practice Evidence-based practice
View of knowledge	
Tacit	Codified
Local, situated, sticky	Generic, cumulative
Context sensitive	Context free
Purpose of research and enquiry	
Innovation, generative activity, professional learning	Replication, hypothesis-testing, outcome measurement, causality
Model of research	
Enlightenment or percolation model	Engineering or problem-solving model
Conceptual (for understanding)	Instrumental (for efficiency), utilitarian
Practice aspiration/orientation	
Person-centred	Evidence-based
Values-driven	Technical, clinical
Craft, art, professional judgement	Technician, teacher-proof
Process of research	
Bottom up – exploratory, iterative (e.g. practice-oriented design experiments)	Outside in – field test best practice techniques (e.g. randomised controlled trials)
Evolving, tinkering, deliberative, critical reflection	Competence now, prescriptive
Dialogue, relational	Distillation and dissemination, rational-linear
Evidence creation with educators	Knowledge utilisation, knowledge management
Role of practitioners	
Practitioner as learner, research translation	Researcher as disseminator, knowledge transfer
Practitioner engaged, co-production	External researchers
User involvement encouraged, inclusive	Expert knowledge

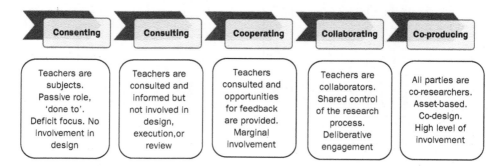

Figure 12.3 The teachers' research participation ladder
Adapted from Tripp (1998: 41)

Drivers and challenges of research engagement

Appeals for 'evidence-based', 'research-aware', or 'evidence-informed' practice need to proceed alongside the development of conditions that support such activity. Schools and teachers will be at different stages in developing their capacity for engaging with research and enquiry. There are a number of significant drivers and barriers to greater research engagement by teachers that need to be addressed if aspirations for research-rich schools are to be realised.

Drivers

- Endorsement of research engagement by professional associations, e.g. the Chartered College.
- Reflective approach embedded in professional standards for teaching.
- Increased use of digital communications technology for networking, e.g. Twitter, Pedagoo, edu-blogs, etc.
- Grassroots movements to promote practice-oriented research, e.g. TeachMeet, ResearchEd.
- Expansion of school-to-school professional learning networks, e.g. Teaching Schools, Research Schools, or the Professional Learning Schools network (Wales).
- Increased attention to knowledge mobilisation by intermediary organisations, e.g. the Education Endowment Foundation.
- Policy commitment to the 'self-improving' school model of self-evaluation.
- Accountability – cost-effectiveness explanation required for how resources have been used for optimal impact, e.g. accounting for pupil premium/development grant spend.

Barriers

- Few opportunities for teachers and school leaders to set the agenda for research.
- Lack of time within the working week and competing priorities for individual teachers to access and discuss the professional applications of research.
- Competing resource pressures restricting capacity for professional enquiry. Few 'research champions' in schools and limited budgets for professional development with external supporters.
- Few opportunities to sustain engagement over time and limited external support for local design experiments or systematic trials.
- Pay walls limit teacher access to high quality primary sources.
- Lack of a national platform (in England) to support teachers to access relevant research digests easily at no cost.
- Under-valuing of close-to-practice research and evaluation activity within national research accountability systems, e.g. the UK Research Excellence Framework (REF).
- Under-investment in close-to-practice educational research and school–university research partnerships within university Schools of Education.

- Insufficient attention to effective communication of research by funders and researchers.
- Insufficient investment in building research literacy in professional education programmes.

The research ecosystem

It is important not to limit our critical appraisal of research to scrutiny of outputs, but to seek also to shape the research that is commissioned, how it is conducted, and how findings of value are communicated. The funders of research increasingly require applicants to detail how they have already or plan to consult with users/stakeholders in deciding what is important, and how it will be investigated and shared for optimal benefit. Rather than looking at research as a linear process in terms of inputs and outputs, it is helpful to conceptualise research engagement as an activity that takes place within a dynamic ecosystem. This perspective takes account of the conditions and opportunities nested within a linked system of relationships and connections. While 2D ecological models, such as Figure 12.4, capture, in part, movement and motivations, they are less well equipped to show differences in power. Whilst national standards and accountabilities are a small part of the research ecosystem diagram, they are the outcome of debate around what matters most in education and what teachers should attend to. It follows that policy literacy is an important counterpart to research literacy.

Critical appraisal ground rules

Developing the ability to appraise research literature critically is an essential step in becoming research literate. You need to be confident that the information you draw on to support decisions about professional practice is robust, before using your professional judgement to assess how transferable it is to your own setting. How do you know that the research you are accessing is from a reputable source, is methodologically robust, and the findings trustworthy? What does rigour (strength and precision) look like in educational research? How can you judge the credibility of the conclusions? What are appropriate quality criteria for the diverse types of educational research? If the findings of descriptive (qualitative) studies are context specific, how do teachers make judgements about the transferability of promising interventions to other contexts?

One of the difficulties you may face when conducting quality appraisal is a tendency for the education media and researchers to report top-line findings and under-report methodological details. As a starting point, establish whether the research has been subject to peer review prior to publication. Remember that the space for detailing the research approach is limited in a short journal article or executive summary of a commissioned research report. It is difficult to evaluate the credibility of research-based guidance when no data or evidence is provided in support of the recommendations. However, you should take care not to discount studies based only on the scope and quality of reporting. As a discerning consumer of research, you have a professional obligation to explore the warrant of

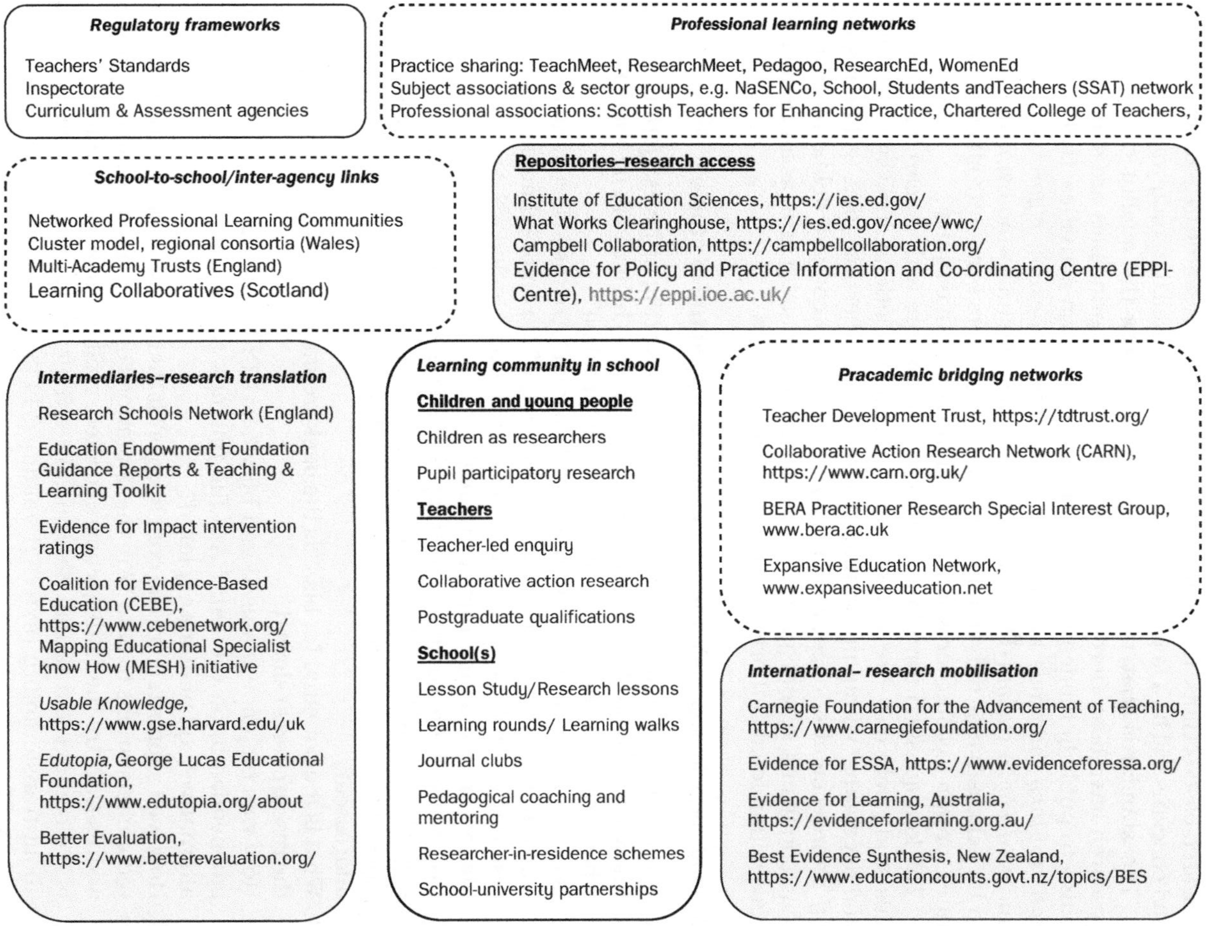

Regulatory frameworks

Teachers' Standards
Inspectorate
Curriculum & Assessment agencies

School-to-school/inter-agency links

Networked Professional Learning Communities
Cluster model, regional consortia (Wales)
Multi-Academy Trusts (England)
Learning Collaboratives (Scotland)

Professional learning networks

Practice sharing: TeachMeet, ResearchMeet, Pedagoo, ResearchEd, WomenEd
Subject associations & sector groups, e.g. NaSENCo, School, Students andTeachers (SSAT) network
Professional associations: Scottish Teachers for Enhancing Practice, Chartered College of Teachers,

Repositories–research access

Institute of Education Sciences, https://ies.ed.gov/
What Works Clearinghouse, https://ies.ed.gov/ncee/wwc/
Campbell Collaboration, https://campbellcollaboration.org/
Evidence for Policy and Practice Information and Co-ordinating Centre (EPPI-Centre), https://eppi.ioe.ac.uk/

Pracademic bridging networks

Teacher Development Trust, https://tdtrust.org/
Collaborative Action Research Network (CARN), https://www.carn.org.uk/
BERA Practitioner Research Special Interest Group, www.bera.ac.uk
Expansive Education Network, www.expansiveeducation.net

International– research mobilisation

Carnegie Foundation for the Advancement of Teaching, https://www.carnegiefoundation.org/
Evidence for ESSA, https://www.evidenceforessa.org/
Evidence for Learning, Australia, https://evidenceforlearning.org.au/
Best Evidence Synthesis, New Zealand, https://www.educationcounts.govt.nz/topics/BES

Learning community in school

Children and young people

Children as researchers
Pupil participatory research

Teachers

Teacher-led enquiry
Collaborative action research
Postgraduate qualifications

School(s)

Lesson Study/Research lessons
Learning rounds/ Learning walks
Journal clubs
Pedagogical coaching and mentoring
Researcher-in-residence schemes
School-university partnerships

Intermediaries–research translation

Research Schools Network (England)
Education Endowment Foundation Guidance Reports & Teaching & Learning Toolkit
Evidence for Impact intervention ratings
Coalition for Evidence-Based Education (CEBE), https://www.cebenetwork.org/
Mapping Educational Specialist know How (MESH) initiative
Usable Knowledge, https://www.gse.harvard.edu/uk
Edutopia, George Lucas Educational Foundation, https://www.edutopia.org/about
Better Evaluation, https://www.betterevaluation.org/

Figure 12.4 The research for practice ecosystem

research-based claims. The value and relevance of the research to your own priorities and concerns will be a key factor, in addition to how well the study was conducted.

The standards that might be applied to assess the quality of educational research have been fiercely debated. Four central principles are suggested as a guide to publicly funded UK research and evaluation activities: that studies are *contributory* (advance knowledge); *defensible in design; rigorous in conduct;* and *credible in claim* (HM Treasury, 2012: 11). The following list is not intended to be exhaustive or universally applicable, but offers some introductory ground rules for you to consider when approaching research outputs.

The key question for all practitioners who engage with research is how does this study help me? Are well-grounded recommendations affordable, available, and acceptable within my setting? These are *not* questions that will be resolved by 'improvement science', rather they will be the outcome of deliberation among teaching teams, school governors, parent and community groups, and senior officials within local authorities and multi-school Trusts.

Ground rules in appraising research reports – qualitative studies

1. Is there a clearly formulated question that is worthy of investigation? Do you know why this study was conducted and why it is believed to be important? On what terms has this issue been deemed a 'problem'?
2. Is the chosen approach appropriate to the aim? Are the selected methods best suited to generate the insights that are sought? Was more than one method for generating data used? Are different data sources included? Are the stages of the research and timeframe provided?
3. How were the participants, setting, and sample size decided (sampling strategy)? What are the inclusion and exclusion criteria? Are significant characteristics of the participants/setting provided? Is non-participation and withdrawal addressed?
4. What is the potential for bias? Is the background and perspective/standpoint of the researcher(s) shared?
5. How was the data analysed and by whom? Did more than one analyst work independently on the data? Are the findings consistent with the data? Were alternative explanations explored?
6. How well supported are the conclusions? It there a coherent trail from top-line recommendations to data? Are the limitations of the evidence and/or approach addressed? Are the findings corroborated, credible, and important?
7. Is the context and setting described in sufficient detail to support judgement about transferability (external validity)? Is the potential for wider inference beyond the study explained well?

Ground rules in appraising research reports – quantitative studies

1. Does the trial have a clearly focused question (rationale, population, intervention, outcome)? Why is this trial needed? What is the 'problem' that is being addressed?
2. Were participants randomly selected and assigned to the intervention and control group?

3. Were the two groups treated equally, apart from the intervention being trialled?
4. Were all the participants who started the study accounted for? Was there any loss of participants?
5. What outcomes were measured? How precise is the estimate of the effect of the intervention?
6. Where repeated measures are used, are the baseline data and subsequent data points appropriate to show trends?
7. Could the results be influenced by extraneous factors, e.g. participant maturation or expectancy effects?
8. Were the study participants and setting similar to my pupils and school context?

Prompt for reflection

Research can support sound decision-making in schools, but how often are decisions evidence-based compared with other sources of authority? Think back to the last guidance material you were offered to support a change in policy and/or practice at your school. How did the presenters support their recommendations? Was sufficient material shared to help you judge the credibility of findings? What did you need to know before reaching a reasonably informed judgement? In approaching the guidance, did you engage in critical appraisal?

Conclusion

It is not unreasonable to suggest that educational change is supported by the best available evidence rather than by 'eminence, charisma, and personal experience' (Goldacre, 2013: 8). Uncontrolled experimentation and educational interventions with no evidential warrant (or worse) are happening in schools across the country. Being professional means taking an ethical responsibility to appraise interventions that affect outcomes for children and young people. Caution should always be exercised in approaching knowledge claims before a rush to action in response to pressure for change. From the discussion above, it should be clear that there are risks, as well as opportunities, in each iteration of the evidence turn. This is most apparent where the motivation to engage with research starts from the premise that educational problems can be 'repaired' through the application of usable knowledge generated elsewhere. At best, this is a naïve science-into-service formula; at worst, it positions the teacher-as-problem and neglects *what does not work*, including sources of educational inequity that lie beyond the classroom and outside the control or choice of teachers and pupils.

Professionals working in the public sector know that the relationship between evidence and policy is seldom direct. A range of factors including the personal preferences of reform-minded ministers and the pressure of the electoral timescale influence policy decisions. The evidence turn is closely allied to a comparative turn. The politics of competitive comparison ratchets up pressure to improve

Table 12.2 Sources of evidence and practice guides

Organisation	Key publications, tools, and networks
Education Endowment Foundation: https://educationendowmentfoundation.org.uk/	Putting evidence to work: A school's guide to implementation (2019a)
The Alliance for Useful Evidence: https://www.alliance4usefulevidence.org/	What counts as good evidence? (2013)
British Educational Research Association: https://www.bera.ac.uk/	Ethical guidelines for educational research (2018)
Chartered College of Teaching: https://chartered.college	*Impact* and *The Profession* magazines
Coalition for Evidence-Based Education: www.cebenetwork.org/	Leading Research Engagement in Education (2017)
National Foundation for Educational Research: https://www.nfer.ac.uk/	Teachers' engagement with research: what do we know? (2019) and 'How To' guides collection. Online self-review tool, https://apps.nfer.ac.uk/SRT/
Nesta: https://www.nesta.org.uk/	Using research evidence: A practice guide (2016)
Institute for Effective Education: https://the-iee.org.uk/	Engaging with evidence (2019)
Mapping Educational Specialist Know How (MESH): http://www.meshguides.org/	MESH Guides, research summaries produced for teachers
Research Schools Network: https://researchschool.org.uk/	A network of schools that supports the use of evidence to improve teaching practice
ResearchEd: https://researched.org.uk/	Events designed to bridge the gap between research and practice in education.
Sense about science: https://senseaboutscience.org/ & Ask for Evidence: https://www.askforevidence.org/index	How do I know what to believe? (2017)

performance indicators in schools and across school systems. Teaching quality is judged using proxy measures including rankings based on national and international tests and surveys, such as the OECD's Programme for International Student Assessment (PISA), and the Teaching and Learning International Survey (TALIS). The requirement for teachers to constantly upskill and push pupil attainment levels ever higher may exert a distorting influence on teachers' attitudes towards, and understandings of, the role of research and its relation to school improvement (see also Chapter 11 on 'Teacher wellbeing and resilience').

To conclude, research literacy is important in fulfilling the ethical work of teaching by promoting deliberation on what matters most (priorities for research), establishing what we know already (the extant knowledge base), planning how an elicited change might be achieved and with whom (for example, collaborative design research), and monitoring impact regularly to assess whether intended outcomes of value are achieved. Research literacy is action-oriented. It entails professional deliberation in communities of enquiry to set local priorities, appraise the quality of available evidence; and the feasibility and acceptability of a range of possible strategies. Educators know that teaching and learning is relational; so too is professional enquiry. Rickinson et al. (2020: 27) suggest that quality in the *use* of evidence involves a combination of 'skillsets', 'mindsets', and 'relationships'. The research literate teacher needs the skills and knowledge to appraise research critically (skillset), a disposition towards enquiry as the foundation of adaptive expertise (mindset), and a commitment to collaborative professionalism (relationships).

Further reading and resources

Bakker, A. (2018) *Design Research in Education: A practical guide for early career researchers.* London: Routledge. A guide to conducting intervention-based design research in schools.

Cain, T. (ed.) (2019) *Becoming a Research-Informed School: Why? What? How?* London: Routledge. Provides information and examples of how teachers use research in schools.

Godfrey, D. and Brown, C. (2019) *An Ecosystem for Research-Engaged Schools: Reforming education through research.* London: Routledge. An overview of key debates in the use of evidence to promote teacher development.

Hattie, J. (2012) *Visible Learning for Teachers: Maximizing impact on learning.* London: Routledge. An introduction to the use of meta-analyses to establish the effectiveness of teaching strategies.

HM Treasury (2012) *Quality in qualitative evaluation: A framework for assessing research evidence.* London: HM Treasury. Available at: https://assets.publishing.service.gov.uk/government/uploads/system/uploads/attachment_data/file/190986/Magenta_Book_quality_in_qualitative_evaluation__QQE_.pdf. A framework for assessing qualitative evaluations.

References

Abel, M. and Bäuml, K.H.T. (2020) Retrieval-induced forgetting in a social context: Do the same mechanisms underlie forgetting in speakers and listeners? *Memory and Cognition*, 48 (1): 1–15.

Abel, M. and Roediger III, H.L. (2018) The testing effect in a social setting: Does retrieval practice benefit a listener? *Journal of Experimental Psychology: Applied*, 24 (3): 347–359.

Agarwal, P. (2020) *Sway: Unravelling unconscious bias.* London: Bloomsbury Sigma.

Ainsworth, S. and Oldfield, J. (2019) Quantifying teacher resilience: Context matters. *Teaching and Teacher Education*, 82: 117–128.

Åkerlind, G. (2007) Constraints on academics' potential for developing as a teacher. *Studies in Higher Education*, 32 (1): 21–37.

Alliance for Useful Evidence (2013) What counts as good evidence? London: Alliance for Useful Evidence. Available at: https://www.alliance4usefulevidence.org/assets/What-Counts-as-Good-Evidence-WEB.pdf.

Alsup, J. (2006) *Teacher Identity Discourses: Negotiating personal and professional spaces.* Mahwah, NJ: Lawrence Erlbaum Associates.

Anderson, L. and Olsen, B. (2006) Investigating early career urban teachers' perspectives on and experiences in professional development. *Journal of Teacher Education*, 57 (4): 359–377.

Anderson, L.W., Krathwohl, D.R., Airasian, P.W., Cruikshank, K.A., Mayer, R.E., Pintrich, P.R. et al. (2014) *A Taxonomy for Learning, Teaching, and Assessing: A revision of Bloom's Taxonomy of Educational Objectives*, Pearson New International edition. Harlow: Pearson.

Armstrong, T. (2012) *Neurodiversity in the Classroom: A strengths-based approach to help students with special educational needs.* Alexandria, VA: ASCD.

Baddeley, A. (2000) The episodic buffer: A new component of working memory? *Trends in Cognitive Sciences*, 4 (11): 417–423.

Baddeley, A.D. and Hitch, G. (1974) Working memory, in G.H. Bower (ed.) *Psychology of Learning and Motivation*, Vol. 8 (pp. 47–89). New York: Academic Press.

Bain, A. (1879) *Education as a Science.* London: Kegan, Trench & Trubner.

Baker, D. (2011) *The Politics of Neurodiversity: Why public policy matters.* Boulder, CO: Lynne Rienner.

Bakker, A. (2018) *Design Research in Education: A practical guide for early career researchers.* London: Routledge.

Banerjee, R., Weare, K. and Farr, W. (2014) Working with 'Social and Emotional Aspects of Learning' (SEAL): Associations with school ethos, pupil social experiences, attendance, and attainment. *British Educational Research Journal*, 40 (4): 718–742.

Barber, J. and Noble, M. (2020) Before the system: The importance of building relationships with your pupils, in E. Overland, J. Barber and M. Sackville-Ford (eds.) *Behaviour Management: An essential guide for student and newly qualified teachers* (pp. 114–128). London: Routledge.

Barber, M. and Mourshed, M. (2007) *How the world's best education systems come out on top.* London: McKinsey. Available at: https://www.mckinsey.com/industries/public-and-social-sector/our-insights/how-the-worlds-best-performing-school-systems-come-out-on-top.

Barrowford Primary School (2019) *Behaviour in schools (relationship management policy).* Available at: http://barrowford.lancs.sch.uk/wp-content/uploads/2020/02/Behaviour-in-schools.pdf (accessed 11 August 2020).

Beauchamp, C. and Thomas, L. (2010) Reflecting on an ideal: Student teachers envision a future identity. *Reflective Practice*, 11 (5): 631–643.

Beauchamp, G. (2017) *Computing and ICT in the Primary School: From pedagogy to practice*, 2nd edition. London: David Fulton/Routledge.

Beauchamp, G. and Kennewell, S. (2010) Interactivity in the classroom and its impact on learning. *Computers and Education*, 54: 759–766.

Beauchamp, G., Burden, K. and Abbinett, E. (2015) Teachers learning to use the iPad in Scotland and Wales: A new model of professional development. *Journal of Education for Teaching: International Research and Pedagogy*, 41 (2): 161–179.

Beltman, S., Mansfield, C. and Price, A. (2011) Thriving not just surviving: A review of research on teacher resilience. *Educational Research Review*, 6 (3): 185–207.

Bennett, N. and Turner-Bisset, R. (2002) Case studies in learning to teach, in N. Bennett and C. Carré (eds.) *Learning to Teach* (pp. 165–190). London: Routledge.

BERA (2018) *Ethical guidelines for educational research*, 4th edition. London: BEERA. Available at: https://www.bera.ac.uk/publication/ethical-guidelines-for-educational-research-2018.

BERA/RSA (2014) *Research and Teacher Education. Building the capacity for a self-improving education system*. London: BERA.

Berger, R. (2003) *Ethic of Excellence*. Portsmouth, NH: Heinemann.

Bernstein, B. (2000) *Pedagogy, Symbolic Control and Identity: Theory, research, critique*, revised edition. Oxford: Rowman & Littlefield.

Bethune, A. (2018) *Wellbeing in the Primary Classroom: A practical guide to teaching happiness*. London: Bloomsbury.

Bibby, T. (2011) *Education – An 'Impossible Profession'? Psychoanalytic explorations of learning and classrooms*. London: Routledge.

Biesta, G. (2010) *Good Education in an Age of Measurement: Ethics, politics, democracy*. Boulder, CO: Paradigm.

Birbalsingh, K. (2016) 'No excuses': Inside Britain's strictest school, *The Guardian*, 30 December. Available at: https://www.theguardian.com/education/2016/dec/30/no-excuses-inside-britains-strictest-school.

Birtwistle, J. (1998) Reading recovery: A problem-solving approach to reading, in R. Burden and M. Williams (eds.) *Thinking Through the Curriculum*. London: Routledge.

Bishop, D. (2010) *What's in a name?* Available at: http://deevybee.blogspot.com/2010/12/whats-in-name.html (accessed 9 June 2020).

Bolton, G. and Delderfield, R. (2018) *Reflective Practice: Writing and professional development*, 5th edition. London: Sage.

Bransford, J.D., Brown, A.L. and Cocking, R.R. (2000) *How People Learn: Brain, mind, experience, and school*. Washington, DC: National Academy Press.

Brett, C.E., Lawn, M., Bartholomew, D.J. and Deary, I.J. (2010) Help will be welcomed from every quarter: The work of William Boyd and the Educational Institute of Scotland's Research Committee in the 1920s. *History of Education*, 39 (5): 589–611.

Britzman, D.P. (2003) *After-education: Anna Freud, Melanie Klein and psychoanalytic histories of learning*. Albany, NY: State University of New York Press.

Brookfield, S. (2017) *Becoming a Critically Reflective Teacher*, 2nd edition. San Francisco, CA: Jossey-Bass.

Brooks, C. (2015) Research and professional practice, in G. Butt (ed.) *MasterClass in Geography Education: Transforming teaching and learning* (pp. 31–44). London: Bloomsbury.

Brooks, R. (2019) *The Trauma and Attachment-aware Classroom: A practical guide to supporting children who have encountered trauma and adverse childhood experiences*. London: Jessica Kingsley.

Brown, P.C., Roediger III, H.L. and McDaniel, M.A. (2014) *Make it Stick*. Cambridge, MA: Harvard University Press.

Cabinet Office (2018) *The What Works Network, five years on.* Available at: https://www.gov.uk/government/publications/the-what-works-network-five-years-on.

Cain, T. (ed.) (2019) *Becoming a Research-Informed School: Why? What? How?* London: Routledge.

Canter, L. and Canter, M. (2001) *Assertive Discipline: Positive behaviour management for today's classroom*, 3rd edition. Los Angeles, CA: Canter & Associates.

Churches, R., Dommett, E.J., Devonshire, I.M., Hall, R., Higgins, S. and Korin, A. (2020) Translating laboratory evidence into classroom practice with teacher-led randomized controlled trials – a perspective and meta-analysis. *Mind, Brain, and Education*, 14 (3): 292–302.

City, E.A., Elmore, R.F., Fiarman, S.E. and Teitel, L. (2009) *Instructional Rounds in Education.* Cambridge, MA: Harvard Education Press.

Clark, A.E., Flèche, S., Layard, R., Powdthavee, N. and Ward, G. (2018) *The Origins of Happiness: The science of well-being over the life course.* Princeton, NJ: Princeton University Press.

Clarke, A.M., Morreale, S., Field, C.A., Hussein, Y. and Barry, M.M. (2015) *What works in enhancing social and emotional skills development during childhood and adolescence? A review of the evidence on the effectiveness of school-based and out-of-school programmes in the UK.* WHO Collaborating Centre for Health Promotion Research: National University of Ireland Galway. Available at: https://www.eif.org.uk/report/what-works-in-enhancing-social-and-emotional-skills-development-during-childhood-and-adolescence.

Clarke, M. and Phelan, A. (2015) The power of negative thinking in and for teacher education. *Power and Education*, 7 (3): 257–271.

Coalition for Evidence-Based Education (CEBE) (2017) *Leading research engagement in education.* York: CEBE. Available at: https://www.cebenetwork.org/projects/leading-research-engagement.

Cochran-Smith, M. and Lytle, S.L. (2001) Beyond certainty: Taking an inquiry stance on practice, in A. Lieberman and L. Miller (eds.) *Teachers Caught in the Action: Professional development that matters* (pp. 45–58). New York: Teachers College Press.

Cochran-Smith, M. and Lytle, S.L. (2009) *Inquiry as Stance: Practitioner research for the next generation.* New York: Teachers College Press.

Coe, R., Aloisi, C., Higgins, S. and Major, L.E. (2014) *What makes great teaching? Review of the underpinning research.* The Sutton Trust, with the Centre for Evaluation and Monitoring and Durham University. Available at: https://www.suttontrust.com/wp-content/uploads/2014/10/What-Makes-Great-Teaching-REPORT.pdf (accessed 20 November 2020).

Coenders, F. and Verhoef, N. (2019) Lesson study: Professional development for beginning and experienced teachers. *Professional Development in Education*, 45 (2): 217–230.

Collaborative for Academic, Social, and Emotional Learning (CASEL) (2015) *Effective social and emotional learning programs.* Chicago, IL: CASEL. Available at: http://secondaryguide.casel.org/casel-secondary-guide.pdf.

Corcoran, R.P., Cheung, A.C.K., Kim, E. and Xie, C. (2018) Effective universal school-based social and emotional learning programs for improving academic achievement: A systematic review and meta-analysis of 50 years of research. *Educational Research Review*, 25: 56–72.

Csikszentmihalyi, M. (2008) *Flow: The psychology of optimal experience.* New York: HarperCollins.

Darling-Hammond, L. (2013) *Getting Teacher Evaluation Right: What really matters for effectiveness and improvement.* New York: Teachers College Press.

Darling-Hammond, L., Flook, L., Cook-Harvey, C., Barron, B. and Osher, D. (2020) Implications for educational practice of the science of learning and development, *Applied Developmental Science*, 24 (2): 97–140.

Davies, P. (2002) Personal communication with the authors, University of Staffordshire, in C. Rust (ed.) *Improving Pupil Learning – Ten years on.* Oxford: OCSLD.

Day, C. (2013) *Resilient Teachers, Resilient Schools.* Abingdon: Routledge.

Del Prete, T. (2013) *Teacher Rounds.* London: Sage.

Department for Education (DfE) (2011) *Teachers' standards.* London: DfE. Available at: https://www.gov.uk/government/publications/teachers-standards (accessed 20 November 2020).

Department for Education (DfE) (2019a) *Early career framework.* London: DfE. Available at: https://www.gov.uk/government/publications/early-career-framework.

Department for Education (DfE) (2019b) *State of the nation 2019: Children and young people's wellbeing.* London: DfE. Available at: https://www.gov.uk/government/publications/state-of-the-nation-2019-children-and-young-peoples-wellbeing.

Department for Education (DfE) (2020) *Early career framework reforms: Overview.* London: DfE. Available at: https://www.gov.uk/government/publications/early-career-framework-reforms-overview/early-career-framework-reforms-overview (accessed 8 October 2020).

Department of Education, Northern Ireland (DENI) (2016) *The learning leaders: A strategy for teacher professional learning.* Bangor: DENI. Available at: https://dera.ioe.ac.uk//25762/.

Department of Education, Northern Ireland (DENI) (2019) *Children and young people's strategy, 2019–2029.* Bangor: DENI. Available at: https://www.education-ni.gov.uk/sites/default/files/publications/education/2019-2029%20CYP%20Strategy.pdf.

Developmental Adult Neurodiversity Association (DANDA) (2006) The make-up of neurodiversity, in M. Colley (ed.) *Living with Dyspraxia: A guide for adults with developmental dyspraxia* (pp. 161–162). London: Jessica Kingsley.

Dewey, J. (1916) *Democracy and Education. An introduction to the philosophy of education.* New York: Macmillan.

Dewey, J. (1933) *How We Think: A restatement of the relation of reflective thinking to the educative process.* Boston, MA: D.C. Heath.

Digital Education Advisory Group (DEAG) (2013) *Beyond the classroom: A new digital education for young Australians in the 21st century.* Available at: https://docs.education.gov.au/system/files/doc/other/deag_final_report.pdf (accessed 15 August 2020).

Dix, P. (2017) *When the Adults Change, Everything Changes: Seismic shifts in school behaviour.* London: Crown House.

Doolittle, P. (2013) How your 'working memory' makes sense of the world, *TED Talk,* June. Available at: https://www.ted.com/talks/peter_doolittle_how_your_working_memory_makes_sense_of_the_world?language=en#t-548976.

Duncan-Howell, J. and Lee, K.T. (2007) M-learning: Finding a place for mobile technologies within tertiary educational settings, in *ICT: Providing choices for learners and learning: Proceedings of ASCILITE Singapore 2007* (pp. 223–231). Available at: http://www.ascilite.org.au/conferences/singapore07/procs/duncan-howell.pdf (accessed 1 February 2020).

Dweck, C. (2007) *Mindset: The new psychology of success.* New York: Ballantine Books.

Ecclestone, K. and Rawdin, C. (2016) Reinforcing the 'diminished' subject? The implications of the 'vulnerability zeitgeist' for well-being in educational settings. *Cambridge Journal of Education,* 17 (1): 1–17.

Education Endowment Foundation (EEF) (2015) *Promoting Alternative Thinking Strategies (PATHS): Evaluation report.* London: EEF. Available at: https://dera.ioe.ac.uk//33115/.

Education Endowment Foundation (EEF) (2019a) *Putting evidence to work: A school's guide to implementation.* London: EEF. Available at: https://educationendowmentfoundation.org.uk/tools/guidance-reports/a-schools-guide-to-implementation/.

Education Endowment Foundation (EEF) (2019b) *Metacognition and self-regulated learning,* Guidance report. Available at: https://educationendowmentfoundation.org.uk/tools/guidance-reports/metacognition-and-self-regulated-learning/.

Education Endowment Foundation (2019c) *Improving social and emotional learning in primary schools.* London: EEF. Available at: https://educationendowmentfoundation.org.uk/tools/guidance-reports/social-and-emotional-learning/.

Education Scotland (2020) *What digital learning might look like: Examples of digital literacy and computing science learning at early, first and second levels*. Available at: https://education.gov.scot/media/uh2jebbs/nih158-what-digital-learning-might-look-like.pdf.

Elliott, J. (2019) What is lesson study? *European Journal of Education*, 54: 175–188.

Ellis, N. (ed.) (2016) *Managing Teacher Workload*. Woodbridge: John Catt Educational.

Ellsworth, E (1997) *Teaching Positions: Difference, pedagogy and the power of address*. New York: Teachers College Press.

Engeström, Y. (2011) From design experiments to formative interventions. *Theory and Psychology*, 21 (4): 598–628.

Estyn (2020) *Effective school support for disadvantaged and vulnerable pupils – case studies of good practice*. Cardiff: Estyn. Available at: https://www.estyn.gov.wales/thematic-report/effective-school-support-disadvantaged-and-vulnerable-pupils-case-studies-good.

European Commission (2011) *Wellbeing in 2030*. Eurobarometer Qualitative Studies. Available at: https://ec.europa.eu/commfrontoffice/publicopinion/archives/quali/wellbeing_aggregate_en.pdf (accessed 8 September 2020).

Fadde, P.J. and Sullivan, P.A. (2013) Using interactive video to develop pre-service teachers' classroom awareness. *Contemporary Issues in Technology and Teacher Education*, 13 (2): 156–174.

Florian, L. and Black-Hawkins, K. (2011) Exploring inclusive pedagogy. *British Educational Research Journal*, 37 (5): 813–828.

Forde, C., McMahon, M. and Reeves, J. (2009) *Putting Together Professional Portfolios*. London: Sage.

Forman, F. (2020) *At home with weaving well-being: A well-being journal for kids*. Outside the Box Learning Resources. Available at: https://www.otb.ie/wwb-home/.

Fox, R. (1998) Thinking and the language arts, in R. Burden and M. Williams (eds.) *Thinking Through the Curriculum*. London: Routledge.

Fretwell, N., Osgood, J., O'Toole, G. and Tsouroufli, M. (2018) Governing through trust: Community-based link workers and parental engagement in education. *British Educational Research Journal*, 44 (6): 1047–1063.

Freud, A. (1930) *Psychoanalysis for Teachers and Parents*, trans. B. Low. Boston, MA: Beacon Press.

Gathercole, S.E., Pickering, S.J., Ambridge, B. and Wearing, H. (2004) The structure of working memory from 4 to 15 years of age. *Developmental Psychology*, 40 (2): 177–190.

General Teaching Council for Northern Ireland (GTCNI) (2011) *Teaching: The reflective profession*. Belfast: GTCNI. Available at: https://gtcni.org.uk/professional-space/professional-competence/teaching-the-reflective-profession (accessed 24 April 2020).

General Teaching Council for Scotland (GTCS) (2012) *Standards for registration*. Edinburgh: GTCS. Available at: https://www.gtcs.org.uk/professional-standards/standards-for-registration.aspx (accessed 1 February 2020).

Geographical Association (2011) *The Geography National Curriculum: GA curriculum proposals and rationale*. Sheffield: Geographical Association. Available at: https://www.geography.org.uk/download/ga_gigcccurriculumproposals.pdf.

Gibbs, G. (1988) *Learning by Doing: A guide to teaching and learning methods*. London: Further Education Unit.

Gilger, J. and Kaplan, B. (2001) Atypical brain development: A conceptual framework for understanding developmental learning disabilities. *Developmental Neuropsychology*, 20 (2): 465–481.

Gilmore, S. and Anderson, V. (2016) The emotional turn in higher education: A psychoanalytic contribution. *Teaching in Higher Education*, 21 (6): 686–699.

Godfrey, D. and Brown, C. (2019) *An Ecosystem for Research-Engaged Schools: Reforming education through research*. London: Routledge.

Godfrey, G., Seleznyov, S., Anders, J., Wollaston, N, and Barrera-Pedemonte, F. (2019) A developmental evaluation approach to lesson study: Exploring the impact of lesson study in London schools. *Professional Development in Education*, 45 (2): 325–340.

Goldacre, B. (2013) *Building evidence into education*. London: Department for Education. Available at: https://www.gov.uk/government/news/building-evidence-into-education.

Goldman, J.D.G. and Grimbeek, P. (2014) Pre-service primary school teachers' self-reflective competencies in their own teaching. *European Journal of Psychological Education*, 30 (2): 189–207.

Goodall, J. (2015) Ofsted's judgement of parental engagement: A justification of its place in leadership and management. *Management in Education*, 29 (4): 172–177.

Goodall, J. (2016a) *Reporting to support. Teacher Toolkit*. Available at: https://www.teachertoolkit.co.uk/2016/08/10/parental-support/ (accessed 28 September 2020).

Goodall, J. (2016b) Technology and school–home communication. *International Journal of Pedagogies and Learning*, 11 (2): 118–131.

Goodall, J. (2018) Learning-centred parental engagement: Freire reimagined. *Educational Review*, 70 (5): 603–621.

Graham, A. and Truscott, J. (2020) Meditation in the classroom: Supporting both student and teacher wellbeing? *Education 3–13*, 48 (7): 807–819.

Griffith, A. and Burns, M. (2012) *Engaging Learners*. London: Crown House.

Griffiths, D. (2020) Teaching for neurodiversity: Training teachers to see beyond labels. *Impact: Journal of the Chartered College of Teaching*, Issue 8 (Spring). Available at: https://impact.chartered.college/article/teaching-for-neurodiversity-training-teachers-see-beyond-labels/ (accessed 26 November 2020).

Guðjónsdóttir, H. and Öskarsdóttir, E. (2016) Inclusive education, policy and practice, in S. Markic and S. Abels (eds.) *Science Education Towards Inclusion* (pp. 7–22). New York: Nova Science.

Guerriero, S. (ed.) (2017) *Pedagogical knowledge and the changing nature of the teaching profession*, Educational Research and Innovation. Paris: OECD Publishing. Available at: http://www.oecd.org/education/pedagogical-knowledge-and-the-changing-nature-of-the-teaching-profession-9789264270695-en.htm.

Gutman, L.M. and Vorhaus, J. (2012) *The impact of pupil behaviour and wellbeing on educational outcomes*, Research report DFE-RR253. London: Department for Education. Available at: https://dera.ioe.ac.uk/16093/1/DFE-RR253.pdf.

Hahn, A. (2019) Facing one's implicit biases: From awareness to acknowledgement. *Journal of Personality and Social Psychology*, 116 (5): 769–794.

Hall, T., Meyer, A. and Rose, D. (2012) *Universal Design for Learning in the Classroom: Practical application*. New York: Guilford Press.

Hargreaves, A. (2007) Sustainable professional learning communities, in L. Stoll and K.S. Louis (eds.) *Professional Learning Communities: Divergence, depth and dilemmas* (pp. 181–196). Maidenhead: Open University Press.

Hargreaves, A. and Dawe, R. (1990) Paths of professional development: Contrived collegiality, collaborative culture, and the case of peer coaching. *Teaching and Teacher Education*, 6 (3): 227–241.

Hargreaves, A. and O'Connor, M.T. (2018) *Collaborative Professionalism: When teaching together means learning for all*. Thousand Oaks, CA: Corwin/Sage.

Haßler, B., Major, L. and Hennessy, S. (2015) Tablet use in schools: A critical review of the evidence for learning outcomes. *Journal of Computer Assisted Learning*, 32 (2): 139–156.

Hattie, J. (2012) *Visible Learning for Teachers: Maximizing impact on learning*. London: Routledge.

Hattie, J. (2013) *Visible Learning*. London: Routledge.

Helliwell, J.F., Layard, R., Sachs, J. and De Neve, J. (eds.) (2020) *World happiness report 2020*. New York: Sustainable Development Solutions Network. Available at: https://worldhappiness. report/ed/2020/.

Hirsch, Jr., E.D. (2016) *Why Knowledge Matters: Rescuing our children from failed educational theories*. Cambridge, MA: Harvard Education Press.

HM Treasury (2012) *Quality in qualitative evaluation: A framework for assessing research evidence*. London: HM Treasury. Available at: https://assets.publishing.service.gov.uk/ government/uploads/system/uploads/attachment_data/file/190986/Magenta_Book_quality_ in_qualitative_evaluation__QQE_.pdf.

Hofstetter, R. and Schneuwly, B. (2006) Introduction. Progressive education and educational sciences: The tumultuous relations of an indissociable and irreconcilable couple?, in R. Hofstetter and B. Schneuwly (eds.) *Passion, Fusion, Tension: New education and educational sciences. End 19th–middle 20th century* (pp. 1–16). Berne: Peter Lang.

Honeybourne, V. (2018) *The Neurodiverse Classroom*. London: Jessica Kingsley.

Honingh, M., Bondarouk, E. and Brandsen T. (2020) Co-production in primary schools: A systematic literature review. *International Review of Administrative Sciences*, 86 (2): 222–239.

Hulme, M., Woodfine, C., Kardas, K. and Griffiths, D. (2020) *Wellbeing strategies and vulnerable group support: Case studies of good practice*. ESRI/Manchester Metropolitan University, Education Achievement Service. Available at: http://e-space.mmu.ac.uk/625809/.

Humes, W. (2015) The educational achievements of a 'great visionary': William Boyd (1874–1962). *Scottish Educational Review*, 47 (2): 37–58.

Institute for Effective Education (IEE) (2019) *Engaging with evidence*. York: IEE. Available at: https://the-iee.org.uk/wp-content/uploads/2019/03/Engaging-with-Evidence.pdf.

Iver, M.A., Epstein, D.B., Sheldon, SB. and Fonseca, E. (2015) Engaging familiars to support students' transition to high school: Evidence from the field. *The High School Journal*, 99 (1): 27–45.

Jeynes, W. (2018) A practical model for school leaders to encourage parental involvement and parental engagement. *School Leadership and Management*, 38 (2): 147–163.

John, P. and Sutherland, R. (2005) Affordance, opportunity and the pedagogical implications of ICT. *Educational Review*, 57 (4): 405–413.

Johnson, B. and Down, B. (2013) Critically re-conceptualising early career teacher resilience. *Discourse: Studies in the Cultural Politics of Education*, 34 (5): 703–715.

Kaplan, B., Crawford, S., Cantell, M., Kooristra, L. and Dewey, D. (2006) Comorbidity, co-occurrence, continuum: What's in a name? *Child: Care, Health and Development*, 32 (6): 723–731.

Kearney, M., Schuck, S., Burden, K. and Aubusson, P. (2012) Viewing mobile learning from a pedagogical perspective. *Research in Learning Technology*, 20: 14406. Available at: https:// doi.org/10.3402/rlt.v20i0.14406.

Kempf, A. (2018) *The challenges of measuring wellbeing in schools*. Toronto: Ontario Teachers' Federation. Available at: https://www.otffeo.on.ca/en/wp-content/uploads/sites/2/2018/02/ The-challenges-of-measuring-wellbeing-in-schools-Winter-2017-web.pdf.

Kennewell, S. and Beauchamp, G. (2007) The features of interactive whiteboards and their influence on learning. *Learning, Media and Technology*, 32 (3): 227–241.

Keogh, J., Garvis, S., Pendergast, D. and Diamond, P. (2012) Self-determination: Using agency, efficacy and resilience (AER) to counter novice teachers' experiences of intensification. *Australian Journal of Teacher Education*, 37 (8): 46–65.

Kohn, A. (1999) *Punished by Rewards: The trouble with gold stars, incentive plans, A's, praise and other bribes*, 2nd edition. Boston, MA: Houghton Mifflin.

Kolb, D.A. (1984) *Experiential Learning: Experience as the source of learning and development*. Englewood Cliffs, NJ: Prentice-Hall.

Kukulska-Hulme, A. (2009) Will mobile learning change language learning? *ReCALL*, 21 (2): 157–165.

Lagemann, E.C. (2000) *An Elusive Science: The troubling history of educational research.* Chicago, IL: University of Chicago Press.

Land, R., Cousin, G., Meyer, J. and Davies, P. (2005) Threshold concepts and troublesome knowledge (3): Implications for course design and evaluation, in C. Rust (ed.) *Improving Pupil Learning: Diversity and inclusivity* (pp. 53–64). Oxford: Oxford Centre for Staff and Learning Development.

Lefstein, A. and Snell, J. (2011) Professional vision and the politics of teacher learning. *Teaching and Teacher Education*, 27 (3): 505–514.

Lemov, D. (2010) *Teach Like a Champion: 49 techniques that put students on the path to college.* San Francisco, CA: Jossey-Bass.

Lendrum, A., Barlow, A. and Humphrey, N. (2015) Developing positive school–home relationships through structured conversations with parents of learners with special educational needs and disabilities (SEND). *Journal of Research in Special Educational Needs*, 15 (2): 87–96.

Lewis, A. and Norwich, B. (2005) *Special Teaching for Special Children? Pedagogies for inclusion.* Maidenhead: Open University Press.

Luckin, R. (2008) The learner centric ecology of resources: A framework for using technology to scaffold learning. *Computers and Education*, 50 (2): 449–462.

Luthar, S.S., Cicchetti, D. and Becker, B. (2000) The construct of resilience: A critical evaluation and guidelines for future work. *Child Development*, 71 (3): 543–562.

Manyukhina, Y. and Wyse, D. (2019) Learner agency and the curriculum: A critical realist perspective. *The Curriculum Journal*, 30 (3): 223–243.

Martinez, A.G. and Hinshaw, S.P. (2016) Mental illness stigma: Theory, developmental issues, and research priorities, in D. Cicchetti (ed.) *Developmental Psychopathology*, Vol. 4: *Risk, resilience, and intervention*, 3rd edition (pp. 997–1040). Hoboken, NJ: Wiley.

Masataka, N. (2017) Implications of the idea of neurodiversity for understanding the origins of developmental disorders. *Physics of Life Reviews*, 20: 85–108.

Mason, J. (2001) *Researching Your Own Practice: The discipline of noticing.* London: Routledge.

Menter, I., Hulme, M., Elliot, D. and Lewin, J. (2010) *Literature review on teacher education in the 21st century.* Edinburgh: The Scottish Government. Available at: https://dera.ioe.ac.uk/1255/1/0105011.pdf.

Meredith, A. (1995) Terry's learning: Some limitations of Shulman's pedagogical content knowledge. *Cambridge Journal of Education*, 25 (2): 175–187.

Metwally, D., Ruiz-Palomino, P., Metwally, M. and Gartzia, L. (2019) How ethical leadership shapes employees' readiness to change: The mediating role of an organizational culture of effectiveness. *Frontiers in Psychology*, 10: 2493. Available at: https://doi.org/10.3389/fpsyg.2019.02493.

Meyer, A., Rose, D. and Gordon, D. (2014) *Universal Design for Learning: Theory and practice.* Wakefield, MA: CAST Professional Publishing.

Meyer, J.H.F. and Land, R. (2003) Threshold concepts and troublesome knowledge (1): Linkages to ways of thinking and practising, in C. Rust (ed.) *Improving Pupil Learning – Ten years on* (pp. 412–424). Oxford: OCSLD.

Meyer, J.H.F. and Land, R. (2005) Threshold concepts and troublesome knowledge (2): Epistemological considerations and a conceptual framework for teaching and learning. *Higher Education*, 49 (3): 373–388.

Middlehurst, T. (2013) *Student Impact in the Redesigned School*, Redesigning Schooling series. London: Schools, Students and Teachers Network.

Mind (2019, May) *Self-esteem.* Available at: https://www.mind.org.uk/media-a/2955/self-esteem-2019.pdf (accessed 24 April 2020).

Moody, C. and Moody, R. (2020) *Unconscious Bias Journal: Change the way you live and work with positive reflection and action*. London: JCRM Journals.

Morton, S. and Wright, A. (2015) *Getting evidence into action to improve Scotland's public services*. Edinburgh: What Works Scotland. Available at: http://whatworksscotland.ac.uk/publications/getting-evidence-into-action-to-improve-scotlands-public-services/.

National Foundation for Educational Research (NFER) (2019) Teachers' engagement with research: what do we know? Slough: NFER. Available at: https://www.nfer.ac.uk/teachers-engagement-with-research-what-do-we-know-a-research-briefing/.

Nesta (2016) *Using research evidence: A practice guide*. London: Nesta. Available at: https://www.nesta.org.uk/toolkit/using-research-evidence-practice-guide/.

Nisbet, J. (2005) What is educational research? Changing perspectives through the 20th century. *Research Papers in Education*, 20 (1): 25–44.

Novak, K. (2016) *UDL Now! A teacher's guide to applying Universal Design for Learning in today's classrooms*, revised and expanded edition. Wakefield, MA: CAST Professional Publishing.

OECD (2005) *Teachers matter: Attracting, developing and retaining effective teachers*. Paris: OECD. Available at: http://www.oecd.org/education/school/34990905.pdf.

OECD (2016) *What makes a school a learning organisation? A guide for policy makers, school leaders and teachers*. Paris: OECD. Available at: https://www.oecd.org/education/school/school-learning-organisation.pdf.

OECD (2017) *Social and emotional skills: Well-being, connectedness and success*. Paris: OECD. Available at: https://www.oecd.org/education/school/UPDATED%20Social%20and%20Emotional%20Skills%20-%20Well-being,%20connectedness%20and%20success.pdf%20(website).pdf.

OECD (2018) *Developing schools as learning organisations in Wales*. Paris: OECD. Available at: https://hwb.gov.wales/api/storage/3c7ac963-4059-4f15-bdf9-368b16c3ecf7/developing-schools-as-learning-organisations-in-wales-highlights_0.pdf.

OECD (2019a) *Changing the odds for vulnerable children: Building opportunities and resilience*. Paris: OECD. Available at: https://www.oecd.org/publications/changing-the-odds-for-vulnerable-children-a2e8796c-en.htm.

OECD (2019b) *PISA 2018 results*, Vol. III: *What school life means for students' lives*. Paris: OECD. Available at: https://www.oecd.org/publications/pisa-2018-results-volume-iii-acd78851-en.htm.

OECD (2020) *How's life? 2020: Measuring well-being*. Paris: OECD. Available at: http://www.oecd.org/statistics/how-s-life-23089679.htm.

Office of the First Minister and Deputy First Minister (2016) *Our children and young people – our pledge: A ten-year strategy for children and young people in Northern Ireland 2006–2016*. Available at: https://www.education-ni.gov.uk/publications/ten-year-strategy-children-and-young-people-northern-ireland-2006-2016-0 (accessed 28 September 2020).

Ofsted (2015) *School Inspection Handbook*. London: Ofsted.

Ofsted (2019) *The Education Inspection Framework*. Manchester: Ofsted.

Ott, M., Hibbert, K., Rodger, S. and Leschied, A. (2017) A well place to be: The intersection of Canadian school-based mental health policy with student and teacher resiliency. *Canadian Journal of Education*, 40 (2): 1–30.

Overland, E., Barber, J. and Sackville-Ford, M. (2020) *Behaviour Management: An essential guide for student and newly qualified teachers*. Abingdon: Routledge.

Pantaleo, S. (2016) Teacher expectations and student literacy engagement and achievement. *Literacy*, 50 (2): 83–92.

Patton, K. and Parker, M. (2017) Teacher education communities of practice: More than a culture of collaboration. *Teaching and Teacher Education*, 67: 351–360.

Pavey, B. (2007) *The Dyslexia-Friendly Primary School: A practical guide for teachers*. London: Sage.

Pearson, R.C. (2014) *Written Reporting: Exploring school approaches and parental understandings*. Auckland: The University of Auckland.

Pernet, C., Dufor, O. and Démonet, J.-F. (2011) Redefining dyslexia: Accounting for variability, *Escritos de Psicologia*, 4 (2): 17–24.

Pollard, A. with Black-Hawkins, K., Hodges, G.C., Dudley, P., James, M., Linklater, H. et al. (2014) *Reflective Teaching in Schools*, 2nd edition. London: Bloomsbury.

Porter, L. (2014) *Behaviour in Schools: Theory and practice for teachers*, 3rd edition. Maidenhead: Open University Press.

Portman, S. (2020) Reflective journaling: A portal into the virtues of daily writing. *The Reading Teacher*, 73 (5): 597–602.

Price, A., Mansfield, C. and McConney, A. (2012) Considering 'teacher resilience' from critical discourse and labour process theory perspectives. *British Journal of Sociology of Education*, 33 (1): 81–95.

Priestley, J.B. ([1945] 2000) *An Inspector Calls*. Harmondsworth: Penguin.

Priestley, M., Biesta, G. and Robinson, S. (2013) Teachers as agents of change: Teacher agency and emerging models of curriculum, in M. Priestley and G. Biesta (eds.) *Reinventing the Curriculum: New trends in curriculum policy and practice* (pp. 187–206). London: Bloomsbury.

Purser, R. (2019) *McMindfulness: How mindfulness became the new capitalist spirituality*. London: Repeater Books.

Pushor, D. (2012) Tracing my research on parent engagement: Working to interrupt the story of school as protectorate. *Action in Teacher Education*, 34 (4/5): 464–479.

Rao, K. and Mao, G. (2016) Using Universal Design for Learning to design standards-based lessons. *Sage Open*, 6: 4. Available at: https://doi.org/10.1177/2158244016680688.

Reitano, P. and Harte, W. (2016) Geography pre-service teachers' pedagogical content knowledge. *Pedagogies: An International Journal*, 11 (4): 279–291.

Rhodes, I. and Long, M. (2019) *Improving behaviour in schools*. London: Education Endowment Foundation. Available at: https://educationendowmentfoundation.org.uk/public/files/Publications/Behaviour/EEF_Improving_behaviour_in_schools_Report.pdf (accessed 24 July 2020).

Rickinson, M., Walsh, L., Gleeson, J., Cirkony, C. and Salisbury, M. (2020) Understanding quality of evidence use. *Research Intelligence*, 144: 26–27.

Roberts, J.E. (2012) *Instructional Rounds in Action*. Cambridge, MA: Harvard Education Press.

Roediger, H.L. and Karpicke, J.D. (2006) Test-enhanced learning: Taking memory tests improves long-term retention. *Psychological Science*, 17 (3): 249–255.

Rogers, B. (2015) *Classroom Behaviour: A practical guide to effective teaching, behaviour management and colleague support*. London: Sage.

Rosenshine, B. (2010) *Principles of instruction*, Educational Practices Series 21. Available at: http://www.formapex.com/telechargementpublic/rosenshine2010a.pdf.

Rosenshine, B. (2012) Principles of instruction: Research-based strategies that all teachers should know. *American Educator*, 36 (1): 12–19.

Rosenthal, R. and Jacobson, L. (1968) *Pygmalion in the Classroom: Teacher expectation and pupils' intellectual development*. New York: Holt, Rinehart & Winston.

Ruby-Davies, C. (2010) Classroom interactions: Exploring the practices of high- and low- expectation teachers. *British Journal of Educational Psychology*, 77 (2): 289–306.

Rusk, R.R. (1929) *Experimental Education*. London: Longmans, Green.

Rusk, R.R. (1932) *Research in Education. An Introduction*. London: University of London Press.

Rycroft, L. and Dutaut, J.L. (2018) *Flip the System UK: A teachers' manifesto*. Abingdon: Routledge.

Sachs, J. (2001) Teacher professional identity: Competing discourses, competing outcomes. *Journal of Education Policy*, 16 (2): 149–161.

Sachs, J. (2003) *The Activist Teaching Profession*. Buckingham: Open University Press.

Sackville-Ford, M. and Baggaley, S. (2020) Being human: Compassionate education rather than behaviour management, in E. Overland, J. Barber and M. Sackville-Ford (eds.) *Behaviour Management: An essential guide for student and newly qualified teachers* (pp. 129–146). London: Routledge.

Sahlberg, P. (2016) The global educational reform movement and its impact on schooling, in K. Mundy, A. Green, B. Lingard and A. Verger (eds.) *The Handbook of Global Education Policy* (pp. 128–144). Chichester: Wiley.

Sannino, A., Engeström, Y. and Lemos, M. (2016) Formative interventions for expansive learning and transformative agency. *Journal of the Learning Sciences*, 25 (4): 599–633.

Schenk, L., Hamza, K.M., Enghag, M., Lundegård, I., Arvanitis, L., Haglund, K. et al. (2019) Teaching and discussing about risk: Seven elements of potential significance for science education. *International Journal of Science Education*, 41 (9): 1271–1286.

Schneider, W. (1985) Developmental trends in the metamemory–memory behavior relationship: An integrative review, in D.L. Forrest-Pressley, G.E. MacKinnon and T.G. Waller (eds.) *Metacognition, Cognition and Human Performance*, Vol. 1 (pp. 57–109). Orlando, FL: Academic Press.

Schon, D. (1983) *The Reflective Practitioner: How professionals think in action*. New York: Basic Books.

Schutz, P.A., Hong, J. and Cross Francis, D. (2018) *Research on Teacher Identity: Mapping challenges and innovations*. Cham: Springer.

Schwab, J.J. (1978) *Science, Curriculum and Liberal Education: Selected essays*. Chicago, IL: University of Chicago Press.

Scott, E. (2020) The benefits of journaling for stress management, *Very Well Mind*. Available at: https://www.verywellmind.com/the-benefits-of-journaling-for-stress-management-3144611.

Scottish Executive (2006) *Scottish schools (parental involvement) act guidance*. Edinburgh: Scottish Executive. Available at: https://education.gov.scot/parentzone/Documents/parental-involvement-act-guidance.pdf (accessed 24 September 2020).

Scottish Government (2011a) *Curriculum for excellence: Health and wellbeing – experiences and outcomes*. Edinburgh: Scottish Government. Available at: https://www.education.gov.scot/Documents/health-and-wellbeing-eo.pdf (accessed 24 September 2020).

Scottish Government (2011b) *Curriculum for excellence: Health and wellbeing across learning: Responsibilities of all – experiences and outcomes*. Edinburgh: Scottish Government. Available at: https://education.gov.scot/Documents/hwb-across-learning-eo.pdf (accessed 24 September 2020).

Scottish Government (2017) *Getting it Right for Every Child update*. Edinburgh: Scottish Government. Available at: https://www.gov.scot/publications/getting-it-right-for-every-child-girfec-update-july-2017/.

Scottish Government (2018) *Understanding wellbeing*. Edinburgh: Scottish Government. Available at: https://www.gov.scot/publications/shanarri/ (accessed 28 September 2020).

Scottish Government (2019) *Scotland's wellbeing – Delivering the national outcomes*. Edinburgh: Scottish Government. Available at: https://nationalperformance.gov.scot/sites/default/files/documents/NPF_Scotland%27s_Wellbeing_May2019.pdf.

Selwyn, J., Magnus, L.I. and Briheim-Crookall, L. (2017) *Our lives, our care: Looked after children's views on their well-being*. Bristol: School for Policy Studies, University of Bristol. Available at: https://research-information.bris.ac.uk/en/publications/our-lives-our-care-looked-after-chidrens-views-on-their-well-bein.

Sense About Science (2017) *How do I know what to believe?* Available at: https://senseaboutscience.org/activities/i-dont-know-what-to-believe/.

Shakespeare, W. ([1606] 2007) *Macbeth*. Harmondsworth: Penguin.

Sherrington, T. (2019) *Rosenshine's Principles in Action*. Woodbridge: John Catt Educational.

Shimamura, A. (2018) *MARGE: A whole-brain learning approach for students and teachers.* Available at: https://shimamurapubs.wordpress.com/marge-a-whole-brain-learning-approach-for-students-and-teachers/.

Shulman, L.S. (1986) Those who understand: Knowledge growth in teaching. *Educational Researcher*, 15 (2): 4–14.

Shulman, L.S. (1987) Knowledge and teaching: Foundations of the new reform. *Harvard Educational Review*, 57 (1): 1–22.

Singer, J. (1999) 'Why can't you be normal for once in your life?' From a 'problem with no name' to the emergence of a new category of difference, in M. Corker and S. French (eds.) *Disability Discourse* (pp. 59–67). Buckingham: Open University Press.

Siugzdaite, R., Bathelt, J., Holmes, J. and Astle, D. (2020) Transdiagnostic brain mapping in developmental disorders. *Current Biology*, 30 (7): 1245–1257.

Smith, J. (2017) *The Lazy Teacher's Handbook: How your students learn more when you teach less.* Carmarthen: Independent Thinking Press.

Smith, M. and Trede, F. (2013) Reflective practice in the transition phase from university student to novice graduate: Implications for teaching reflective practice. *Higher Education Research and Development*, 32 (4): 632–645.

Snowling, M. and Hulme, C. (2012) Annual research review: The nature and classification of reading disorders – a commentary on proposals for DSM-5. *Journal of Child Psychology and Psychiatry*, 52 (5): 593–607.

Stenhouse, L. (1981) What counts as research? *British Journal of Educational Studies*, 29 (2): 103–114.

Storrs, A. (2012) Keeping it real with an emotional curriculum. *Teaching in Higher Education*, 17 (1): 1–12.

Sweller, J. (2010) Cognitive load theory: Recent theoretical advances, in J.L. Plass, R. Moreno and R. Brünken (eds.) *Cognitive Load Theory* (pp. 29–47). Cambridge: Cambridge University Press.

Sweller, J. (2011) Cognitive load theory and e-learning, in G. Biswas, S. Bull, J. Kay and A. Mitrovic (eds.) *Artificial Intelligence in Education*. AIED 2011. Lecture Notes in Computer Science, Vol. 6738 (pp. 5–6). Heidelberg: Springer.

Takahashi, A. and McDougal, T. (2016) Collaborative lesson research: Maximising the impact of lesson study. *Mathematics Education*, 48 (4): 513–526.

Taljaard, J. (2016) A review of multi-sensory technologies in a Science, Technology, Engineering, Arts and Mathematics (STEAM) classroom. *Journal of Learning Design*, 9 (2): 46–55.

Tarrant, P. (2013) *Reflective Practice and Professional Development.* Thousand Oaks, CA: Sage.

Taylor, R.D., Oberle, E., Durlak, J.A. and Weissberg, R.P. (2017) Promoting positive youth development through school-based social and emotional learning interventions: A meta-analysis of follow-up effects. *Child Development*, 88: 1156–1171.

The Children's Society (2020a) *The Good Childhood Report 2020.* London: The Children's Society. Available at: https://www.childrenssociety.org.uk/sites/default/files/2020-11/Good-Childhood-Report-2020.pdf (accessed 8 July 2020).

The Children's Society (2020b) *Life on hold: Children's well-being and COVID-19.* London: The Children's Society. Available at: https://www.childrenssociety.org.uk/information/professionals/resources/life-on-hold.

Timperley, H. (2011) *Realizing the Power of Professional Learning.* Maidenhead: Open University Press.

Timperley, H. (2015) *Professional conversations and improvement-focused feedback.* Melbourne, VIC: Australian Institute of Teaching and School Leadership (AITSL). Available at: https://www.aitsl.edu.au/docs/default-source/default-document-library/professional-conversations-literature-review-oct-2015.pdf?sfvrsn=fc2ec3c_0.

Tinker, R. (2015) *Stakeholder schools: Why collaboration is key to the next phase of school reform.* London: Fabian Society. Available at: https://fabians.org.uk/wp-content/uploads/2015/09/Stakeholder-schools-Sept-151-2.pdf.

Tobin, B. (2017) Understanding the direct involvement of parents in policy development and school activities in a primary school. *International Journal for Transformative Research,* 4 (1): 25–33.

Tripp, D. (1998) Critical incidents in action inquiry, in G. Shacklock and J. Smyth (eds.) *Being Reflexive in Critical Educational and Social Research* (pp. 36–49). London: Falmer Press.

Tschannen-Moran, M. and Gareis, C. (2015) Principals, trust and creating vibrant schools, *Societies,* 5: 256–276.

Turner-Bisset, R. (1999) The knowledge bases of the expert teacher. *British Educational Research Journal,* 25 (1): 39–55.

Ungar, M., Ghazinour, M. and Richter, J. (2013) Annual research review: What is resilience within the social ecology of human development? *Journal of Child Psychology and Psychiatry,* 54 (4): 348–366.

UNICEF (2007) *Child poverty in perspective: An overview of child well-being in rich countries,* Innocenti Report Card No. 7. Florence: Unicef Innocenti Research Centre.

Valli, L. (1997) Listening to other voices: A description of teacher reflection in the United States. *Peabody Journal of Education,* 72 (1): 67–88.

van Es, E.A. and Sherin, M.G. (2002) Learning to notice: Scaffolding new teachers' interpretations of classroom interactions. *Journal of Technology and Teacher Education,* 10 (4): 571–596.

Vincent, C. (2017) The children have only got one education and you have to make sure it's a good one: Parenting and parent–school relations in a neoliberal age. *Gender and Education,* 29 (5): 541–557.

Vincent, C. and Maxwell, C. (2016) Parenting priorities and pressures: Furthering understanding of 'concerted cultivation'. *Discourse: Studies in the Cultural Politics of Education,* 37 (2): 269–281.

Vrikki, M., Warwick, P.D. Vermunt, J., Mercer, N. and Van Halem, N. (2017) Teacher learning in the context of Lesson Study: A video-based analysis of teacher discussions. *Teaching and Teacher Education,* 61: 211–224.

Wang, J. and Hartley, K. (2003) Video technology as a support for teacher education reform. *Journal of Technology and Teacher Education,* 11 (1): 105–138.

Waples, D. and Tyler, R.W. (1930) *Research Methods and Teachers' Problems. A Manual for Systematic Studies of Classroom Procedure.* New York: The Macmillan Company.

Welsh Government (2008) *The digital competence framework.* Cardiff: Welsh Government. Available at: https://hwb.gov.wales/curriculum-for-wales-2008/digital-competence-framework-curriculum-for-wales-2008-version.

Welsh Government (2016) *Statutory guidance to the governing bodies of maintained schools in Wales regarding the duty to hold meetings with parents.* Cardiff: Welsh Government. Available at: https://gov.wales/sites/default/files/publications/2018-03/statutory-guidance-to-the-governing-bodies-of-maintained-schools-in-wales-regarding-the-duty-to-hold-meetings-with-parents.pdf (accessed 24 July 2020).

Welsh Government (2017) *Professional standards for teaching and leadership.* Cardiff: Welsh Government. Available at: https://hwb.gov.wales/professional-development/professional-standards/ (accessed 24 July 2020).

Welsh Government (2019) *Professional standards for teaching and leadership.* Cardiff: Welsh Government. Available from: https://hwb.gov.wales/professional-development/professional-standards/ (accessed 24 July 2020).

Wertsch, J.V. (1991) *Voices of the Mind: A sociocultural approach to mediated action.* Hemel Hempstead: Harvester Wheatsheaf.

White, J. (2018) The weakness of 'powerful' knowledge. *London Review of Education*, 16 (2): 325–335.

Whitehead, J., Telfer, H. and Lambert, T. (2013) *Values in Youth Sport and Physical Education*. London: Routledge.

Wigelsworth, M., Verity, L., Mason, C., Humphrey, N., Qualter, P. and Troncoso, P. (2020) *Primary social and emotional learning: Evidence review*. London: Education Endowment Foundation. Available at: https://educationendowmentfoundation.org.uk/public/files/Social_and_Emotional_Learning_Evidence_Review.pdf.

Wilcox, K.C. and Lawson, H.A. (2018) Teachers' agency, efficacy, engagement, and emotional resilience during policy innovation implementation. *Journal of Educational Change*, 19 (2): 181–204.

Wilder, S. (2014) Effects of parental involvement on academic achievement: A meta-synthesis. *Educational Review*, 66 (3): 377–397.

World Health Organization (WHO) (2020) *Spotlight on adolescent health and wellbeing*. Geneva: WHO. Available at: https://www.euro.who.int/en/health-topics/Life-stages/child-and-adolescent-health/health-behaviour-in-school-aged-children-hbsc/hbsc-2020.

Young, M. (2008) *Bringing Knowledge Back In: From social constructivism to social realism in the sociology of education*. Abingdon: Routledge.

Zenner, C., Herrnleben-Kurz, S. and Walach, H. (2014) Mindfulness-based interventions in schools – a systematic review and meta-analysis. *Frontiers in Psychology*, 5: 603. Available at: https://doi.org/10.3389/fpsyg.2014.00603.

Appendix: Checklist for ethical professional enquiry

- ✓ Is your enquiry really needed? Who else thinks this? What do we already know about this topic? What are the potential benefits of this enquiry for teachers, pupils, parents, etc.? How will the insights you generate deepen understanding and/or support improvement? Who is the intended audience for your findings?
- ✓ Does your school, Trust, or local authority have a formal review policy for teacher research? Who needs to know about the enquiry you are planning? What is the process for obtaining ethical approval?
- ✓ Are there any risks to participants, e.g. may current pupils be disadvantaged for possible future benefit?
- ✓ What kinds of information will you gather? Does this include information beyond your normal practice? What are the ethical implications of this? Why do you want to gather this information? Do you have explicit permission to access and record this information for research purposes?
- ✓ What exactly does the research involve for participants? Is your choice of methods appropriate? Are you including a range of perspectives and opportunities? Have you spelt out the time commitment required, the activities involved, how you will use the information that is produced?
- ✓ Does your professional enquiry involve people with less power than yourself, e.g. pupils, co-workers, and parents?
- ✓ How will you obtain fully informed consent? What are the procedures for opting in and opting out? Does your enquiry rely on a gatekeeper to access information or participants? How does consent/assent vary for very young children? How will you revisit consent at the different stages of your project? How will you manage withdrawal of consent? What are the implications of this for your project?
- ✓ Have you considered the accessibility of all your project materials, e.g. the language level and age appropriateness? Have you considered if any of your materials carry a cultural or gender bias?
- ✓ How long will you retain the information you gather? Will project files be stored securely? Who will have access to this information?
- ✓ Are you familiar with the provisions of the Data Protection Act and GDPR? Have you discussed your plans with your school or Trust data manager?
- ✓ Have you considered possible adverse reactions to your methods? How will this be handled?
- ✓ How will you manage privacy and confidentiality? Are there limits to how far anonymity can be assured? How will you protect the identity of participants or settings, if relevant?

✓ How will you address potential for bias when conducting your analysis and interpretation of findings? How will you know if you are seeing what you hope to see (confirmation bias)?

✓ Do you plan to share your findings with the participants? If so, at what stage and in what form? How will you respond to participant feedback?

✓ How will you communicate your findings? How will your findings be subject to professional scrutiny? How will you protect participant anonymity during dissemination?

✓ Have you planned for the end of your project? Have you planned for the disposal of project files that contain information that you do not have permission to retain?

Glossary

ABC questioning method – Add anything, Build on the answer, Challenge then answer.

Adaptive expertise – the capacity to adapt professional practice to the needs of new settings and emergent circumstances.

Ambitious expectations – having and communicating a positive belief in and expectation from each student you are teaching.

Assumed compliance – the assumption that a pupil will comply with an instruction. This can be implied in tone, using an imperative. Alternatively, the use of 'thank you' rather than 'please' suggests compliance.

Cognitive behaviourism – examines the role of cognitive processes influencing a child's behaviour.

Cognitive load – an instructional design, cognitive theory that proposes cognitive processes become overwhelmed when the capacity of the working memory system is exceeded.

Cognitive taxonomy – a way of organising knowledge according to higher-order and lower-order cognitive skills. This can help teachers and pupils make sense of the level of challenge of different knowledge in the subject area.

Cultural myth – a falsehood of expectation or impression created as a result of social and cultural beliefs of what teaching is and what teachers do.

Curriculum – carries many meanings, such as a body of knowledge, a process of learning, the route taken through a subject/topic, a process of inducting novices into an area of expertise.

Cycle of reflection – typically involves describing an experience; recording how you feel; making sense of the experience; identifying what you have learned; and using the new knowledge generated to adapt practice in the future.

Deliberate practice — the specific devotion of time and resources to engaging in professional development, usually of one particular pedagogical skill.

Discipline – concepts and ways of thinking and practising in an academic subject.

Early career teachers – teachers within their first five years of teaching, following teacher training.

Educational autobiographical experiences – past experiences of education and being educated through personal engagement.

Encoding – in the context of memory processes, this refers to sensory information being processed and converted into a construct that can then be stored and retrieved later.

Episodic memory – a long-term memory process that involves the recall of contextual information from past personal events or autobiographical information.

Equifinality – the idea that similar levels of resilience can result from very different processes of interaction between risk and protective factors.

Guidance approaches – built on humanist theories, assert that behaviour that is disruptive is associated with an unmet need.

Learning rounds (also called instructional or teacher rounds) – a professional learning technique conducted by groups of teachers to explore an authentic problem of practice at department, school, or school cluster level.

Lesson Study – iterative cycles of collaborative planning of a research lesson (development phase), live lesson observation (enactment), followed by reflective discussion and revision of the lesson plan (professional learning).

Liminality – a state of transition between one phase and the next.

Logic model – planning tool used by professionals to think deeply about the specific goals, required resources, processes, and intended (as well as any possible *un*intended) outcomes that may result from an intervention.

Long-term memory – a cognitive process that allows us to perceive and process (encode), store and then subsequently retrieve information; the capacity is theoretically limitless.

Meta-analyses – pooling of all available results from research in a particular area and the use of statistical methods to summarise findings.

Metacognition – knowledge and skill relating to optimum learning, including planning, monitoring, and evaluating one's progress on cognitive tasks.

Metamemory – a type of metacognition that refers to the self-monitoring and self-control of memory processes.

Methodological approach – the specific procedures or techniques used to identify, select, process, and analyse information about a topic.

M-learning – learning mediated by a mobile device.

Multifinality – a term used to describe the process through which the same risk factor can lead to very different resilience outcomes across individuals.

Neurodiversity – the natural variations in human brains reflected in their unique profiles of learning and other mental functions.

Pedagogical content knowledge – the mixture of both content knowledge and pedagogical knowledge that teachers bring together in their teaching and planning of lessons.

Pedagogy – how knowledge and skills are imparted in an educational context; the act of teaching.

Positive recognition – having given a clear instruction to a class, the use of targeted praise to those complying reiterates the instruction in a positive manner.

Positive repetition – following the statement of a clear instruction to a class, asking a compliant pupil to repeat the instruction reiterates the expectation in a positive manner.

Pragmatic behaviourism – the use of reward and sanctions to regulate pupil behaviour, aligned with assertive discipline.

Praxis – putting theory into practice; enactment.

Pupil agency – the potential in a learning situation for pupils to act and affect the nature of that situation by exercising their creative and critical capacities.

Qualified teacher status – the officially recognised award and status given to a teacher on successful completion of their first year of teaching.

Qualitative data – descriptive data; data that does not take a numerical form (e.g. text, images, audio).

Quantitative data – units of measurement in the form of numbers (e.g. quantity or range).

Radical behaviourism – the idea that environmental and contextual factors should be taken into account when managing behaviour.

Randomised controlled trial – a study where two or more groups are randomly assigned (at individual or cluster level) to an intervention/treatment group or a non-treatment/control group; or groups access different versions of a programme tackling a common problem.

Reflection-in-action – decisions made by teachers in the classroom as events occur, tacitly drawing on professional knowledge accumulated over time.

Reflection-on-action – thinking about actions after the moment has passed, considering reasons for what happened.

Retrieval – in the context of memory processes, this refers to previously stored information being reactivated and remembered.

Semantic memory – a long-term memory process that involves the recall of factual information.

SLANT – rules used in a class: Sit up, Lean forward, Ask and answer questions, Nod your head, and Track the speaker.

Substantive and syntactic content knowledge – the literacy and grammar of a school subject.

Targeted questions – directing specific questions, perhaps differentiated by challenge, to specific students in a hands-down classroom environment

Theory of change – planning tool that explores all the possible activities that might be undertaken to realise a desired change, and shows how and why the desired change is expected to come about.

Unconscious bias – processing of various external stimuli in the subconscious mind resulting in subtle adjustments in our outward behaviour.

Universal Design for Learning (UDL) – a framework for teaching and learning that offers flexibility in the presentation of learning, of methods of student engagement, and of media for expression of students' knowledge, skills, and understanding.

Widgets – a visual picture-symbols communication system.

Working memory – a system that stores and simultaneously processes information; it has a very limited capacity.

Index

Page numbers in italics are figures; with 't' are tables; with 'g' are also glossary terms.